LIVINGSTONE'S
LAST
JOURNEY

LIVINGSTONE'S LAST JOURNEY

SIR REGINALD COUPLAND

K.C.M.G., C.I.E., HON. D.LITT. (DURHAM)
Fellow of All Souls College
Beit Professor of Colonial History
in the University of Oxford

London 1947

Readers Union / Collins

This volume was produced in 1947 in Great Britain in complete conformity with the authorized economy standards. First published in 1945 by Wm. Collins Sons & Co. Ltd., it is set in Baskerville 12 on 13 point and was reprinted in London by Keliher, Hudson & Kearns, Ltd. It is one of the books produced for sale at a reduced price to its members only by Readers Union Ltd., of 38 William IV Street, London, and of Letchworth, Hertfordshire. Particulars of Readers Union are obtainable from either of these addresses

MAPS

Showing Livingstone's Journeys

	PAGE
March 1866 to March 1869	44
July 1869 to October 1871	76
February 1871 to May 1872	160
August 1872 to February 1874	226

GENERAL MAP OF THE TERRITORY

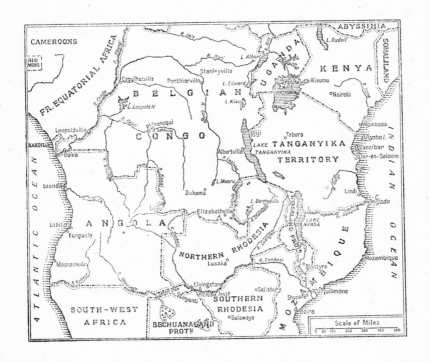

NOTE

Most of this book was written several years ago as a sequel to *Kirk on the Zambesi* and was then laid aside while I made a full-scale study of East African history. That work was completed in the summer of 1939, and this book would also have been finished that autumn but for the war. The delay has proved profitable since in the course of it new and valuable documentary material, in particular the Kirk and Waller Papers, has become available.

The references to these and other documents and to the secondary sources will be found at the end of the book. It has not seemed necessary to give references to the two books most often cited, Livingstone's *Last Journals* and Stanley's *How I Found Livingstone*, because, the narrative in each case being in chronological sequence, readers who want to look up the passages quoted will have little difficulty in finding them.

ON March 24, 1866, David Livingstone disembarked from H.M.S. *Penguin* in which he had sailed from Zanzibar and landed on the shore of East Africa near the mouth of the River Rovuma. A few days later he disappeared into the bush with his little caravan of coloured folk and baggage animals. From that time till he died in 1873 at a village in the heart of the continent, about 700 miles from the coast, only one white man was to see him again.

The broken record of his wanderings—the occasional letters that reached his friends in England, the long intervals of silence, the report of his death and its correction, how he was ' found ' and ' lost ' again, till the last news came that his body was being carried down to the sea— all this excited the keenest interest in Britain. For Livingstone had become a national hero. So great, indeed, was his fame among all classes of the British people, so powerful his influence on public opinion, and so far-reaching the effect of what he said and did on the destiny of Africa that he must be ranked among the greatest of the great Victorians. If he had pursued to the end the vocation he chose in his youth, he would have won a high place, no doubt, in the roll of heroic missionaries ; but he did more than that because he was more than a missionary. Within ten years, indeed, of his first arrival in the South African mission-field in 1841, he ceased to be a missionary in the normal sense of the word. He still prayed and preached as he went his way. He believed that what he was doing was the best he could do to promote the spread of Christianity in Africa. But his primary task, his immediate objective, was not evangelism and conversion. He had become in the first place an explorer. A few more years, and he had become also a kind of statesman, a man who had set himself to save the Africans from something worse than paganism.

It is difficult to realise to-day that, less than a hundred years ago, the whole central mass of the African continent was still as much a blank on European maps as it was in the days of Herodotus. On the West the course of the Niger had been traced from source to sea by 1830 ; but nobody knew whence the Congo flowed. Northwards the source of the Nile was similarly unknown. On the East white men had reached the slopes of the snow-capped mountains Kilimanjaro and Kenya ; but, though there was an old tradition among Africans and Arab traders that somewhere in the interior stretched a vast inland sea, no white man had set eyes on any of the Great Lakes. It is easy to understand how strongly this vast geographical and human mystery appealed to a man of Livingstone's temperament. Restless, vigorous, intensely individualistic, impatient of the routine, the harness, the control involved in the work of a mission station, he had been barely a year at his first post at Kuruman when he hailed ' with inexpressible delight ' the decision of the London Missionary Society's directors ' that we go forward to the dark interior.'[1] In 1842 he was at Mabotsa, 200 miles north of Kuruman ; in 1846 at Chonaune 40 miles further ; in 1847 at Kolobeng, another 40 miles on. Those were small advances, and they were dwarfed by the tremendous project which had now captured Livingstone's mind. ' *Who will penetrate through Africa ?* ' he had asked,[2] and, God willing, he knew the answer.

In 1849 he made the first of his longer journeys, accompanied by two big-game hunters, W. C. Oswell and Mungo Murray, and, traversing the dry belt of the Kalahari, discovered Lake Ngami. In 1851, pressing on northwards in search of healthier country for a mission-station than the flat malarious surroundings of the Lake, he crossed the Chobe and came at last to ' a glorious river ' which, though he was unaware of it at the time, was the Upper Zambesi. This was a long step forward—some 450 miles from Kolobeng—and it seemed a most suitable neighbourhood for planting an advanced mission-post. Not far off, the Batoka

highlands promised a tolerable climate, and the chief of
of the Makololo, the tribesmen of the district, was so
favourably impressed by the first white man he had seen
that he warmly welcomed the suggestion of a mission
among his people.

This first visit to Makololand was the turning-point in
Livingstone's life. When he arrived there the first stage of
his metamorphosis had been reached. When he left, the
second stage had begun. He had heard a new kind of call,
conceived a new sense of his mission in the world. For,
during his stay in Makololand, he had come face to face,
as it happened, with the African Slave Trade ; and this
chance encounter had sown the seed of what was soon to
become and to remain his cardinal purpose—the destruction of the Trade.

The shocking facts of the European Slave Trade in West
Africa had long been known to the British public at this
time.* It was less than fifty years since the British Parlia-
ment by the Act of 1807 had prohibited British subjects
from sharing any longer in the greatest crime committed
by one race against another in the annals of mankind. It
was less than a generation since the death of Wilberforce
in 1833. It was a bare decade since the British Government
had dispatched the ill-fated Niger Expedition of 1841 to
prepare the way for the execution of Buxton's ' positive '
doctrine—the doctrine that the Slave Trade could never
be completely stamped out by preventive action at sea and
that the only effective policy was to establish colonial
settlements on African soil which would attack the Trade
at its source directly by the promotion of ' legitimate '
commerce and indirectly by the spread of Christianity and
civilisation. The Expedition proved a tragic failure ;
malaria decimated its members and put the survivors to
flight : and the Government, rebuked for having sent so
many Englishmen to a certain death, put the ' positive '
policy on the shelf. So the atrocious business of stealing

* For an account of the Trade and its abolition, see the author's *The British Anti-
Slavery Movement* (Home University Library, 1933).   A2

men, women and children from the interior and smuggling them over the Atlantic continued. It did not stop till, from 1863 onwards, Slavery itself was stopped in the trans-Atlantic world.

The European Slave Trade was not confined to West Africa. Cargoes of slaves were obtained on the coast of Portuguese East Africa and shipped thence round the Cape to South America ; and, when this branch of the business was more or less effectively dealt with by British treaties and patrols, there remained the Arab traffic to the northward. Long before Europe took a hand in the game in the fifteenth century, Asia had been steadily filching Africans from Africa to stock the plantations and staff the households and harems of the Middle East and India ; and, if the numbers taken were less, the methods were even more cruel. The British Government had not neglected this field of its crusade against the Trade. By prohibitory regulations in British India, by agreements with the chiefs of the Arabian seaboard and especially by treaties with the Arab Sultan of Zanzibar, the central *entrepôt* of the Trade as a whole, a persistent effort was made to limit and control it. But the complete suppression of the Trade in this predominately Moslem area was not yet regarded as practical politics ; and the famous slave-market at Zanzibar was still packed with Africans of both sexes and all ages, awaiting purchase and transportation over the Arabian Sea.

When Livingstone entered the field, the Arab Slave Trade was beginning to penetrate further westwards than it had ever done before, and he was shocked to discover that, not long before his arrival, his friendly Makololo had become involved in it. They had combined with a neighbouring tribe to raid another tribe for slaves wherewith to purchase firearms from the Arabs. The story of West Africa —inter-tribal warfare, devastation, depopulation—was beginning to be told again in the very centre of the continent, and what was the use of suppressing the scourge in the West if it was allowed to spread over from the East ? To Livingstone it seemed that the need for action was urgent and that the only effectual action was to revive in Central Africa the ' positive ' policy which had been dropped in the West since 1841. Thus the plan for a mission-station in the Batoka uplands acquired in his mind a new importance and a wider scope. It must be a settle-ment of farmers and traders as 'well as missionaries. It must be a little British ' colony.'*

It was this idea that inspired the feat of exploration which suddenly made Livingstone a famous man. The practicability of European settlement in Africa in those days was determined by two primary factors—climate and communications. Livingstone believed he had already found a healthy area : it remained to find a way to it. The path he had taken himself from the Cape across the fringes of the Kalahari Desert was clearly unsuitable. Apart from the danger of drought it was much too long. Safer and shorter access to the sea-coast, west or east, must be dis-covered, and in order to discover it Livingstone made his historic march across the width of Africa. Leaving Makolo-land at the end of 1853, he reached the Atlantic at Loanda in a little less than seven months. The return journey in 1854-55 took just a year. Those times sufficed to show how hard it was to traverse the bush-covered backlands of Angola, and towards the end of 1855 Livingstone turned east. He reached the sea at Quilimane in less than five months. He had followed, for most of the time, the course of the Zambesi. Might this not be the ideal route to the interior, a water-route far shorter and cheaper and less laborious than any land-route could be ?

With this notion in his mind Livingstone arrived in England at the end of 1856. The news of his crossing of Africa had preceded him, and he found himself the lion of the day. Universities, cities, learned societies, chambers of commerce vied with each other to do him honour. But

* Livingstone, of course, never contemplated full-scale British colonisation of the Canadian or Australian type. ' The idea of a colony in Africa,' he noted in 1864, ' as the term " colony " is usually understood, cannot be entertained. English races cannot compete in manual labour of any kind with the natives.' W. G. Blaikie, *Personal Life of David Livingstone* (6th ed., London, 1925), 279.

' the end of the geographical feat,' as he had said, ' is only
the beginning of the enterprise ' ; and more to his purpose
than the honorary degrees and the F.R.S. and the cheering
audiences was the warm sympathy accorded by the
Government to his project of establishing a colonial settlement by way of the Zambesi. Towards the end of 1857
it was announced that £5000 was to be spent on a
Government expedition to explore the Zambesi valley
under Livingstone's command.

2

THE Zambesi Expedition* lasted over five years (1858-
1863). It was the central experience of Livingstone's life,
but its results seemed at the time disappointing, and its
course was overshadowed by personal tragedy.

The first set-back was the discovery that the Zambesi
was too full of sandbanks and shallows to be easily navi-
gable and that well to the east of the healthy central uplands the waterway was blocked by the Kebrabasa rapids.
For a time this seemed to be more than compensated by
the exploration of the River Shiré and the discovery of
Lake Nyasa. The project of a colony on the Shiré
Highlands began to shape itself in Livingstone's mind,
and it was given substance when the United Universities
Mission to Central Africa sent out the brilliant young
C. F. Mackenzie as the first Missionary Bishop to establish
a mission-station under Livingstone's guidance. But from
that moment the fortunes of the Expedition steadily
declined, partly owing to the effect on its members of the
tropical climate and malaria, but mainly owing to the
Slave Trade. For, as the explorers ascended the Shiré,
they found that the country on both its banks, hitherto
immune from the scourge, was being torn and wasted by
slave-raids and the inter-tribal warfare they invariably

* The Expedition is described in Livingstone's *The Zambesi and its Tributaries*
(London, 1865), and in the author's *Kirk on the Zambesi* (Oxford, 1928). The former
is based on Livingstone's journal, the latter on Kirk's.

provoked. Livingstone and Mackenzie themselves were involved in a skirmish with the militant Ajawa—the first time, the former sadly commented, that he had been attacked by Africans and forced in self-defence to fight them. And it soon became clear that there was no means of stopping the spread of strife and pillage throughout the area in which the mission-station had been founded. When the explorers made their last trip up the Shiré, the results of the slave-raids were hideously apparent—cornfields reduced to a wilderness, emaciated natives by the river-side, children starving to death, corpses floating downstream.

It was not surprising, therefore, though Livingstone deplored it, that after Mackenzie's death (to be recorded presently) his successor, Bishop Tozer, decided to withdraw his mission from the mainland altogether and locate it for the time being at Zanzibar. Nor was it surprising that the Foreign Office similarly decided in 1863 to recall the Expedition. It had lasted much longer and cost much more than had been anticipated, and as regards its primary task of exploration it had by now done all it seemed likely to do. Livingstone, naturally enough, was deeply disappointed and dejected. He could not know that his discovery of Nyasaland was to lead before long not only to the foundation of missionary and trading settlements beside the Lake but to the establishment of a British protectorate. All he could see was the frustration of his hopes and the abandonment of all the fine fertile country he had been the first white man to penetrate to the horrors of the Slave Trade.

And that country was the grave of more than his hopes. His friend and comrade, Mackenzie, sickened of malaria on his way down the Shiré in 1862 ; by a fatal mischance his stock of the indispensable quinine was lost when his canoe ran on a shoal and overturned : within a fortnight he was dead. Three of the six missionaries who had accompanied him also died. ' This will hurt us all,' said Livingstone, when he heard of Mackenzie's death ; but a far heavier

blow soon fell. His wife, Mary, had come out to join him
—so bright seemed the Expedition's prospects—but she
got no farther than Shupanga on the Lower Zambesi when,
in April 1862, she too succumbed to malaria. 'For the
first time in my life,' wrote Livingstone in his private
journal, ' I feel willing to die.'

On his march across Africa Livingstone had been
accompanied by Africans only, and the record of it, therefore, had been Livingstone's alone—that fascinating ' best-
seller,' *Missionary Travels and Researches in South Africa.* Of
the Zambesi Expedition also Livingstone published his
own account, *The Zambesi and its Tributaries* ; but this
time there were white men with him, the members of the
Expedition and the staff of the Mission ; and the journals
some of them kept—especially John Kirk's*—and the
letters they wrote home supplement Livingstone's narrative with an invaluable body of evidence, most of which is
now available to students of African history.

What, then, is the picture of Livingstone's personality
which emerges from the record ? On all the major points,
of course, it is the same Livingstone who had already shown
the world what he was like. The qualities which had
enabled him to do what he had done on the fringes of the
Kalahari Desert and in the wild backlands of Angola stand
out again in high relief—his faith, his courage, his strength
of will, his humanity, his powers of endurance. There is
scarcely a page of his private journal which does not betray
his unshakable belief that, wherever he went, he was
watched and guided by his Maker. ' You know,' he wrote
to a friend after the discovery of the Shiré Highlands, ' how
I have been led on from one step to another by the overruling providence of the great Parent, as I believe, in
order to [achieve] a great good for Africa.'[1] Expressions
of this faith will recur from time to time in the pages of
this book, couched often in a language which has grown a

* The manuscript of this has been presented by his son, Lt.-Col. J. W. C. Kirk,
to the Bodleian.

little strange to modern ears. But the reader must not be misled. When Livingstone prays aloud, as it were, in his journal, he is utterly unselfconscious. He is not ranting; still less, of course, is he a humbug; he is just an honest mid-Victorian Scot of humble parentage and simple up-bringing, who has no doubt that God means him to do what he is doing and will help him to do it. And if the conviction that his life was thus dedicated to Africa was strengthened as those years in Zambesia went by, so also was his belief that it would not last long. As early as 1852, on his second journey to Makolololand, he had asked: ' Am I on my way to die?'[1] And the appeal with which he ended his famous lecture at Cambridge in 1857 had been linked with the same mystical presentiment. ' I know that in a few years I shall be cut off in that country which is now open; do not let it be shut again.'[2] More than once in the course of the Zambesi Expedition this sombre note is repeated. Three weeks after his wife's death in 1862 he comments in his journal on the beautiful surroundings of her grave and reflects that in the course of his journeying he may have passed the spot which was to be his own last resting-place. ' I have often wished that it might be in some far-off still deep forest, where I may sleep sweetly till the resurrection morn.'[3] Again, a few months later: ' I suppose that I shall die in these uplands, and somebody will carry out the plan I have longed to put into practice. I have been thinking a great deal since the departure of my beloved one about the regions whither she has gone. . . . There will be work there as well as here.'[4] Again in 1863: ' I feel very often that I have not long to live, and say " My dear children, I leave you. Be manly Christians, and never do a mean thing. Be honest to men, and to the Almighty One." '[5]

In this profound faith in the working of God's will on earth and in the life to come his courage and his deter-mination were rooted. ' He did not know what fear was,' said his lieutenant, Kirk, who of all his companions stood nearest him in strength of mind and body; and no leader of less unflinching resolution could have kept the Expedition going so long through all its ups and downs. He sometimes took the most formidable risks in order to reach the goal he had set himself. Nor would he listen to any plea of caution or even of common sense when once he had made up his stubborn mind. ' If I risk nothing,' he said on one such occasion, ' I shall gain nothing.'[1]

To Livingstone's humanity, likewise, to his gentleness with Africans and his tact in dealing with them, there is ample witness in the story of the Expedition. In the instructions Livingstone drafted for its members, no obligation was more clearly and forcibly expressed than that of ' treating the people with kindness ' and exercising ' the utmost forbearance' towards them. Guns would be carried, but mainly for the purpose of obtaining food and scientific specimens. ' It is hoped that we may never have occasion to use our arms for protection from the natives, but the best security from attack consists in upright conduct.'[2] Livingstone's regret in being forced to open fire on the Ajawa has already been recorded ; and it is worth noting here how fully Kirk shared his leader's feelings. Once, on the River Rovuma, the boat in which the two of them were sitting was fired on by some robber tribesmen, four bullets passing through the sail. Seeing a couple of them waiting to let fly at a point where the current would bring the boat close to the bank, Kirk shot one of them dead. It was an act of self-defence, yet it is clear from Kirk's account of it that the taking of a life, which he had never done before and never did again, lay hardly on his conscience.[3] And it may be observed in passing that almost all the great British explorers of Africa showed the same reluctance to use their rifles against Africans even in a dangerous situation.[4] It would have been better for the repute of the European peoples in Africa, at that time and after, if every white man who went there had shared those scruples.

Lastly, while the Zambesi Expedition gave further proof of its leader's unusual capacity for physical endurance, it also showed that the strongest white man cannot work hard in the Tropics for years at a stretch without paying for it. Unquestionably those five years told on Livingstone's physique. He had frequent bouts of malaria, a tiresome attack of eczema, and, more disquieting, several attacks of dysentery, the last of them serious. His natural powers of recuperation, however, were not as yet abated ; and for most of the time he was as full of energy, as tireless, as contemptuous of tropical conditions as he had always been. In one of his letters Mackenzie took, so to speak, a snap-shot of him, climbing the Shiré highlands, which readers of the forthcoming pages of this book may profitably keep in mind. ' You would like to see our picturesque appear-ance on the march . . . Livingstone in his jacket and trousers of blue serge and his blue cloth cap. . . . I with trousers of Oxford grey and a coat like a shooting coat, a broad-rimmed wideawake with white cover, which Livingstone laughs at, but which, all the same, keeps the sun off. *He* is a salamander. . . .'[1] Another letter con-tains this little masterpiece of description—' Livingstone tramping along with a steady, heavy tread which kept one in mind that he had walked across Africa.'[2]

The main difference between that walk across Africa and the Zambesi Expedition was that on the former, Livingstone had been alone with his Makololo and on the latter he had six companions of his own race. And he had not been long on the Zambesi before he began to regret this difference. To begin with, he felt that he could have gone faster alone. Kirk excepted, the other members of the party were by no means his equals in physical strength: they could not keep up his pace. When, moreover, danger had to be faced, he could not hazard the lives of others as fearlessly as he hazarded his own. And there was another reason for his discomfort. He was a born leader of men, but of black men, not of white. His solitary life had made him shy and silent among his own kind, and he seems to have been altogether lacking in the good leader's

ability to combine tact with firmness, to share his mind
with his subordinates, to imbue their comradeship with
faith in himself and in one another. This was doubly
unfortunate in the circumstances of the Expedition—the
delays and disappointments and the sense of frustration
they provoked, the psychological effects of the tropical
climate and of the fever which attacked them all from time
to time, the strain of living, year after year, so close together
and so far from home. Livingstone himself, like lesser
mortals, was brusque and moody when he was unwell or
galled by some exasperating hitch in his plans. Kirk
jotted down a delightful comment on this theme during a
rough voyage between the Zambesi and the Rovuma.
'Dr. L. is uncomfortable at sea and looks so. When the
weather gets foul or anything begins to go wrong, it is
well to give him a wide berth, most especially when he
sings to himself. But the kind of air is some indication. If
it is " The Happy Land," then look out for squalls and
stand clear. If " Scots wha hae," then there is some grand
vision of discovery before his mind.'[1] But it was not
mainly Livingstone's fault that the Expedition proved to
be, as Kirk put it, ' an unfortunate expedition for quarrels.'
The worst misfit among the six men Livingstone had chosen
for his staff was his own brother Charles. It was he who
began all the quarrels—with Bedingfeld, the naval officer,
with Baines, the artist and storekeeper, with Thornton, the
mineralogist. It was Charles who persuaded his brother
that Baines—unmethodical, careless, unselfish, loyal,
plucky Baines—was a petty thief.[2] 'Although Dr. L.,'
Kirk notes, ' may know the truth of his brother's insinuations . . . still they have a powerful influence as I have
more than once observed,'[3] Lastly, while David's bearing
towards other members of the party was sometimes stiff
and cold, it was only with Charles that on more than one
occasion he completely lost his temper.[4]

The personal discord in his little party, the quarrels and
the scenes, and his own incapacity to keep the peace helped
to convince Livingstone that, while companions might be

needed for river-transport or for intensive scientific research,
he could do the primary job of exploring best alone and
best on foot. There were other reasons, of course. During
the last gloomy months on the Shiré, Livingstone frankly
discussed the subject with E. D. Young, an ex-naval officer,
who had joined the Expedition just when it had begun to
peter out. ' Constantly,' Young relates, ' has he asserted
his belief that for a man to succeed as a traveller in Africa
he should go unaccompanied by other white men.' A
party, however small, is encumbered with extra baggage,
excites more suspicion among the natives, and is liable to
constant halts owing to the sickness of one or other of its
members.[1] All sound reasons for Livingstone preferring
solitude ; but it was the personal reason, the friction with
his companions, that, more than any other, made him
wish at times he was alone again with his Makololo.

That does not mean that Livingstone was at odds with
all his party, that he kept himself to himself, that he had
no real friends. With one of the missionaries, Horace
Waller, he had become acquainted at home, and in Africa
the acquaintance ripened into intimacy. With Waller,
who was nearly twenty years younger than Livingstone,
it was a case of pure hero-worship ; and the older man
responded with all the warmth of heart that lay beneath
his outward stiffness and reserve. His letters to Waller are
full of affectionate badinage. He ' rags ' him for his
bachelordom, his decorum, and especially, as a good
Scottish Presbyterian should, for his Anglican addiction to
bishops. And there was one member of the Expedition,
other than his brother, with whom, if he was not quite so
intimate as with Waller, he made a close and lasting
friendship in those testing days in Africa. John Kirk will
figure prominently in this book, and a few words of introduction must be accorded him.

He was born, a ' son of the manse,' in Forfarshire in
1832—the same year as Waller—and he went in due course
to Edinburgh University where he obtained his M.D. and
also acquired an exceptional knowledge of botany. After

serving for a year as a resident at the Royal Infirmary, with Joseph Lister as a colleague, he was one of the fifty chosen from the hundreds who answered the call for volunteers to make good the shocking shortcomings revealed in the first winter of the Crimean War. Back at home in 1857, he was thinking of deserting medicine for botany and actually on the point of standing for a vacant chair of natural history at a Canadian university when he received Livingstone's offer of the double post of medical officer and botanist on his staff. He had no domestic ties. He had all the scientist's zest for the exploration of a new world and all the young man's liking for a venture into the unknown. He accepted the appointment at once, little knowing that it was to prove the first step in a great career, that he was destined, like Livingstone, to spend the best part of his life in Africa and to render a service to its people only less valuable than Livingstone's.*

He proved his quality on the Zambesi and the Shiré. Of all the little band he was the only one, besides its leader, who stood the physical and moral test from beginning to end. However tense the atmosphere, it seems to have been as difficult to quarrel with the unassuming young Scot as it was easy to be friends with him. All his colleagues, except Charles Livingstone, were on the best of terms with him throughout. So were the staff of the Mission. 'As for Dr. Kirk,' wrote the valiant Mackenzie in a letter home, 'we are the greatest possible cronies.'[1] One of the Mission's annual reports spoke of the professional aid which Kirk rendered as 'a kindness which will never be forgotten.'[2] Even with Charles Livingstone Kirk never had an open quarrel, though he thoroughly disliked him. 'The character of the two brothers,' he observes, 'is in no respect alike'—the one 'straightforward, honest, rather shy, the other . . .' That the good man could be so influenced in his judgment of others by the bad was what surprised Kirk most in Livingstone's behaviour through

---

* Kirk's work at Zanzibar is described in the author's *The Exploitation of East Africa* (London, 1939).

all those years. He noted, too, as has been seen, that he was sometimes irritable and morose, and he saw, what was plain to see, that he could not, as he put it, ' get on with white men under him.' But he never lost his deep respect for him and never wavered in his loyalty. When the two years he had agreed to serve were up, it was Livingstone's wish that kept him on the Zambesi. ' Dr. L. desired me to remain,' says the diary ; ' I had intended going home, but at once agreed to stop.'[1] And in the later stages of the Expedition, when Kirk was getting thoroughly worn out and more and more desperately homesick, he only stayed because Livingstone begged him to stay and because he believed that Livingstone really needed him. In all those years they had no serious dispute till, not long before the end, Livingstone—incited, one suspects, by his brother— expressed his dissatisfaction with the results of Kirk's botanical researches.[2] Kirk firmly defended himself and Livingstone withdrew his charges. Thus the tie between the older and the younger man, which had stood so many strains, remained happily unbroken ; and, as it chanced, just before they parted, it was knitted even tighter than before. It had been at last decided that Kirk and Charles Livingstone should go home, and they were on the point of starting for the coast when ' the Doctor,' who was staying behind with Young to wind up what remained of the Expedition, fell ill. It was a serious attack of dysentery, more serious than any he had yet had, and beyond his power to cope with by himself. ' I wish I were off,' wrote Kirk ; but of course he stayed and tended Livingstone till, in three weeks' time, he was sufficiently recovered to be safely left. Conceivably Kirk had saved his life as he had certainly saved the lives of more than one member of the Mission party ; and the letters which he received from Livingstone while waiting at Quilimane for a ship were warmer and more intimate than any of his previous com- munications.[3] Now fully convalescent, Livingstone writes at length about the details of the daily round, freely dis- cusses the plans and character of the new bishop, reports

the news he has had of his family in Scotland, and so
forth, ' Ever yours with sincere affection, David Livingstone.'

3

BEFORE returning to England himself Livingstone embarked
on a last adventure. He had to dispose of the Expedition's
launch, the *Lady Nyassa*, and, since the best market seemed
to be Bombay, he decided, without the slightest hesitation,
to sail the boat himself across the Indian Ocean. She was
a seaworthy craft, but only some forty feet long, with a
small steam-engine amidships and an awning over the
stern.* Into this cockleshell Livingstone packed three
white men besides himself—a stoker, a carpenter and a
sailor—seven African volunteers from the Zambesi country
who had never seen the sea, and two Waiyau boys in their
early ' teens,' Chuma and Wikitani by name, who had
been rescued from the slave-raiders in the Shiré highlands.
The voyage from Zanzibar was expected to take about
eighteen days ; but, since he carried only fourteen tons
of coal, Livingstone was bound to trust mainly to his sail,
and for long periods he was becalmed among the porpoises
and sharks and flying fish ; and it was not till the forty-
fifth day that ' the forest of masts ' was seen looming
through the haze in Bombay harbour. ' We had sailed
over 2500 miles. The vessel was so small that no one
noticed our arrival.'[1]

In the summer of 1864 Livingstone was home at last,
and again he found himself the lion of the day. The great
ladies begged him to honour their drawing-rooms. The
great men wanted to shake his hand. He dined with the
old Prime Minister who of all British statesmen since
Wilberforce had fought hardest and longest to kill the

---

* A photograph taken by Kirk of the *Lady Nyassa* afloat on the Zambesi is
reproduced in *Kirk on the Zambesi*, 237.

Slave Trade, and attended Lady Palmerston's reception
(' My lady very gracious—gave me tea herself.') He found
Russell ' very cold as all the Russells are,' and Gladstone
' very affable.'[1] But, as soon as he could, he broke away
from London to Scotland and his family. It was six years
since he had seen them. ' Mother did not know me at
first.' Nor did he recognise his eldest son, Thomas ; ' he
has grown so much.' His third son, Oswell, now nearly
13, was also there, and his elder daughter Agnes, ' very
tall,' and, last but not least, five-year-old Anna Mary,
" a nice little girl," whom he now saw for the first time.[2]
In September he lectured to the British Association at
Bath, and then settled down to write his account of the
Zambesi Expedition. Most of the work was done at a place
with amusingly incongruous associations—Newstead Abbey,
now the home of his old friend, W. F. Webb, once, more
notoriously, Byron's. Charles Livingstone collaborated—
his name appeared on the title-page as joint author with
his brother—and Kirk was also called in to help. It proved
a fairly long task, and the book, a stout volume of over
six hundred pages, was not finished till the spring of 1865.
It was as warmly greeted and as widely read as its prede-
cessor.

Meantime Livingstone had been chafing to get back to
Africa. Physically he was not the man he had been in
1858. Those years of toil and disease had induced internal
trouble for which a surgeon he consulted advised an operation ; but major operations in those days were more
dangerous than they are now, and it was decided not to
risk it. In any case Livingstone refused to worry about his
health. He was only 52, after all, and the idea of his
settling down quietly at home was inconceivable. Nor did
he greatly care whether or not the Government continued
to employ him. ' I don't know,' he had written to Waller
at the close of the Zambesi Expedition, ' whether I am to
go on the shelf or not. If I do, I make Africa the shelf.'[3]
Back to Africa, then, it was always certain he would go.
And, had he wanted a new incentive, he would have found

it in the great feats of African exploration which had been achieved during the last few years northwards of the area in which he himself had been engaged. Early in 1858, about a month before he had sailed from England for the Zambesi, Burton and Speke, pushing inland by way of Unyanyembe, had reached Lake Tanganyika at Ujiji, and in the summer of the same year Speke had seen and named Lake Victoria Nyanza. At the end of 1860 Speke had returned to this neighbourhood accompanied by Grant ; and on July 28, 1862—the year of tragedy on the Zambesi —they had stood at the Ripon Falls a few miles below the point at which the principal stream of the Nile flows out from Lake Victoria.* Then, in 1864, a few months before Livingstone came home, Baker had found what seemed to be a second source of the Nile in Lake Albert. These were great discoveries, but they had laid the heart of Africa only half-open. No one yet knew where the central watershed lay. Did the Nile enter Lakes Victoria and Albert in the south as well as leave them in the north ? If so, its true source or sources might lie far southwards, perhaps in the latitude of Lake Tanganyika. And Tanganyika itself, might it not discharge its overflow northwards or westwards ? And somewhere in that area surely the source of the Congo, still quite unknown, was to be found.

These were highly exciting questions for any one with the lust for exploration in his blood ; and, long before the book was done, Livingstone had made up his mind to have a try at solving them. The same idea had occurred to others. At the beginning of 1865, Livingstone's old friend, Sir Roderick Murchison, President of the Royal Geographical Society, which had taken the lead in organising the Burton-Speke-Grant expeditions, wrote to ask him about his plans and wishes. He described the question of the watershed as one ' of intense geographical interest,' and suggested that Livingstone might be able to settle it by cutting across from the upper Rovuma to Lake Tanganyika

* Speke came home in 1863 and accidentally shot himself in 1864. The funeral was near Bath at the time of the British Association's meeting, and Livingstone attended it.

and thence exploring westward. This would be a ' purely
geographical ' enterprise, and ' if you do not like to under-
take it, I am of opinion that no one, after yourself, is so
fitted to carry it out as Dr. Kirk.'[1] Livingstone replied
that he had already decided to make just such a journey
as Murchison had proposed, but that he could not go as
a scientist and nothing else. He must have intercourse
with the people and do what he could ' by talking to
enlighten them on the Slave Trade and give them some
idea of our religion.'[2] With this Murchison could not
quarrel, and in a few weeks' time the project had taken
solid shape. In the preface to his book Livingstone
announced that he was about to make ' another attempt
to open Africa to civilising influences.' ' I propose to go
inland, north of the territory which the Portuguese in
Europe claim, and endeavour to commence that system
on the East which has been so eminently successful on the
West Coast ; a system combining the repressive efforts of
H.M. cruisers with lawful trade and Christian missions.
. . . I hope to ascend the Rovuma or some other river
north of Cape Delgado, and, in addition to my other work,
shall strive, by passing along the northern end of Lake
Nyassa and round the southern end of Lake Tanganyika,
to ascertain the watershed of that part of Africa.'[3]

The Foreign Office was prepared to back this project
on the cheap. Livingstone was to be given consular
authority to deal with African chiefs anywhere between
the frontiers of Portuguese East Africa and Abyssinia ; but
Russell refused to promise him a salary till he should have
settled down somewhere, and the Government's contribu-
tion to the finances of the expedition was only £500. The
Royal Geographical Society provided another £500. James
Young, who had begun a lifelong friendship with Livingstone when he taught him the use of mechanical tools
at Glasgow University and had since acquired fame and
fortune by the preparation of petroleum for domestic use,*
gave £1000. That was all, and, of course, not nearly

* Hence nicknamed by Livingstone ' Sir Paraffin.'

enough. Such parsimony, indeed, can only be explained by the belief, apparently shared by Livingstone himself, that the projected journey would not take very long—a year or two, perhaps. Nor did Livingstone worry then— or ever—about money. He had crossed Africa with nothing in his purse, and the new venture was to be quite unlike the last. Writing to tell Kirk about it all, ' I would be delighted,' he said, ' if we could go together, but I fear the money won't reach a salary.' Couldn't Kirk try to raise it in some other quarter ? Failing him, ' I would rather go alone than take any one untried. I suffered too much from Bedingfeld, etc.' And he would travel light : he wouldn't take ' many goods . . . nor go in grand array.'[1]

Kirk's reply to this letter has not been preserved, but it seems improbable that, even if the salary had been available, he would have wanted to go. For he had fallen in love, and in the course of this year he became engaged. With no money of his own he could not afford to marry till he had obtained a regular and reasonably secure means of livelihood, and he was planning to start on the professional career for which he had been preparing when Livingstone diverted him to the Zambesi. Clearly he was not so free now as he had been then to go wandering in Africa with no certainty whatever as to what his prospects would be after it. In any case nothing came of the proposal, and from what has been said above it seems probable that, however much he liked and trusted the young fellow-Scot, Livingstone was not sorry to be setting out alone.

He left England in mid-August. Kirk and Waller went down to Folkestone to say good-bye. ' This is very kind,' noted Livingstone in his diary. ' The Lord puts it into their hearts to show kindness, and blessed is his name.'[2] They never saw him again.

4

LIVINGSTONE went first to Bombay where he was warmly
greeted by the Governor, Sir Bartle Frere, one of the
ablest and most high-minded of the British proconsuls of
his day. For the last sixty years the Bombay Government
had been closely concerned with the Arab Slave Trade,
not only in preventing its victims being smuggled into
British India but in combating it at its source ; and
mainly for the latter purpose it had maintained since 1841
a Political Agent at Zanzibar, who also acted as British
Consul. Naturally, therefore, Frere had watched Livingstone's operations in East Africa with the deepest interest
and was anxious to help in his new enterprise. ' The
Governor is a brick,' wrote Livingstone to Waller, ' and
will do all he can for me.'[1]

There were two main things to be done at Bombay.
First there was the disposal of the *Lady Nyassa*. Livingstone
was hoping that its sale would greatly strengthen his
meagre financial resources ; but, though it had cost over
£6000, he got only £2300 for it ; and unfortunately he
was advised to invest the money in the shares of an Indian
bank which shortly afterwards crashed.

His second task was to recruit the personnel for his
expedition—a matter of crucial, of supreme importance.
For the problem which confronted an explorer of Livingstone's day was not so much the problem of moving himself
from place to place—though that alone might be none too
easy at times—as the problem of moving other things as
well. He had to carry with him not only his tent, his
clothes, his arms, his pots and pans, and such necessary
luxuries as tea and coffee and sugar and, above all,
medicine, but also the bales of cloth and bags of beads
wherewith to purchase—since there was virtually no
current coin—his supplies of fresh food and, at need, his
right of way. And since baggage-animals were almost

useless—they suffered too much from variations of climate
and from marauding lions and leopards at night, while in
areas infested by the tsetse fly they could not live—nearly all
these goods and chattels had to be carried on men's heads;
so that the length of the traveller's journey was determined
not only by the length of his purse in terms of cloth and
beads, but also by the number of porters he could hire—
and their efficiency. A hundred porters might be of less
use than ten, if they were lazy and disobedient, if they
dawdled on the path, if they damaged or pilfered from
their loads, if they distrusted their leader or shied from
the dangers into which he led them, if in the last resort
they simply ran away. And that they should act otherwise
was, after all, a good deal to expect of them, however much
they wanted their wages and desired to honour their bond.
It meant confiding themselves, body and soul, to a strange
white man who led them far from home into unknown
places for a purpose which they could hardly understand.
Could even his magic powers be trusted to protect them
from hostile tribes, to feed them when supplies ran short,
to bring them back safely in the end to their wives and
children ?

Livingstone's previous experience in this vital matter
had been highly encouraging, but the circumstances had
been quite different from what they would be now. The
men who had followed him so devotedly across Africa had
not been hired at a coastal town. His march had started
from Makololand, and his Makololo porters had been
raw tribesmen who, after discussion in the tribal council,
had been deputed to accompany the explorer to the coast
and back.[1] On the Zambesi the long hauls had been made
by water ; and most of the few porters needed had again
been Makololo. But this time those faithful tribesmen were
out of reach, and Livingstone could scarcely hope to find
other Africans as simple and unspoiled and as ready to
follow him into the unknown. His first recruits, as it
happened, were not Africans of any kind. At Frere's
suggestion he applied to the Bombay Marine Battalion,

and twelve sepoys with a *havildar* in charge were permitted
to volunteer to go to Africa under Livingstone's command
on the same sort of terms as if they had been dispatched on
a military expedition oversea. Livingstone next visited the
school at Nassick which consisted mostly of African boys
who had been rescued from slavery and were being trained
to earn a living as free men. ' I found some of the Africans,'
he wrote to his daughter Agnes, ' to have come from parts
I know—one from Ndonde on the Rovuma—and all had
learned some handicraft, besides reading and writing etc.,
and it is probable that some of them will go back to their
own country with me.'[1] But most of the ' Nassick boys '
seem to have been contented with their lot. Only nine of
them took the chance of going home. ' Two or three are
Ajawas,' Livingstone told Waller : ' I have taken every
pains to let them know that work, not play, is intended.'[2]

Livingstone was also to take back with him the two
lads, Chuma and Wikitani, who had shared in his long and
perilous voyage from Zanzibar. When he left Bombay for
England in 1864, he had entrusted them to the care of
Dr. Wilson of the Scottish Free Church Mission, and he
was delighted to learn how well they had done in his
absence. They could read simple English, like Aesop's
Fables, and ' speak it too, but not very well.' Waller had
not forgotten them since the Zambesi days and had sent
Livingstone a gift of money for them. ' As they wish to
be baptised,' wrote the latter, ' the Dr. consulted me, and,
as they have a general knowledge of our faith and desire
it, I see no reason to object. . . . Chuma invested in a
suit of greys with your money, and Wiko in a coat and
blanket. They are to write to you by next mail. Chuma
goes with me as servant up to Government House on
Monday next. They have both given great satisfaction in
every way. . . . Chuma is a very sharp fellow ; never got
into any quarrel at school ; I expect his appearance put
the fear of death into the Hindoos, but Dr. Wilson thinks
it is his goodness.'[3]

So much for the human personnel ; but Livingstone

had also decided to make an experiment in animal transport. ' I intend to take some buffaloes as beasts of burden,'
he wrote to his friend A. H. Layard at the Foreign Office,
' and I am indulging the hope that they may withstand
the poison of the tsetse, and if they do we shall confer a
great boon on East Africa. The brutes are as like our wild
African ones as two peas except the horns. . . . The men
of the Marine Batn., being Indians, know how to manage
them.'[1]

All that was needed now was some African porters, and
Livingstone was intending to obtain these at Zanzibar
which he meant to make the starting-point of his expedition. There was more than one reason for this choice of
a base. About twenty miles from the coast and three
hundred north of the Rovuma, it was the nearest important
town outside Portuguese territory to the scene of his
operations. It was also the station of a British official who,
since he was Consul as well as Political Agent, was in
regular communication both with the Bombay Government and with the Foreign Office. He could be counted
on, therefore, to do all he could to keep Livingstone in
touch with the outer world, to send letters and supplies
after him, and to forward his own letters home. Zanzibar,
moreover, was the seat of the Sultan's government ; and,
though the present Sultan, Seyyid Majid, had less prestige
and authority than his great father, Seyyid Said,* he
exercised a kind of suzerainty over the neighbouring mainland and claimed, and usually obtained, the loyal obedience
of those of his Arab subjects who were trading there. It
was desirable, therefore, that Livingstone should secure
the Sultan's approval of his invasion of his African
' dominions ' and be able to rely on his support in his
relations with the Arabs he might meet inland.

It chanced that, while Livingstone was at Bombay,
Colonel Playfair, who held the double post at Zanzibar,
had asked to be relieved of it on grounds of health, and

---

* For the life and achievements of this outstanding Arab prince, see R. Coupland,
East Africa and its Invaders (Oxford, 1938).

the Government was considering the appointment of his successor. When Livingstone heard of it, he instantly thought of Kirk. It was, indeed, precisely for a position of that kind somewhere on the East African coast that he had been urging Kirk's claims in official quarters in London. ' I wish Kirk could get that post,' he now wrote to Oswell, his old companion of Kalahari days: ' he would be invaluable there.'[1] But it was not to be expected that the Bombay Government, to whom the Foreign Office was accustomed to leave the choice, would prefer the young stranger to one of their own tried officers ; and in due course Dr. G. E. Seward, the agency surgeon, was appointed to act in Playfair's place. This left the surgeon-ship vacant, and so, as it happened, opened the door to what was to prove in course of time Kirk's great career. ' Many happy returns of this day to you, my dear Kirk,' wrote Livingstone on New Year's Day, 1866. ' The Governor sent for me yesterday. . . . He said that he wished to ask me about you. He knew that I had always spoken very handsomely about you, but there were some-times private circumstances in a man's character which, unless called upon to reveal, no one would think of men-tioning ; there may be something (here I put in the word " cranky "), yes, something that, though not prominent, might render him an inconvenient public servant. I replied, in terms that I need not repeat, that I knew no defect of character or temper ; you got on well with people, but were firm in doing your duty, etc. ; and I felt certain that from your hatred of the Slave Trade and knowledge of the whole subject you would be invaluable at Zanzibar. He said that it was a great recommendation that I wished you to be there, and he would have much pleasure in telegraphing to you to-day.'[2]

Kirk was tempted by the offer. He was drawn to Africa by the same threads that drew Livingstone. It was not merely the fascination which the African tropics have exerted over so many European travellers : it was the desire to take a hand in the fight with the Slave Trade—

a desire which any one of ordinary humanity who had
seen at close range what the Slave Trade was doing to the
African people was bound to feel. But would the post
solve his domestic problem ? If the salary was modest, it
was safe, and there would be prospects of promotion as
time went on. But was it fair to ask a young woman who
had never left home to start her married life in such distant
exile and so dangerous a climate ? After full discussion it
was decided to take the risk. Early in June the new agency
surgeon, now 34 years of age, arrived at Zanzibar—some
ten weeks after Livingstone had left it. In the following
spring Helen Cook came out and married him.

Thus, at the core of the growing group of Britons who
were sharing in greater or less degree in the crusade
against the Slave Trade in East Africa—ministers, proconsuls, divines, missionaries, geographers, business men,
journalists and a host of nameless folk—a little triple
alliance had been formed. Livingstone, its spearhead,
penetrating the black veil that still concealed so much of
Africa and letting in the light of public knowledge. Kirk,
his tried and trusted lieutenant, at his island base. Waller,
the closest of all the friends he had made in Africa, in
London, with his hand on all the strings of the humanitarian movement.

And now the period of waiting was nearly over. Only
the final preparations at Zanzibar remained, and four
days after his talk with Frere about Kirk Livingstone
sailed from Bombay. For the last few weeks, to judge from
his letters home, his spirits had been steadily rising. It
would be fanciful to say, in view of what we know was
coming, that he was ' fey.' But he was full of confidence
—if he dared to hum at Government House, it was
certainly ' Scots wha hae '—and full of fun. ' My dearly
beloved Waller,' he writes, '. . . Walla means " a fellow "
here ; buggywalla, for instance, is a cabby, patiwalla a
flunkey. I make no comment.' And he goes on to have a
ribald fling at Bishop Tozer whom he never forgave for
deserting the mainland and whose ecclesiastical get-up—

'holding fast to his crozier and swathed in his muslins'
—irritated him. 'You may fancy me falling into Tozer's
arms [at Zanzibar] and kissing him. He has turned over
a new leaf; scrubs the boys with his sleeves tucked up.'
'You will never be a man till you are wedded,' he writes
in another letter to Waller. 'I only wish I had you *in
extremis* and a nice girl willing to take you by the hand.
Wouldn't I marry you! . . . If offended, you might
expose me in a novel, *Married above him*.'[1] And so on. . . .

5

LIVINGSTONE sailed from Bombay in the *Thule*, a steamship
which the Bombay Government was giving to the Sultan,
and he had been commissioned to make the formal pre-
sentation, 'to show,' as he says, 'in how much estimation
I was held and thereby induce the Sultan to forward my
enterprise.' He also bore a letter in which Frere requested
Majid to 'direct every aid to be given within your Highness' dominions' to Livingstone's philanthropic designs,
viewed as they were 'with the warmest interest by Her
Majesty's Government both in India and in England.'
Livingstone arrived at Zanzibar on January 28, and paid
his first official call at the Palace next day. 'His Highness
met us at the bottom of the stair, and, as he shook hands,
a brass band, which he got at Bombay, blared forth " God
save the Queen." This was excessively ridiculous, but I
maintained sufficient official dignity. After coffee and
sherbet we came away, and the wretched band now struck
up " The British Grenadiers " as if the fact of my being
only 5 feet 8 . . . ought not to have suggested " Wee
Willie Winkie " as more appropriate.'[2]
   The Sultan can scarcely have been overpleased at
Livingstone's return to East Africa and his openly avowed
objective. Many of his subjects were deeply engaged in the
Slave Trade. A large part of his own revenue was derived

from the customs dues it paid. But, like Said before him, Majid did not underrate the value of British friendship, and his courteous reply to Frere's request was all that could be desired. 'Your honoured letter borne by Dr. Livingstone duly reached me, and all that you said about him I understood. I will show him respect, give him honour, and help him in all his affairs ; and that I have already done this I hope he will tell you.'[1] And he certainly did the most helpful thing he could do. He gave Livingstone a signed document, a sort of passport, calling on any subject of his who might come into contact with the bearer to render him any assistance he might need.

Seven weeks elapsed before H.M.S. *Penguin* arrived from its southward station to take Livingstone to the Rovuma. It was a tedious time—its only relief the ' very great kindness ' of Dr. Seward and his wife—and Livingstone's impatience was whetted by the disagreeable conditions of life at Zanzibar. He was particularly disgusted at the lack of any sort of sanitation and at the stench arising from the filth on the beach. ' At night it is so gross and crass one might cut out a slice and manure a garden with it.' And he hated the lazy self-indulgence of a community that battened on the Slave Trade. ' It is the old, old way of living—eating, drinking, sleeping ; sleeping, drinking, eating. . . . Slaving-dhows* coming and slaving-dhows going away.'[2] One day he visited the famous slave-market. He found about three hundred slaves exposed for sale, most of whom he recognised from their faces and markings as coming from the Nyasa country. ' One woman said that she had heard of our passing up Lake Nyasa in a boat, but she did not see me. . . . All who have grown up seemed ashamed at being hawked about for sale. The teeth are examined, the cloth lifted up to examine the lower limbs, and a stick is thrown for the slave to bring and thus exhibit his paces. Some are dragged through the crowd by the hand, and the price called out incessantly. . . .'

* Arab sailing ships.

Meantime Livingstone was filling up his complement of servants and porters. Three of them were men who had worked for him on the Zambesi and who chanced to be at Zanzibar—Susi and Amoda, from the Shupanga district, who had been employed to cut fuel for the *Pioneer*, and Musa, a Moslem native of Johanna, one of the Comoro Islands, who had served in the *Lady Nyassa* on her voyage up the Shiré. The last-named had not earned a good character. E. D. Young, indeed, who had him under his orders for more than a year, described him roundly as a liar and a thief.[1] And that or something like it had long been the general reputation of Johanna men. Captain Owen, surveying East African waters in 1823, described them as 'little thieves, great rogues, and enormous cowards.'[2] Nearly fifty years later, Burton, who always painted in strong colours, described the Comoro people, ' especially the Johanna men,' as '*facile principes* among Eastern imposters.' ' The singular scoundrels have completely mastered the knack of cajoling Europeans. . . . They are as cowardly as they are dishonest.' ' It was not without astonishment,' he adds, ' that I heard of Dr. Livingstone engaging a party of them for exploration in the African interior.'[3] But Livingstone seems to have thought that at any rate these islanders were preferable to the riff-raff of Africans at Zanzibar, morally contaminated, as he believed them all to be, by contact with the slave-ships thronging the harbour and the slave-gangs toiling on the clove plantations ; and he had written three times from Bombay to William Sunley, the British Consul at Johanna, asking him if he could get some men to go with him.[4] No reply had reached him, and the ten Johanna men, headed by Musa, whom he did obtain, were picked up at Zanzibar. A last addition to his labour-force was made after he had landed on the mainland. A local Indian trader engaged twenty-four more porters for him. That brought the total strength to sixty. And there were sixteen animals : for, besides three buffaloes and a calf, Livingstone had bought six camels, four donkeys and two mules.

One other item of Livingstone's preparations must be recorded owing to the importance that was to be attached to it later on. His new journey was not going to be a sequence of forced marches. ' We were always in too great a hurry last expedition,' he had written to Kirk before he left England.[1] He meant to establish an advanced post in the interior, and ' work quietly west ' from there. Since he might well be away from the coast for a year or two and since the cost of a caravan to carry all the supplies needed for that length of time was far beyond his resources, he planned to take a relatively small quantity with him and to have more sent up to the post from Zanzibar. For the site of the post he first thought of the highlands above the Rovuma near Lake Nyasa, but he finally decided on Ujiji. It seemed a sensible choice. It lay on Lake Tanganyika at the head of a well-known Arab trade-route which started at Bagamoyo just opposite Zanzibar and passed through the Arab trading ' colony ' at Unyanyembe. It was a longish journey, about 620 miles from the coast in a straight line and considerably more than that for caravans. Burton and Speke took eight months over it in 1857-58. But, if the way was long, at least it was well-known and—at that time—safe. Speke reported ' the Zanzibar route to Ujiji ' as ' constantly travelled over by Arabs.'[2] And Ujiji itself in his day was a bustling, flourishing place. In view of Livingstone's experience eleven years later his account of how he ' revelled in the good living afforded by the market at Ujiji ' deserves to be quoted. ' The facilities of the place giving us such a choice of food, our powers in the culinary art were tried to their fullest extent. It would be difficult to tell what dishes we did not make there. Fish of many sorts done up in all the fashions of the day—meat and fowl in every form—vegetable soups and dishes of numberless varieties—fruit-preserves, custards, custard-puddings and jellies—last, but not least, buttered crumpets and cheese—formed as fine a spread as was ever set before a king.'[3]

Clearly, it seemed, Ujiji was the right place ; and it

was even more obvious who should be commissioned to send supplies there. For many years past the business of stocking the Arab caravans going inland had been mainly in the hands of the Hindu firm of Jairam Sewji, hailing from Bombay. It was a prosperous firm and highly respectable. It added substantially to its ordinary trading profits by farming the customs revenue on the Sultan's behalf.[1] Its leading member at Zanzibar at this time was the venerable Ludha Damji whose immense wealth and snowy beard figure in several of the contemporary travel-books. The junior manager was Kooverji Valabdhas (Koorji). Livingstone's contact with them both is recorded in his journal. ' We visited an old man to-day [March 6], the richest in Zanzibar, who is to give me letters to his friends at Tanganyika, and I am trying to get a depot of goods for provisions formed there, so that when I reach it I may not be destitute. . . . I have arranged [March 18] with Koorji, a Banyan,* who farms the custom-house revenue here, to send a supply of beads, cloth, flour, tea, coffee and sugar to Ujiji on Lake Tanganyika. The Arab there, with whom one of Koorji's people will remain in charge of the goods, is called Thani bin Suelim.'[2]

Koorji's firm had a good reputation among British residents and travellers at Zanzibar. Burton bought provisions and hired a ship from him in 1857.[3] Speke employed him to obtain porters in 1860. Neither of them complained of any dishonesty or slackness. Nor was it only for the sake of the profits that these Indian traders were willing to do business with British explorers. They were mostly British subjects, having come from British India, and they were well aware how much their business owed to the protection of the British flag and how desirable it was to keep on good terms with the British authorities. Nevertheless, whatever assurances Koorji might give to Livingstone, face to face, in his office at Zanzibar, could he be trusted to carry out that vital part of the plan effi-

* The Hindu caste of traders, many of whom were settled at Zanzibar and the towns on the coast.

ciently and expeditiously when Livingstone, deep in the interior, had lost all contact with him ? It was a risk, and Livingstone, as usual, took it.

Meantime H.M.S. *Penguin* had at last arrived and its commander, Lieutenant Garforth, had at once agreed to take Livingstone down to the Rovuma. On March 18 he took leave of the Sultan. ' He offered me men to go with me, and another letter if I wished it.' Next morning the *Penguin* sailed, accompanied by a dhow in which Livingstone had stowed his little menagerie. On March 22 they anchored off the mouth of the Rovuma, and on the 24th the *Penguin* departed, leaving Livingstone and his men and his animals—the last ' all very much the worse for being knocked about in the dhow '—on the shore of Mikindani bay. The great adventure had begun. Squalid Zanzibar lay behind and forgotten. And Livingstone, his spirits once more at their highest, jotted down in his journal that well-known passage which, in the light of what was coming, provides in almost every sentence a rare example of dramatic irony.

Now that I am on the point of starting on another trip into Africa I feel quite exhilarated : when one travels with the specific object in view of ameliorating the condition of the natives any act becomes ennobled. Whether exchanging the customary civilities or arriving at a village, accepting a night's lodging, purchasing food for the party, asking for information, or answering polite African inquiries as to our objects in travelling, we begin to spread a knowledge of that people by whose agency their land will yet become enlightened and freed from the slave-trade.

The mere animal pleasure of travelling in a wild unexplored country is very great. When on lands of a couple of thousand feet, brisk exercise imparts elasticity to the muscles, fresh and healthy blood circulates through the brain, the mind works well, the eye is clear, the step is firm, and a day's exertion always makes the evening's repose thoroughly enjoyable.

We have usually the stimulus of remote chances of danger either from beasts or men. Our sympathies are drawn out towards our humble hardy companions by a community of interests and, it may be, of perils, which makes us all friends. Nothing but the most pitiable puerility would lead any manly heart to make their inferiority a theme for self-exaltation ; however, that is often done, as if with the vague idea that we can, by magnifying their deficiencies, demonstrate our immaculate perfections.

The effect of travel on a man whose heart is in the right place is that the mind is made more self-reliant : it becomes more confident of its own resources—there is greater presence of mind. The body is soon well-knit ; the muscles of the limbs grow as hard as a board and seem to have no fat ; the countenance is bronzed, and there is no dyspepsia. Africa is a most wonderful country for appetite, and it is only when one gloats over marrow bones or elephant's feet that indigestion is possible. No doubt much toil is involved, and fatigue of which travellers in the more temperate climes can form but a faint conception ; but the sweat of one's brow is no longer a curse when one works for God : it proves a tonic to the system and is actually a blessing. No one can truly appreciate the charm of repose unless he has undergone severe exertion.

The curtain is up. The tragedy has begun. The hero has made the happy self-confident opening speech which warns the audience of his approaching doom.

6

WHAT sort of country was it that Livingstone was starting to explore ?

He had first to cross the belt of more or less level land which fringes all the coast of mid-East Africa. About a hundred miles from Mikindani it rises fairly steeply to the great central plateau which stretches right across the continent from Ethiopia to the neighbourhood of the Cape. Its average height is about 3000 feet, but there are one or two blocks of still higher country, as in Kenya, and at two

or three points it throws up mountains so high that their
crests are capped with ice and snow even under the tropical
sun. A few hundred miles inland—about 200 from
Mikindani, about 600 from Bagamoyo—the plateau is
split by the so-called ' Great Rift Valley ' which, running
southwards from the Red Sea, forms the deep clefts in
which lie the chain of great inland lakes, Albert Nyanza,
Tanganyika and Nyasa.

The vegetation of all this central area is broadly
uniform. There are local varieties, of course—one of the
most curious is the arid thorny region inland from Bagamoyo which constituted, as will appear on later pages of
this book, a nasty obstacle to travellers before the railway
came and bridged it—but the general aspect of the country,
league after league, is much the same. It is mostly savannah
country, rough, droughty, infertile. Vast areas of poor
grass are interspersed with vast areas of poor woodland.
Among the mountains or on those lakes the scenery is
superb ; but elsewhere often the only beauty in the land-
scape is the radiant African light that bathes it. Sometimes, it is true, the interminable steppe or interminable
woodland is varied by the result of some slight local change
of climate—maybe a stretch of well-watered parklike
country with succulent grass and spreading trees and
browsing herds of antelope or zebra : maybe, and more
likely, a bare, sandy, stony plain, not far removed from
desert. There is little, in fact, in the eastern half of Central
Africa which accords with romantic stories of tropical
adventure. Its explorers rarely had to hack their way
through a jungle of poisonous thorns and strangling
creepers. The belts of ' rain-forest ' with its gigantic trees
and riotous undergrowth are few and narrow, and the
woods through which Livingstone made his way were
mostly little more than huge copses, growing to some
twenty feet and looking in the dry season like an endless
thicket of dead poles and sticks with now and again a
solitary evergreen to break the dull monotony.

It is only in the wet season that this kind of country is

difficult to cross on foot ; but, when the ' greater rains ' fall from March to May or the ' lesser rains ' in October or November, it becomes in places wellnigh impassable. The dry stream-beds on the hillsides are filled with raging torrents. The rivers surge furiously along and overflow their banks. Great stretches of level land are waterlogged or transformed into shallow lakes. But in the dry season the walker can make his way, slowly perhaps, if only because of the hot sun, but steadily, along the paths that wind from village to village through the wilderness. Between June and October, therefore, and again between December and February, one must imagine Livingstone plodding along those tracks, behind him a straggling line of porters with bundles on their heads, on either hand a screen of coarse grass, often rising shoulder-high, or of little leafless trees and shrubs. Of his progress in the wet season there will be more anon.

Nor were the fauna of the country an impediment to travel. The lion and the leopard, the elephant, the buffalo and the rhinoceros are not much more dangerous, if left alone, than the gazelle or the giraffe. It was a hunted and wounded lion that crunched Livingstone's shoulder away in the south in 1844. Only at night were wild beasts likely to be troublesome, and only then if the camp fire was allowed to burn low. The insects, indeed, were a far more serious nuisance, the swarms of ants and flies and midges and mosquitoes—especially, in certain areas, the tsetse fly, bearing death to baggage-animals, and, in all moist low-lying places, the anopheles mosquito, inoculating humans with malaria.

And, lastly, the people. In all the area covered by Livingstone's explorations the native population belonged to the great negro race, the Bantu, which inhabits most of Central Africa. In a few districts—Uganda, for example, or Usambara—a relatively elaborate political and social system existed at this time ; but, wherever Livingstone went, the natives were living a primitive tribal life, some of them in more or less isolated groups, others coalescing

B2

under some paramount chief. One or two concentrations of population at the 'capital' of such a chief might deserve the name of 'town'; but the vast majority of Africans lived in innumerable villages—little huddles of small round huts of clay and wattle with only the low doorway for the egress of its inmates, human and animal, and the smoke and the foul air, the whole surrounded by a stockade to keep the cattle and the children safe from marauders, and beyond that the green belt of cultivated ground.

Except along one track—the track followed by the German explorer, Roscher, who reached the northern end of Lake Nyasa in 1859 a few weeks after Livingstone reached its southern end and was murdered on his way back to the coast*—these African villagers had never seen a white man; and, when they did, to judge from the accounts of Livingstone and other travellers, they were astonished at the strange phenomenon, usually intensely and often tiresomely inquisitive—the white man's ablutions, especially the tooth-brushing, were a great public spectacle—sometimes suspicious or frightened, but never in normal circumstances hostile, provided, of course, that the white man behaved himself. The abnormal circumstances—and in a steadily expanding area they were now becoming all too normal—were the conditions brought about by slave-raiding. Though the Portuguese connived at it in the Nyasa country, the actual raiders were almost always Arabs or half-castes; but, in a neighbourhood on which the blight had once descended, any stranger, whatever his colour, was instantly suspect and the attitude towards him instinctively bellicose. In the rest of the country the white man's reception—provided again that he behaved with courtesy and patience—might vary with the character and propensities of the local chief: he might be arrogant and impudent, he might levy extortionate *hongo* for permission to traverse his territory, he might fail to provide the food the traveller wanted or to furnish extra porters or a trust-worthy guide for the next stage of the journey: but in

* See *The Exploitation of East Africa*, 109-10.

most parts of the country such unfriendly reactions were unusual, and nowhere—except in those slave-raided areas—was there open and unprovoked hostility. Is it fully realised nowadays how well on the whole the Africans received the first Europeans who broke uninvited into their secluded life and how strong the additional obligation it imposed on the newcomers' humanity?

If there were no Europeans in all this African world, there were some thousands of Asiatics. Most of the ports along the coast were little Arab townships, controlled and sometimes garrisoned by the Sultan of Zanzibar, and at all of them the local trade was mainly in the hands of Indians. But the Indian merchants rarely ventured far from the sea, whereas the Arabs had spread a network of trade far over the interior. The ' colony ' they established at Unyanyembe, where several trade-routes met, has already been mentioned ; and between Unyanyembe and other little settlements and the coast Arab caravans were constantly on the move in the dry season, usually about 200 strong, sometimes, when forces were joined for safety, rising to 2000 or even to 4000, with a troop of gunmen for escort and the Sultan's scarlet flag at their head. Already in Livingstone's day these tentacles of Asiatic exploitation were beginning to feel their way into the very heart of Africa—northwards over the borders of Uganda, westwards across Lake Tanganyika towards the upper reaches of the Congo, southwards across Lake Nyasa to the fringe of the Katanga copper-belt. And it was exploitation in its most sinister sense. It was not only African ivory and copper the Arabs were after, but also, and in some districts mainly, African men, women and children.

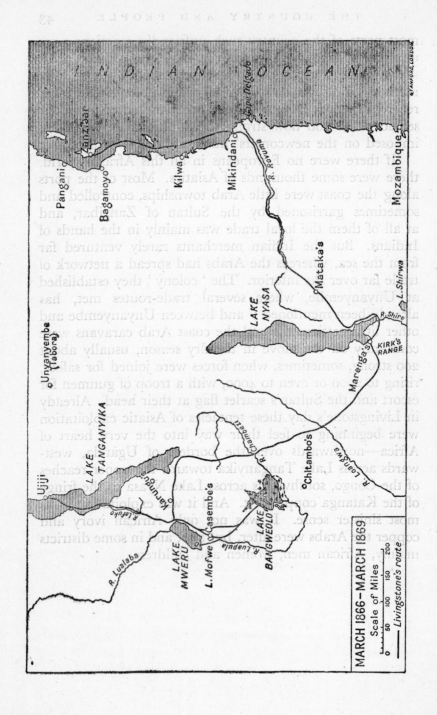

INDIAN OCEAN

Panganí

Zanzibar

Bagamoyo

Kilwa

Mikindani

R. Rovuma

Cape Delgado

Mozambique

Mataka's

LAKE NYASA

L. Shirwa

R. Shire

Marenga's

KIRK'S RANGE

Unyanyembe (Tabora)

Ujiji

LAKE TANGANYIKA

R. Chambezi

Chitambo's

R. Loangwa

Karungu's

LAKE BANGWEOLO

Casembe's

L. Mofwe

LAKE MWERU

R. Luapula

R. Lotulo

R. Lualaba

STANFORD, LONDON

MARCH 1866 — MARCH 1869

Scale of Miles

0   50   100   150   200

——— Livingstone's route

7

LIVINGSTONE's troubles soon began. He left Mikindani on April 6, and, striking south to the Rovuma and then following its left bank westwards, arrived on May 13 at the point at which he and Kirk had turned back in 1862. Thence he continued up the course of the Rovuma to the fringes of the Waiyau country where he bent south-west, and on July 14 he reached Chief Mataka's ' town ' about fifty miles east of Lake Nyasa. But, long before that first stage of his journey was completed, the note of elation had quite died out from his journal. There was reason enough for depression, no doubt, in passing again through country ransacked by the Slave Trade. Grim traces of the slavers' brutal methods were visible everywhere along the track— ' a slave-woman shot or stabbed through the body and lying on the path . . . because she was unable to walk any longer ' ; ' a man dead from starvation ' ; ' a number of slaves with slave-sticks on, abandoned by their master from want of food . . . too weak to be able to speak or say where they had come from ' ; ' a woman tied by the neck to a tree and dead ' : and traces likewise of the effects on the countryside—deserted villages, garden-ground fast going back to jungle, neighbouring communities raiding one another for slaves, the kidnapping of casual wayfarers along the forest-paths, and such a superfluity of trade cloth everywhere as the price of these unholy dealings that ' it is quite a drug in the market, we cannot get food for it.' But Livingstone had seen those harrowing sights before in the Shiré country. And if it was an unpleasant surprise to find the Mazitu raiding in the Rovuma uplands so far east of their usual haunts, killing and burning and spreading terror through the country—' they shake their shields and the people fly like stricken deer '—this, too, was no new experience. Livingstone had come upon the tracks of these barbarous marauders on the western shore of Lake

Nyasa in 1863 ; and he was no more afraid of them now than he had been then.[1] His real trouble was nothing external. It came from within the ranks of his own caravan.

On June 11, nearly two months from the start, the porters hired at Mikindani refused to go farther. ' They say they fear being captured here on their return.' So Livingstone paid them off and sent them back. Thus, at a stroke, his powers of transport were reduced by one-third ; and it was not easy and often involved delay to make the loss good by hiring porters for short stages from the villages he passed. But that was the least of his difficulties. He always maintained that slavery destroys its victim's character, that an emancipated slave rarely recovered his morale with his freedom ; and already, before he left the coast, he had noticed that ' a few of the Nassick boys have the slave-spirit pretty strongly.' One of them openly refused the easy task allotted him and impudently told Livingstone to shoot him, whereupon Livingstone, breaking a rule of his life he very rarely broke, laid his stick across his shoulders. But the effect of this example soon wore off. As they proceeded up-country, their laziness became more marked and more exasperating. At last, early in June, ' I was obliged to tell the Nassick boys that they must either work or return ; it was absurd to have them taking up [i.e. consuming] our goods and not even carrying their own things.' There is something ominous in these complaints. Was it the taint of slavery in these Nassick boys ? Or had their heads been turned at school ? Or was it the contagion of the sepoys ? In any case here were Africans for whom, it seems, the spell of Livingstone's personality had lost its strength.

That Livingstone should fail to manage the sepoys is less surprising. They were not Africans but Asiatics of whose life and language he knew nothing, and accustomed to a military discipline he was incapable of exercising. That they had little, if any, respect for him was soon painfully clear. The caravan was barely a month out from

Mikindani when Livingstone confessed that ' sepoys are a mistake.' Two days later he wrote : ' I went on with the Johanna men and twenty-four carriers, for it was a pleasure to get away from the sepoys and Nassick boys ; the two combined to overload the animals. I told them repeatedly that they would kill them, but no sooner had I adjusted the burdens and turned my back than they put on all their things. It was, however, such continued vexation to contend with their sneaking spirit that I gave up annoying myself by seeing matters, though I felt certain the animals would all be killed.' He was not far wrong. Not only did the sepoys overload the beasts and overdrive them and leave them standing loaded in the sun at rest-places ; but they flogged and goaded and sliced and stabbed them with such ferocious cruelty that Livingstone believed they were deliberately trying to kill them. His experiment, at any rate, was frustrated. All the camels and most of his other animals were soon dead, and it was impossible to say whether they had died of the bite of tsetse flies or of exhaustion and the festering wounds inflicted on them. And the sepoys had other vices. Their habits were filthy. They lightened their loads by throwing part of the precious contents away. They dawdled incorrigibly. The final stage of Livingstone's march to Mataka's took him just over seven days : it was a fortnight later before the last of the sepoys had trickled in. Worst of all, they were detected trying to persuade the Nassick boys to desert and return with them to the coast. And what could Livingstone do ? Once, in the case of the two most flagrant offenders, he reluctantly broke his rule again. ' As the *havildar* said that they would not obey him, I gave Perim and the other some smart cuts with a cane, but I felt that I was degrading myself, and resolved not to do the punishment myself again.' Severity so half-hearted and coming so late in the day did nothing, of course, to stop the rot ; and at last there was nothing for it but to dismiss the sepoys as the porters had been dismissed. Before he left Mataka's on July 28, Livingstone gave them cloth for journey-money

and commended them to the care of a ' respectable ' Arab
trader bound for the coast. ' The *havildar* begged still to
go on with me, and I consented though he is a drag on
the party.' Some weeks later, having not been ' of the
smallest use,' he decamped, or, as Livingstone gently puts
it, ' remained behind.'[1]

The departure of the sepoys seems to have eased
Livingstone's mind. At any rate there is a happier tone
again in the journal when he embarks on the second stage
of his journey and, descending from the highlands, reaches
the shore of Lake Nyasa (August 8). ' It was as if I had
come back to an old home I had never expected again to
see ; and pleasant to bathe in the delicious waters again,
hear the roar of the sea, and dash in the rollers. . . . I feel
quite exhilarated.' But his hopes of crossing the lake were
disappointed. He was now on one of the main routes of the
Arab slave-trade, and, as he had observed in 1863, dhows
were frequently crossing the lake, in one of which, with
the help of the letter of commendation he had obtained
from Sultan Majid, he expected to obtain a passage for
his party. But he had not reckoned with the alarm which
rumours of his and Mackenzie's doings in the Shiré highlands had spread throughout the slave-trading community.
Before reaching the lake, he had tried to get in touch with
the Arab leaders of two slave-caravans—one of them with
several hundred slaves herded in pens of 80 or 100 each
for the night—but, as soon as they heard of his approach,
they had made off into the wilderness. And so it was at
the lake-side. ' All the Arabs flee from me, the English
name being in their minds inseparably connected with
recapturing slaves ; they cannot conceive that I have any
other object in view ; they cannot read Seyyid Majid's
letter.' Naturally, therefore, no dhow was obtainable.
And there was another awkward result of Arab aloofness.
' I cannot transmit letters to the coast.' So near was
Livingstone already to being quite cut off from the world
he had left behind at Zanzibar.

Obliged, therefore, to circumvent the lake on foot, he

slowly made his way down to its southern end. On
September 13 he sighted the Shiré, whence he and Kirk
and their companions had emerged five years before, the
first white men to navigate the waters of Nyasa ; and six
days later, having crossed Lake Pamalombe in canoes, he
arrived at Mponda's village. Here he lost Wikatani. His
old home had been in this district, and, happening to meet
one of his brothers who told him that another brother and
two sisters were living some twenty miles off, he begged
and obtained Livingstone's permission to leave the caravan
and go and live with them.[1] It did not seem much of a
loss : for Wikatani and Chuma likewise, though devoted
to Livingstone, were too young and lighthearted to be
depended on. They were ' very good boys,' wrote Livingstone to Waller later on,[2] ' but still boys utterly.' He had
had to stop employing them as his personal servants when
he found that they had mislaid almost all his forks and
spoons and that, unless he shouted for it, he would get no
breakfast till the afternoon. Wikatani, too, was somewhat
irritating company. He was always giggling or smoking
—and, when he smoked, he screamed—or ' singing
Dididy dididy or weeweewee.' Maybe, then, Livingstone
was not altogether sorry to see the last of him, and certainly his departure was a far less serious matter than the
blow that fell a few days later at Marenga's. So far the
journal has made little mention of the Johanna men, but
it now appears that their conduct had been only less bad
than that of the sepoys. Abetted by their leader, Musa,
they had consistently pilfered from their loads. ' One
stole fifteen pounds of fine powder . . . another left six
tablecloths out of about twenty-four.' But, though their
loads grew lighter, at least they had carried them—so
far. On September 25, however, on hearing from a passing
Arab that ' the country in front was full of Mazitu,' they
refused to go farther. Threats, perhaps, of the whip might
have driven them on. But that was not Livingstone's way.
He argued with them. He enlisted the help of Chief
Marenga. ' I explained to Musa that we should avoid the

Mazitu. Marenga added, ' There are no Mazitu near where you are going.' But Musa's eyes *stood out* with terror, and he said, ' I no can believe that man. . . . No, no, I no go. . . . I want to see my father, my mother, my child at Johanna. I no want to be killed by Mazitu.' What more could Livingstone say ? What could he do ? These men were not faithful Makololo, and again his impotence was manifest. When he gave the order for the march, ' all the Johanna men walked off, leaving the goods on the ground.'[1]

The original porters, the sepoys, the Johanna men—all had now gone ; and Livingstone was left with a remnant of unsatisfactory Nassick boys, with Chuma, Susi and Amoda, and the few porters he was able to hire from village to village. But, if Livingstone was often depressed, he was never daunted ; and, as on the Zambesi Expedition, so now, he could calmly accept rebuffs and reverses as part of God's unquestionable purpose and ' make the best of a bad job.' ' They have been such inveterate thieves that I am not sorry to get rid of them . . . though my party is now inconveniently small.' And so, more or less cheerfully, he continued his march, past ' Mount Mulundini of Kirk's Range,'[2] on through what is now the district of Fort Jameson and over the bush-covered highlands of north-east Rhodesia and down into the valley of the Loangwa. But now the conditions of travel had worsened. On October 29 Livingstone noted ' the first rain—a thunder shower ' ; and a few weeks later the ' set-in ' rains were steadily falling, ' the paths were running with water,' and level spaces were coated thickly with ' excessively adhesive mud.' Progress on foot became slower and slower ; and, more serious, there was difficulty in getting food. They crossed one tract of country into which the Slave Trade, either from Kilwa or from Tete, had not yet penetrated. ' The chief said no Arabs came this way, nor Portuguese native traders.' But, a fortnight later, the journal reports : ' The black traders come from Tete to this country to buy slaves, and as a consequence here we

come to bugs again, which we left when we passed the
Arab slave-traders' beat.' Inevitably, therefore, the natives
were suspicious of the strangers and disinclined to deal
with them. To make matters worse, the villages themselves
were short of food. Musa's fears had not been groundless
after all. The ubiquitous Mazitu were plaguing all this
country as their kinsmen, the Matabele, were plaguing it
to the south. In the last week of October Livingstone was
only prevented from marching straight into them by
meeting a stream of fugitives, 'making a path for themselves through the forest,' while away northwards the
smoke of their burning villages darkened the sky. Weeks
later, it was still the same story. 'The people were all
afraid of us,' says the journal on December 13, 'and we
were mortified to find that food is scarce. The Mazitu
have been here four times, and the fear they have inspired,
though they were successfully repelled, has prevented
agricultural operations from being carried on.' The loss
of four goats, stolen or strayed, provokes this sorry entry
for Christmas Day : ' The loss affected me more than I
could have imagined. A little indigestible porridge of
scarcely any taste is now my fare, and it makes me dream
of butter.' And a few days later : ' We get nothing but a
little *maëre* which grates in the tooth and in the stomach.'
Ominous again. For Livingstone's digestive system had
long been gravely impaired by the dysentery from which
he had suffered during his crossing of Africa and on the
Zambesi. Already on this journey he had had one attack,
at Mataka's, in July. And now on December 6 comes the
first of those brief entries which were soon to become all
too frequent : ' Too ill to march.' That he could live at all
without better food is astonishing. But the disease, though it
was steadily sapping his powers of recovery, had not yet
by any means destroyed them. The physician could still
heal himself. He knew exactly, from long experience, what
drugs to use. The very next day after that brief entry he
continued his march ; and by the end of the year he had
crossed the Loangwa and was pressing steadily northward

towards Lake Tanganyika, undeterred by rain or mud, by hunger or disease. ' I shall make this beautiful land better known,' he wrote on December 30, 'which is an essential part of the process by which it will become " the pleasant haunts of men." It is impossible to describe its rich luxuriance, but most of it is running to waste through the slave-trade and internal wars.' On New Year's Eve the entry runs : 'We now end 1866. It has not been so fruitful or useful as I intended. Will try to do better in 1867 and be better—more gentle and loving ; and may the Almighty, to whom I commit my way, bring my desires to pass and prosper me.'

Three weeks later the worst, the fatal, blow fell. At the beginning of December Livingstone had come across two Waiyau ' boys ' who had been sold into slavery in that country but had been freed by the death of their masters at the hands of the Mazitu. They had volunteered to accompany Livingstone and had been ' very faithful all the way.' ' No one thought they would desert, for they were free men.' On the morning of January 20, apparently by the merest chance, one of them had exchanged his load with another man whom Livingstone had specially en-trusted with his medicine chest ' because he was so careful.' In the course of the day both the Waiyau made off. Heavy rain obliterated their footsteps. Pursuit was attempted, but without result. They had taken other goods, including ' the flour we had purchased dearly to help us as far as the Chambezi, but the medicine-chest was the sorest loss of all.' None could know better what it meant. ' I felt,' Livingstone confesses, ' as if I had now received the sentence of death, like poor Bishop Mac-kenzie.'* And indeed he had received it, though a few years might pass before its execution. He was certain to suffer from dysentery as long as good food was unobtain-able. He was certain to suffer from malaria wherever the country was low-lying and infested with mosquitoes. Unchecked by drugs, the intensity of the diseases would

* See p. 13 above.

certainly and steadily increase until even his incomparable constitution was so completely undermined that, even when drugs were again available, it could not long continue to survive the strain and exposure of African exploration. It is not too much to say that Livingstone's decision to go on into the unknown without his medicine-chest proved, in the long run, suicidal.[1]

Why, then, it has been asked, did he make it? Why did he not return on his tracks to Lake Nyasa whence the main Arab trade-route led to the coast and send at least for some quinine either by Arab agency to Kilwa or by some messenger of his own to Zanzibar? The chances, it is true, were against his getting it unless he went all the way himself; but this, as the sequel shows, he did not fully realise; and in any case, being the sort of man he was, he could not go back, however dire the need, when he had come so far. By point-to-point measure on the map he had walked about 800 miles from Mikindani. He had taken more than nine months over it. And, perhaps, his goal was now not very far ahead. A few more weeks of endurance and he might cross at last the watershed and find a river-system draining not south nor west, nor even east, but north—the sources of the Nile! No, nothing would induce him to turn back now. And he was fortified in his wilful defiance of misfortune and disease by the fatalism which had steadily been growing on him since the death of his wife in 1862. He was still haunted by the belief that he would die in Africa, and before long. And he was quite ready for it if only he might be permitted first to make his last, his crowning discovery. Once before, on the Rovuma in 1862, he had shown to what dangerous lengths this kind of fatalism could lead him. This time the danger was far more definite; but, as before, he just set his teeth and went on. He even tried to find a beneficent intent in the loss of ' the precious quinine.' ' Everything of this kind happens by the permission of One who watches over us with most tender care; and this may turn out for the best by taking away a source of suspicion

among more superstitious, charm-dreading people farther
north.' But for once he could not serenely acquiesce. On
the next page of his journal he confesses, ' This loss of the
medicine-box gnaws at the heart terribly.'[1]

8

THE inevitable sequel was not long delayed. Good food
and dry weather might have held it off for a time, but
the rain was now falling almost without a break, and food
of any sort was almost unobtainable. ' I took my belt up
three holes to relieve hunger,' says the journal shortly
before the loss of the drugs ; and again soon after it, ' We
all feel weak and easily tired, and an incessant hunger
teases us . . . real biting hunger and faintness.' On
February 3 came a gleam of encouragement. A party of
Arab slave-dealers was encountered which had come from
the east near Bagamoyo by a new, direct and relatively
easy route, west-south-west—a route which, so Livingstone
suggests, had been deliberately concealed from him by the
Arabs when he was at Zanzibar. The party was now
returning, and Livingstone seized the opportunity of
regaining contact with the outer world. He gave the
leader ' a packet of letters for which he is to get Rs. 10 at
Zanzibar.' One of them was addressed to Consul Seward
and must be quoted.[2] After describing the dismissal of
the sepoys and the defection of the Johanna men, it continues : ' We have lately had a great deal of hunger, not
want of fine dishes, but want of all dishes except mushrooms. . . . I have had no information whatever from the
coast. If you can send anything more to Ujiji at Tanganyika, 50 lbs. of coffee, a small box of candles, a stick of
sealing-wax, a cheese in tin, a small box of soap, some
French preserved meats, half a dozen bottles of port wine,
well-packed, and some quinine, and calomel, and resin
of jalap [please do so]. Don't exceed these things, please,

for heavy things we cannot carry. Please pay [for] them with what you have in hand. The severest loss I ever sustained was that of my medicines ; every grain of them, except a little extract of hyoscyamus. We had plenty of provisions after we left Lake Nyasa, but latterly got into severe hunger. Don't think, please, that I make a moan over nothing but a little sharpness of appetite. I am a mere ruckle of bones. . . . If Dr. Kirk is with you, will you give him all the information with kind regards.'

Unlike all the other letters Livingstone had written since he left the coast, this packet reached its destination. But it took time. Addressed to Seward it was received by his successor, H. A. Churchill, on January 24, 1868, nearly a year from the date of its dispatch. And, though it may have been some consolation to Livingstone to know that the drugs were actually ' on order,' he needed them at once and badly. On February 17 he was laid up with rheumatic fever. ' This is the first attack of it I ever had—and no medicine ! ' Only three days' rest, and he was on the move again defying the fever and the rain. ' Every step I take jars in the chest, and I am very weak ; I can scarcely keep up the march, though formerly I was always first. . . . I have a constant singing in my ears, and can scarcely hear the loud tick of the chronometer.' Still he struggled on, and on April 1 attained his immediate goal, the southern end of Lake Tanganyika. At once his spirits rose again. He had forged another link in his chain of exploration, and the beauty of the lake bewitched him. ' I never saw anything so still and peaceful as it lies all the morning.' But he had been unable to walk the last few miles ' without tottering,' and in a few days he had ' a fit of insensibility which shows the power of fever without medicine.' ' I found myself floundering outside my hut and unable to get in. I tried to lift myself from my back by laying hold of two posts at the entrance, but when I got nearly upright I let them go and fell back heavily on my head on a box.'

For some weeks he lay dangerously ill ; and, when at

the end of April he moved on again, he was still far from well. Without quinine he could not rid himself of intermittent fever, and he was troubled with dizziness and a constant ' singing in the ears.' Moreover, as no reader of the journal can fail to observe, the physical disorder had had its mental or psychological effects. The record of travel, the scientific observations, the descriptions of the country and the natives—all that part of the narrative, though breaks in it occur more often, is as full and interesting as before. But the central figure is changed. He does not suffer, it is true, from the moral languor or weakness of will that commonly affects the victims of protracted fever. Far from it. His determination to achieve his end is as obstinate as ever. None the less, it is not the old Livingstone. There is something strange, something wrong. If it is not inertia, it is indecision. His purpose is still strong, often heroically strong ; yet now it seems often blind or even passive. He wavers in his plans. ' I am rather perplexed how to proceed,' he says. He resigns himself to prolonged delay and inactivity. He allows himself to be diverted and obstructed as he never did in the old days. His fatalism deepens. It is almost, at times, as if he was letting his course be shaped, not by his own deliberate plan, but by the play of circumstance—or by the hand of God. ' I am deeply thankful at having got so far,' he had written when he reached Lake Tanganyika. ' I am excessively weak . . . but the Highest will lead me further.'

This does not mean, of course, that he had no plan at all. He had made up his mind not to make for his new base at Ujiji, some 300 miles to the north, until he had tested the reports he had heard of Lake Mweru and ascertained whither its waters flowed. His first move, therefore, was west and north along the heights above Lake Tanganyika, and then due west to Chitamba's. There he fell in with a large party of Arab traders, who, impressed perhaps by Sultan Majid's letter which he showed them, were by no means as aloof or unfriendly as those others had been near Lake Nyasa.

'They are connected,' says the journal, 'with one of the most influential native mercantile houses in Zanzibar. Hamees [the leader] has been particularly kind to me in presenting food, beads, cloth, and getting information.' Thus began that close association with the Arabs which has puzzled some of Livingstone's admirers. A curious association, certainly : but it must be remembered that Livingstone's supplies were now running low and that good fresh food was still almost unobtainable. Rightly or wrongly, he had decided not to go yet to Ujiji to replenish his stock. Could he afford then to look askance at gifts that helped him on his westward way? Always responsive to personal kindness and courtesy, might he not let himself regard these kind and courteous men, steeped though they were in the evil he had made it his life's chief purpose to destroy, as instruments thrown in his path for the furtherance of his immediate aim? What is more surprising, surely, is that Livingstone now allowed his movements to be more or less decided by these Arab associates. A band of them, as it happened, had recently run foul of Nsama, a powerful chief who lived to the westward of Chitamba's. There had been fighting and bloodshed ; and the Arabs warned Livingstone that he would be murdered if he continued his march to the west. 'Hamees,' he notes, ' is certainly very anxious to secure my safety.' He is ' not well pleased' at Livingstone suggesting a southward detour. He counsels patience. Let Livingstone wait till peace has been restored. . . . So he waited while the tedious business of negotiation dragged along—content, it seems, to be an onlooker, leaving it all to the Arabs, making no attempt to use his own influence with Nsama on his own account. He waited from May 20 till August 30 ! ' We marched to-day from Chitamba's village after three months and ten days' delay,' says the journal, without further comment.[1]

Nor when the motley caravan had started did it move at a good or steady pace. At Karungu's, about 100 miles from Chitamba's, the Arabs dallied for three weeks, and then ' authority is found in the Koran for staying one day more.' No wonder Livingstone at last grows restive. ' Nothing can be more tedious,' he exclaims, ' than the Arab way of travelling.' But either his supplies, now very low, or his strength was inadequate : he could not or would not go on alone. And so he was still in Arab company when at length, on November 8, at the end of another 100 miles, he reached Lake Mweru, through which now runs the frontier between Northern Rhodesia and the Belgian Congo. Thence, passing the ' farthest west ' and burial place of the Portuguese explorer, Lacerda, he came (November 21) to Casembe's, the headquarters of a powerful hereditary chieftainship. He had been told *en route* by an Arab from Ujiji that the supplies he had ordered to be sent there before leaving Zanzibar had safely arrived ; and now, it seems, having added Lake Mweru to his ' finds,' he had made up his mind to proceed to his base and refit. But he still felt dependent on Arab escort ; and finding at Casembe's one Mohamad bin Saleh, who was also bound for Ujiji and had ' waited when he heard of our coming in order that we might go together,' he gladly accepted his proposal. Indeed he was beginning to weary of his wanderings and his exile. ' I am so tired of exploration,' he wrote in a draft dispatch to Lord Clarendon, ' without a word from home or anywhere else for two years, that I must go to Ujiji for letters before doing any-thing else.'[1] But a month went by before he could escape from Casembe's. The chief, it appears, though he professed respect for the Sultan's letter and anxiety to help Livingstone on his way, required many words and gifts before he would permit the departure of Mohamad with whom he cherished an obscure blood-feud. This delay was the more aggravating because Livingstone was suffering again from fever. ' I am always ill when not working. I spend my time writing letters to be ready when we come to Ujiji.' But on December 22 they were off, and, after splashing waist-deep through streams and plunging through swamps of foul-smelling black mud on the fringes of Lake

Mweru, they arrived (March 17, 1868) at Mpweto's, near the effluence from the lake of the river named by Livingstone Webb's River, but known to the natives as the Lualaba, and in reality, though Livingstone was never to know it, the upper reaches of the Congo. So far, so good. They were now about one third of the way from Casembe's to Lake Tanganyika. And then another check ! The heavy rains had so flooded the country northward as to make it quite impassable. But this time Livingstone was not content to sit and wait. He had heard at Casembe's— and it was true—that Lake Bemba or Bangweolo, some 80 miles to the south, flowed out to the north-west in a river which linked it with Lake Mweru. Here, then, was an essential part of his river-system to be explored and mapped ; here was something to do while the floods on the northward road were falling. Not unnaturally, perhaps, his companions were loath to turn their backs on Ujiji. Mohamad bin Saleh vigorously opposed the plan : and most of Livingstone's own men, who had given no serious trouble since the desertion of the Waiyau, stubbornly refused to accompany him. ' They were tired of tramping, and so verily am I.' And for a day or two Livingstone wavered. ' Were my goods not nearly done, I would go.' In the end he went. Weary though he was, and fever-ridden, it was the old self-reliant Livingstone that struck back on his tracks, alone, with only four 'faithfuls,' and, passing Casembe's, crossing the hilly country beyond it, wading through marsh-land, escaping death from a body of hostile natives only by the utter fearlessness of his demeanour, floundering at the last through tracts of ' spongy ooze ' infested with leeches, arrived on July 18 at Lake Bangweolo. It was an exploit in the old style.[1]

9

TO-DAY a European traveller can reach the neighbourhood
of Lake Bangweolo from Zanzibar in little more than a
week by steamship, rail and motor-car ; and, all the way,
he would be within at most a hundred miles of other white
men.* But Livingstone, in that summer of 1868, was
utterly cut off from his own world. There was not a single
white man between him and the coast ; and to communicate with the coast, as has been seen, was rarely possible,
and, when possible, took at least a year. If it cannot be
said that Livingstone had lost himself, certainly his friends
had lost him. In a dispatch from the banks of the Rovuma
in May, 1866, he had spoken of standing at ' the threshold
of the unknown ' : ' it is best to say little of the future.'[1]
And then it was as if a curtain had fallen behind him, only
to be lifted at long intervals when one of his letters had
the luck to reach its destination or some trader from the
interior reported having seen him. Nor, even when they
heard from him, could his friends reply. They might
learn, a year after the event, that he had been at this
place or was going to that. From time to time, no doubt,
he would be at his base at Ujiji. But where he was or
would be at any given moment they had no notion. For
all they knew he might be dead.

As it happened, the first account of him to penetrate
that veil of African darkness was an account of his death.
On December 6, 1866, Musa and his fellow-renegades,
having crossed Lake Nyasa with some Arab slavers and
followed the trade-route to the coast at Kilwa, arrived at
Zanzibar. Well aware that, if the fact of their desertion
were revealed, they would not only lose their promised pay
but be liable to severe punishment, they had concocted a
circumstantial story ; and with calculated effrontery they

* The writer made the journey from Dar-es-Salaam *via* Dodoma, Iringa, Mbea,
and Abercorn to the Chitambo Mission in nine days in 1928. It would take only
a few hours nowadays by air.

went straight to the British Consulate and told it. Up to the point of the sepoys' dismissal they kept to the truth—assuming, no doubt, that those sepoys had returned to Zanzibar ahead of them. Then the invention began. Their party, they declared, had reached Lake Nyasa, apparently towards its unexplored northern end, and, crossing it in canoes, had proceeded some days' march further into the interior when they suddenly encountered a band of marauding Mazitu. Livingstone, as usual, was walking at the head of the caravan, accompanied by the African ' boys.' The Johanna men, as usual, were behind, and it happened that they had grounded their loads and were resting—a convincing touch—some way behind their leader. Musa had walked on ahead of them and suddenly heard Livingstone cry out that the Mazitu were coming. He saw what followed through the long grass and trees. The savages came on with a rush, shouting their war-cry and rattling their spears on their shields. Livingstone shot two of them down, and then, as he was reloading his rifle, he fell to a blow from an axe on the back of his neck. Musa rushed back to warn his companions and they all made good their escape into the bush. Creeping back at sunset, they had found Livingstone's body and buried it. The bodies of several ' boys ' were lying near. There was no trace of any survivor. All the baggage was gone. Nothing was left to bring away for identification. . . . A clever story, it must be confessed ; but of course neither Seward nor Kirk, whom he at once consulted, was inclined to swallow it at a gulp. One queer point was too obvious to be missed—all the Johanna men had escaped and they alone. But Musa and his eight accomplices had doubtless rehearsed their story in all its picturesque detail again and again on their long march to the coast ; and under the closest examination no serious discrepancy or hesitation was apparent. The route across Lake Nyasa was the route which Livingstone had frequently declared his intention of taking ; and if the account of geographical particulars was confused and contradictory, that was only to be

expected of natives. On personal questions, on the conduct
of the caravan, and especially the order of march on the
fatal day, their statements accorded with Kirk's experience
of Livingstone's previous expedition. And why, if they
were lying, had they come straight to Zanzibar instead of
keeping hid in their homes in Johanna? Were they
capable of putting up so big and dangerous a bluff for the
sake of their pay? Reluctantly the critics were convinced.
'I regard the sad story as true,' wrote Kirk, 'when
stripped of what was obviously meant to conceal or apolo-
gise for cowardice.' 'I send you the saddest news,' began
Seward's dispatch to Lord Stanley. At Zanzibar on the
Sultan's palace, on all the Consulates, and on the shipping
in the harbour, flags were flown at half-mast. But, though
it was thus officially accepted, Seward and Kirk decided
to test the story still further. The Sultan of Johanna and
William Sunley, who had recently retired from the British
Consulate there, were asked to examine the men again on
their arrival home. The Sultan, it appeared, believed the
deserters' story; and a few months later he wrote to
Zanzibar asking that their wages should be paid up to the
date of Livingstone's death as they were 'very much in
need of money.' Sunley—and this was more decisive—
came to the same conclusion as Seward and Kirk. In every
detail the tale he heard at Johanna was the same as the
tale told at Zanzibar. 'If for a moment I question the
truth of [it],' he wrote, 'it is only because I am unwilling
to believe that Livingstone, after going through so many
perils, should perish so miserably.'[1]

Accepted on the spot, the tragic story could scarcely be
questioned in England. Ten days before Seward's dispatch
was delivered at the Foreign Office, one of the secretaries
of the Royal Geographical Society received the news in a
letter from Kirk, and on March 7 this letter was communicated by its President, Sir Roderick Murchison, to *The
Times*. 'If this cruel intelligence should be substantiated,'
he wrote, 'the civilised world will mourn the loss of as
noble and lion-hearted an explorer as ever lived.'[2] That

the story was true Murchison was almost, but not quite, convinced. ' I can now scarcely cling to the hope,' he wrote in a second letter to *The Times* on March 18, ' that my dear friend should still be alive.' On March 25 the question was argued at a sorrowful meeting of the R.G.S. More letters from Zanzibar were read. Seward and Kirk had gone down the coast to Kilwa, the terminus of the Arab trade-route from Lake Nyasa, on the chance of picking up some evidence which might throw doubt on Musa's story. They got nothing. ' I fear the tale is true,' wrote Kirk to Murchison, ' much as I could wish to think it was otherwise. You may imagine how I feel, being the first to communicate the sad news regarding my leader, whom I had known, I may say, far more intimately during the Zambesi Expedition than any other member of it. On all occasions I was his companion when there was rough work to do. I could never wish a better leader.' If only he could believe that the story was untrue ! ' It may be so, I hope indeed it is, but I confess that it is hope against hope all the while.'[1]

Murchison echoed Kirk in opening the discussion. ' There might still be some hopes—he would not say very sanguine hopes—that their illustrious friend was not dead.' Sir Samuel Baker, on the other hand, was ' perfectly certain that they would see Livingstone's face no more.' More valuable was Waller's opinion. He had known Musa and he did not trust him. But Kirk, too, he pointed out, knew Musa ; and he relied on Kirk's ' sagacity.' ' Whatever opinion Dr. Kirk entertained with regard to the fate of Livingstone he must entertain.'[2]

But another of Livingstone's friends was more sceptical. E. D. Young, as recorded above, had been in charge of some Johanna men, including Musa, during the last stage of the Zambesi Expedition. All of them, he now declared, were liars and thieves, and Musa was utterly untrustworthy.[3] He refused to believe a word of the story ; and he offered to go himself to Lake Nyasa and prove it false by inquiries among the natives. Murchison jumped at the

offer, for Young's stark disbelief had strengthened the
doubt that had lingered in his own mind and he agreed
with Young that ' doubt was not to be endured.'[1] So a
small-scale expedition was quickly organised by the Royal
Geographical Society with more than ample financial
assistance this time from the Government. On June 11
Young sailed for the Cape with Lieutenant H. Faulkner
(late 17th Lancers), John Reid, who had served as carpenter on the Zambesi Expedition, and Patrick Buckley,
artisan. In the light of his previous experiences of the river
route to Lake Nyasa, he had had constructed an open
steel boat, with mast and oars, 30 feet long by 8 broad,
drawing only 18 inches of water, and made in detachable
sections small enough to be carried on men's backs. On
July 25 the Expedition was off the Luabo mouth of the
Zambesi, and on August 19, just two months from the
start, the *Search* arrived at the foot of the Murchison Falls.
For Young it had been a familiar and a melancholy
journey. He had passed and tended the graves of Mrs.
Livingstone, Mackenzie, Scudamore, Dickinson and Thornton.[2] He had seen again the hundreds of villages left
desolate by the Portuguese Slave Trade. And if the Makololo had greeted him with the wildest delight, it had been
partly because they needed a protector. One point in
Musa's story was true. The Mazitu were out. All along
the left bank of the Shiré they had driven the Ajawa and
Manganja in panic across the river. At the moment, it
was said, a band of them were camped at Magomero, the
tragic site of Mackenzie's mission. Such, indeed, was the
general alarm that Young would certainly have failed to
enlist the services of the Makololo if it had not been for the
devotion they still bore to Livingstone. As it was, he succeeded in securing 240 of them for the heavy task of
carrying the sections of the *Search* past the Murchison
Falls, and in the first week of September it was afloat on
Lake Nyasa. And now the work of inquiry began. There
was little chance, of course, of discovering where Livingstone was at that time, still less of getting into touch with

him. As a matter of fact he was then wandering with the Arabs more than 500 miles to northward. All Young could hope to do was to disprove Musa's story of his death. And that he quickly did. If Musa had told the truth, Livingstone had crossed the lake at its northern end ; but no sooner had Young reached its south-east corner than he came on traces of the passage of some European traveller— a spoon, a knife, a razor, a cartridge-case, a looking-glass, and other trifles which had been given in exchange for food. Who could this have been if not Livingstone ? But it was not till Young crossed to the west side of the lake that certainty was attained. First, he met some natives who had seen Livingstone and served him as porters and who now described his appearance with exactitude, identified his photograph, and closely mimicked his method of taking observations. Next, he saw Chief Marenga who had entertained Livingstone for two days, produced men who had carried for him for several days' march to the north-west, and described how the Johanna men had returned through his village, soon after Livingstone's departure, saying that they had decided to leave him because their term of service was up and the Mazitu were ahead. Last, he visited the village where Wikatani —who was absent at the time—had made his new home, and interviewed his brother.* It was evidence enough, and since the Makololo, still terrified of the Mazitu, refused to help in exploring the lake to its northern end, the Expedition returned on its tracks and reached the sea on November 11. There they waited, until, on December 2, H.M.S. *Racoon* arrived, as arranged, to take them to the Cape. The first news they heard on board confirmed the results of their own investigation. Reports of Livingstone had arrived overland at Zanzibar.[1]

In the previous February, it will be remembered, Living-

---

* Young met Wikatani when he visited Nyasaland again in 1875 and employed him as an interpreter. He found that he had forgotten most of his English. One night he was surprised to hear someone singing in the hut next his own. It was Wikatani singing a four-line bedtime hymn which, he said, Livingstone had taught him. *Nyassa, a Journal of Adventures,* (London, 1877), 63, 184.

stone had encountered north of the River Chambezi a party of Arab traders bound by a direct route for Bagamoyo. Toward the end of September—just about the time that Young was finding his proofs near Lake Nyasa—a Swahili slave attached to this Arab party came to Zanzibar and told Churchill, who had succeeded Seward at the Consulate in the summer of 1867, that he had seen a white man in the interior, 'quite alone and engaged in no trade.' Churchill and Kirk at once crossed over to Bagamoyo where they found two other eyewitnesses who confirmed the slave's account and said, moreover, that the white man had given letters to a certain Bundouky to bring to Zanzibar. In November came further news. Sultan Majid was informed, and sent the information on to Churchill, that a chief from the Nyasa country, who had recently arrived at Kilwa, reported that a white man had been seen northwards of the Lake some eight months ago. Another month passed, and another, and then, on January 24, 1868, the aforesaid Bundouky appeared at Zanzibar and delivered the packet of letters into Churchill's hands. So, at last, the whole truth was out. The letter to Seward, which has been already quoted, related, *inter alia*, the simple facts of the Johanna men's desertion. It is satisfactory to record that Seward, though he had believed their story, had cautiously refused to pay them their wages until it was confirmed. Their punishment was a matter for the Sultan of Johanna who expressed his ' mortification ' at any subjects of his being guilty of ' such base treachery ' and kept Musa for eight months in irons.[1]

Young's return to England early in 1868, soon followed by Livingstone's letters to his friends at home, enabled Murchison to communicate the ' glorious tidings ' to the Royal Geographical Society in May and to remind his colleagues, with a touch of exaggeration, of his ' utter disbelief ' in Musa's story. There was now, he went on, nothing to do but wait patiently for Livingstone's emergence. If the water-system he was exploring proved to be connected with the Congo (which was, indeed, the fact),

he might appear one day on the west coast. If, on the
other hand, it proved to be connected with Lake Albert
Nyanza and so with the Nile, he might either strike straight
back from the Lake to Zanzibar or make his way down the
river to Egypt and the Mediterranean. In any case, he
warned his hearers, years might elapse before he was seen
again by white men.[1] The curtain, in fact, had fallen again.
And it was harder than ever now to penetrate it. It was
not only distance that for the next few years secluded
Livingstone from the outer world. Throughout the intervening space war and rumours of war were abroad, and
presently, to make it still more difficult to cross, disease.

10

MEANTIME, far away back behind the curtain, Livingstone
was pursuing his devious course, wholly unaware of
his friends' anxieties and efforts on his behalf. It was
not till 1870 that he heard of the Young Expedition.
It was, indeed, his growing sense of isolation, his longing
for the news he never got, that spurred him northwards
from Lake Bangweolo. In the early autumn of 1868
he was back in the neighbourhood of Mpweto's, where
he found the deserters awaiting him and penitent. ' I
have taken all the runaways back again : after trying
the independent life they will behave better. . . . I
have faults myself.' Mohamad bin Saleh had also made
no move during Livingstone's seven-months' absence :
but he was talking now of going to Manyema, the country
westwards of the northern part of Lake Tanganyika ; and
the idea of striking the Lualaba again in that district and
proving, perhaps, that it was the Nile so excited Livingstone that Ujiji again fell into the background. ' The way
seems opening out before me and I am thankful.' But the
plan evaporated, and Livingstone, reverting to Ujiji, sought
anxiously for the Arab escort of which he was now in

greater need than ever. His 'journey-money' was practically exhausted. His exploration of Lake Bangweolo had been curtailed by his inability to hire a canoe. 'I had only my coverlet . . . and it was very cold; the few beads would all be required to buy food on the way back.' Fortunately more than one Arab trader was in the neighbourhood bound for Ujiji. There was Syde bin Habib, with 'an enormous number of tusks and bars of copper' and troops of slaves. And there was Mohamad Bogharib, who was particularly friendly and hospitable to Livingstone and was actually ready to start in the first week of November. But then, at the last moment, a quarrel between Arabs and natives over runaway slaves threw the country into such a ferment that it seemed impossible to move without fighting. On November 28 there was talk of 'going and forcing our way to the north if possible,' but it was only talk. 'The detention,' says Livingstone on December 2, 'is excessively vexatious to me.' Before long, however, the trouble died down; and, at last, on December 11, in company with Mohamad Bogharib, he took the Ujiji road.

Their route lay north-west to the mouth of the River Lofuko on Lake Tanganyika, whence they hoped to proceed by water to Ujiji. But before they were halfway to the Lake, Livingstone was incapacitated by the gravest illness that had yet attacked him. The entry in the journal for New Year's Day, 1869, omits the usual hopes and prayers. It briefly records that on the previous day, though feeling very ill, he had waded through a river with the cold water up to his waist. 'I have been wet times without number, but the wetting of yesterday was once too often.' A few days later he was down with pneumonia, coughing day and night and spitting blood. From time to time, since he had left the coast, he seems to have felt again, as in the Zambesi days, that his end was not far off. A year before this illness, in his prayer for 1868, he had written, 'If I am to die this year, prepare me for it.' And in June the sight of a native grave on the way to Lake Bangweolo had reawakened the thought that had haunted him after the death of his wife. 'We came to a grave in the forest; it was a little rounded mound as if the occupant sat in it in the usual native way : it was strewed over with flour, and a number of the large blue beads put on it : a little path showed that it had visitors. This is the sort of grave I should prefer : to lie in the still, still forest, and no hand ever disturb my bones. The graves at home always seemed to me to be miserable, especially those in the cold damp clay, and without elbow room ; but I have nothing to do but wait till He who is over all decides where I have to lay me down and die. Poor Mary lies on Shupanga brae, " and beeks furnent the sun." ' And now, not so very far from Shupanga, it seemed the call had come. 'I saw myself lying dead in the way to Ujiji,' he wrote when he had the strength to write, ' and all the letters I expected there useless.' 'Cannot walk,' he goes on, ' pneumonia of the right lung, and I cough all day and all night : sputa rust of iron and bloody : distressing weakness. Ideas flow through the mind with great rapidity and vividness in groups of twos and threes : if I look at any piece of wood, the bark seems covered with figures and faces of men, and they remain, though I look away and turn to the same spot again.'

That was not far from delirium, and almost certainly Livingstone would have died at this time if he had been left alone, with only his own followers, unable to buy food. It was Mohamad Bogharib who saved his life. He rigged up a litter and had him carried along with his caravan. He watched over him, cooked his food, treated him with Arab medicines. 'I am so weak,' wrote the patient at the start, ' that I can scarcely speak.' And even in the litter the journey tried him hard. 'Carriage is painful : head down and feet up alternates with feet down and head up.' He tries to shelter his face from the blistering sun with a bunch of leaves—'dreadfully fatiguing in my weakness.' But always the good Mohamad is 'very kind ' to him, and, after more than a month of anxious marching, he brings him to the lakeside, exhausted, ' greatly emaciated,' but still alive.

For the next and last stage of the journey Livingstone was again dependent on Arab aid. The only canoes available belonged to the wealthy Syde bin Habib : so ' I sent to Syde to say that all the Arabs had served me except himself . . . and if I did not get to Ujiji to get proper food and medicine, I should die.' The prayer was granted and Livingstone was soon afloat, still seriously ill, but hoping now ' to hold out to Ujiji ' and craving desperately for the drugs and better food and, above all else, the letters he hoped to find there. ' Patience is never more needed than now,' he says on March 8 : ' I am near Ujiji, but the slaves who paddle are tired.' There was no further check. On March 14, 1869, he reached his goal.

II

THERE were many disappointments in Livingstone's life, but none more bitter than that which met him at Ujiji.

Only a remnant of the goods he had ordered was awaiting him : the rest had been stolen. There was no medicine : and he had been without quinine or any other drug save a little hyoscyamus for more than two years. There were no letters or papers : and he had had no scrap of news from Zanzibar or England for nearly three years.

It will be remembered that Livingstone had himself, before leaving Zanzibar in March, 1866, arranged with Koorji, the manager of the leading Indian firm, for goods to be sent to Ujiji. A further supply of provisions and medicines was dispatched by Seward in the following July.[1] In January, 1868, Livingstone's request for yet more goods, and especially medicine, reached Zanzibar ; but Churchill apparently did not act on it since he inferred from the letter that Livingstone would have come to Ujiji and gone again long before another caravan could get there. 'It is little likely,' he wrote to the Foreign Office, 'that further provisions sent to him now, reaching Ujiji as they probably would a year after his expected arrival there, would ever be received, particularly as no direction of his course is given after that place.'[1] In August, 1868, two more letters from Livingstone arrived, written in the Casembe district in September and December, 1867, and carried by friendly Arabs. They repeated his previous request for supplies ' to be sent to Ujiji, exactly the same as those already sent by Koorji.' ' Koorji's books will guide you as to the sort of goods needed. The medicines are the most important want.' This time Churchill at once complied, for the letters had revealed Livingstone's change of plan, and the later of the two had stated that he was starting for Ujiji in two days' time. Since Koorji's books contained no record of the goods dispatched in 1866, Churchill, after consulting Kirk, sent off such supplies as they thought would be most useful in the Tanganyika country.[2] It may be taken for granted that Churchill and Kirk (to whom Livingstone had sent his ' love ') wrote letters to him to go with those supplies and forwarded also such letters and newspapers from England as had arrived for him at Zanzibar. Of these, however, there were probably few, since for nearly a year from the spring of 1867 most of Livingstone's friends in England believed that he was dead.

It appears, then, at first sight as if a more than ample supply of cloth and beads and tinned foods and drugs should have been waiting for Livingstone when he reached Ujiji on March 14, 1869. But what did he find ? Cloth, beads, coffee and tea had arrived and were in charge of the appointed agent, but it was only a quarter of the cloth that had been ordered and much of it was useless for barter. Koorji or some subordinate of his had fraudulently provided ' stuff for packing instead of calico used in trade.' The other three-quarters of the cloth and the best of the beads had been stolen. ' Medicines, wine and cheese had been left at Unyanyembe, thirteen days east of this.' And, as has been seen, there were no letters or newspapers at all.[1]

Livingstone's biographers have pointed out how severely this blow was felt by ' a man shattered in health and craving for letters and stores,' and the truth of this is manifest from his own journal. Yet surely he must have realised from the first that the establishment of his depot at Ujiji was a risky business ; surely he cannot have expected to find all his stores intact. He knew that the goods carried in any caravan were liable to theft on the road. If his own men had constantly pilfered from their loads, almost under his own eyes, what chance was there of the bales which Koorji had sent him by Arab and African agents reaching their destination inviolate ? And, if the goods or some of them had arrived at Ujiji, as they might well have done, about the end of 1866, was it probable that no thief would get at them there when two whole years and more went by and their owner did not come to claim them ? If the report of his death had been believed at Zanzibar in 1867, might not the Arabs of Ujiji have doubted, two years later, if he were still alive ? Is it not, on cool consideration, more surprising that any goods at all were left than that some had been stolen ? If Livingstone had been himself in body and mind, would he not have foreseen and steeled himself against the disappointment ?

What had happened to his correspondence must have been even more plain. ' I have been busy writing letters home,' he writes in his journal on April 27, ' and have finished forty-two, which in some measure will make up for my long silence.' He also wrote to Kirk asking for porters and more supplies to be sent up to him, and to the Arab Governor of Unyanyembe ' to make inquiries about the theft of my goods.' But he very soon discovered that the old difficulty of finding trusty postmen was greater at Ujiji than it had ever been elsewhere. ' The people here,' he wrote to Kirk, ' are like the Kilwa traders—haters of the English. . . . They dread exposure by my letters. No one will take charge of them.' He had heard, he goes on, that the members of a caravan that had recently left for the coast were warned by their master not to take any of his letters, ' because I might write something he did not like.'[1] The journal reports another influential Arab sending round ' to warn all the Ujijians against taking my letters to the coast.' These Arabs' fears would have been confirmed if they could have read what Livingstone was writing in his journal at this time. ' This is a den of the worst kind of slave-traders; those whom I met in Urungu and Itawa were gentlemen slavers : the Ujiji slavers, like the Kilwa and the Portuguese, are the vilest of the vile. It is not a trade, but a system of consecutive murders.' Not without reason, then, these Arabs regarded Livingstone as their enemy and were determined to make it difficult for him to expose their slaving methods or make trouble about the theft of his goods. Undeterred by his protests—he was a British Consul, he told them, a ' Government man,' and the Sultan at Zanzibar had ordered them to treat him with respect—they did their best to cut him off completely from communication with the coast. And they were not unsuccessful. No letters came in. None of those forty-two got out. Only the letter to Kirk slipped through to Zanzibar.

There was at this time a further obstacle to the safe passage of goods or letters between Ujiji and the coast. The Mazitu raids had set in motion a ripple of alarm and disorder through all East Africa. ' Certain it is,' wrote Seward some six months after Livingstone had started from Mikindani, ' that there is a general restlessness of the tribes between the East African coast and the interior, and that trade is becoming less and less possible.' Already, by the end of 1866, Arab traders were being attacked and murdered within a few miles of Kilwa.[2] Farther south, in 1868, the natives of Mozambique were in open revolt against the flaccid Portuguese government. It was reported at Zanzibar that a strong force organised to repress them had been almost wiped out, that Sofala had fallen, and that Lourenço Marques was besieged.[3] It has been seen

C2

how Livingstone's movements were obstructed to the north-west of Lake Nyasa by little local wars in 1867 and 1868 ; and when he arrived at Ujiji in 1869 he found the road to Unyanyembe ' blocked up by a Mazitu or Watuta war.' Again, then, he ought not to have been disappointed when ' two light boxes ' and no more came safely to Ujiji in May. Again, surely, it is surprising that at that time anything came at all.

A month or two later, as it happened, the last and most formidable barrier between Livingstone and the coast was temporarily removed. A caravan from Unyanyembe arrived at Zanzibar in August, reporting that the way to Ujiji was now open and ' safe even to small bodies of men.' Was Livingstone ignorant—perhaps deliberately kept in ignorance—of this lull in the fighting ? If he had been aware of it, would he not have made an effort to obtain his medicines ? They were lying, he believed, at Unyanyembe, and that was only three or four weeks' march from Ujiji.* Surely, if he had thought it possible, he would have tried to obtain those vital drugs ; and, if no trusty agents could be found, he would have gone himself to get them. Within two months he might have been back at Ujiji, protected from those attacks of fever which had already caused and were again to cause far longer waste of time. But the journal does not raise this question. It only records Livingstone's rapid recovery of health—on March 28, after only a fortnight at Ujiji, it observes, ' Flannel to the skin and tea very beneficial in the cure of my disease : my cough has ceased, and I walk half a mile '—and, as a result, the renewal of his old impatience to be up and doing. He soon decided what it was he had to do. The mystery of Manyema had tempted him when he was down south. He was nearer to it now : he had only to cross the Lake at his feet and then push on a hundred miles or so westward. And it was of this intention that he informed Kirk in the letter he wrote on May 30, asking for porters

* Burton and Speke left Ujiji on May 26, 1858, and reached Unyanyembe on June 19. Livingstone's '13 days' (p. 72 above) seems an underestimate.

and more goods, the letter which did actually reach
Zanzibar. ' I have written to Seyd Majid,' he says, after
enumerating his needs, ' begging two of his guard to see
to the safety of the goods here into Thani bin Suellim's
hands or into those of Mohammed bin Saleh. As to the
work to be done by me it is only to connect the sources
which I have discovered from 500 to 700 miles south of
Speke and Baker's with the Nile. The volume of water
which flows north from latitude 12° south is so large, I
suspect I have been working on the sources of [the] Congo
as well as of the Nile. I have to go down the eastern line
of drainage to Baker's turning-point ; Tanganyika, Uziga,
Chowambe (Baker's) are one water, and the head of it is
300 miles south of this. The western and central lines of
drainage converge into an unvisited lake, west or south-
west of this. The outflow of this, whether to Congo or
Nile, I have to ascertain. The people west of this, called
Manyema, are cannibals if Arabs speak truly. I may have
to go there first, and down Tanganyika, if I come out
uneaten, and find my new squad from Zanzibar. I ear-
nestly hope that you will do what you can to help me with
the goods and men.'[1]

It is clear from this letter and from the journal that
Livingstone did not propose to wait for his ' new squad.'
He hoped to find it at Ujiji on his return from Manyema
and use it for further exploration. The only thing that
delayed his start was the effect of the recent rains. ' I am
thankful to feel getting strong again,' he notes on the day
after he had written to Kirk, ' and wish to go down
Tanganyika but cannot get men : two months must elapse
ere we can face the long grass and superabundant water
on the way to Manyema.' Two months—more than time
enough to fetch that quinine from Unyanyembe over
highland country which cannot have been waterlogged.
But, after those first *cris de coeur*, the journal never mentions
medicine. And Livingstone still had none of the vital
drugs when on July 12, before the second month was
halfway through, he set out again into the unknown.

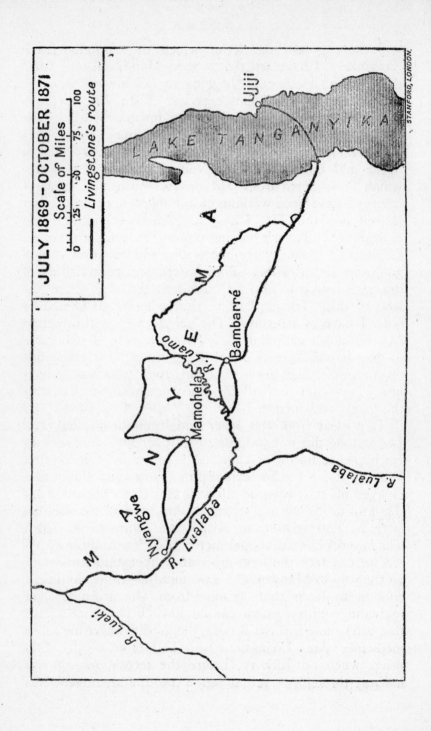

JULY 1869 – OCTOBER 1871

Scale of Miles

0   25   50   75   100

—— Livingstone's route

LAKE TANGANYIKA

Ujiji

M A N Y E M A

Bambarré

R. Luamo

Mamohela

Nyangwe

R. Lualaba

R. Lualaba

R. Lueki

STANFORD, LONDON.

12

LIVINGSTONE did not expect this Manyema expedition to take a very long time—four or five months, he reckoned. In fact it took over two years : he returned to Ujiji on October 16, 1871. And the main reason why his time-table proved so much too sanguine in this second phase of his last campaign was the same as in the first phase. His vitality was failing. Disease, unchecked by drugs, had too deeply undermined it for any real and lasting recovery to be achieved by that brief rest at Ujiji ; and when disease recurred, as it was bound to do, it found his powers of resistance weakened and left him each time less capable, in mind as well as in body, of mastering his fate, of breaking through by force of will the series of obstacles that thwarted and delayed him.

The first fortnight was easy going—southwards by canoe along the lakeside for about fifty miles and then straight across to the west shore. But then Livingstone had to take to his feet, and at the end of the very first day he was obliged to record that some three hours' marching had proved ' very fatiguing in my weakness.' ' Any ascent,' he notes a week later, and he is crossing undulating country, ' though gentle, makes me blow since the attack of pneumonia ; if it is inclined to an angle of 45°, 100 or 150 yards makes me stop to pant in distress.' But he would not spare himself—he never did—and for a time nature humoured him. ' My strength increased,' notes the journal, ' as I persevered.' On September 21 he pitched his camp triumphantly at Bambarré, a place of some importance in eastern Manyema about 100 miles west of Tanganyika. And then came the inevitable set-back. The cold and wet of that highland country soon induced a sharp attack of fever, and it was not till November 1 that he was able to resume his westward search for the Lualaba.

His first effort was a failure. When, after three weeks'

marching, he reached the Luamo, a deep-flowing river
some 200 yards broad, at a point about 25 miles from its
confluence with the Lualaba, he was brought to a dead
stop. It was not illness this time, but another old trouble
—the antagonism which the Arab traders and their slave
agents had created among the natives towards all strangers.
Just as Livingstone's discovery of the Shiré highlands in
1863 had been instantly followed by the expansion of the
Portuguese slave-trade into that area, dogging his footsteps
and wrecking his plans of peaceful settlement, so now his
exploration of Manyema coincided with its first commercial
penetration by the Arabs. Bambarré had hitherto been
their 'farthest west'; but, while Livingstone was on his
way thither, he met, as it chanced, the first exploiter of
the virgin field beyond, one Hassani Dugumbé, who was
returning towards Ujiji with no less than 18,000 pounds
of ivory, obtained at much less than the normal price.
And, unhappily, he and his slaves had pursued their
lucrative trade with needless violence. The natives had
been insulted, plundered, and in some villages done to
death. Naturally, therefore, when Livingstone appeared
not many weeks later, he was met with fierce suspicion.
The natives collected in force as he went by, armed ' with
their large spears and huge wooden shields.' It was evidence, perhaps, that Livingstone had not lost all his
influence over Africans that they did not attack his little
party. They simply ' showed us out of their district.' If
they did not stop them going west, they would not help
them. A canoe was unobtainable to cross the Luamo, even
at a price : and, though Dugumbé would doubtless have
got one if he had wanted it, Livingstone could not. Once
more, therefore, he was baffled. Once more he had wasted
his time. On December 19 he was back at Bambarré.

(And there he found a ' horde of Ujijians . . . all eager
to reach the cheap ivory of which a rumour had spread
far and wide.' So numerous were they and so militant—
' they numbered 500 guns '—that little hope seemed left
of peaceful exploration westward. A detour seemed to offer

the only chance of reaching the Lualaba, and on December
26 Livingstone set off due north. But already his time-
table is lengthening. ' I must try with all my might,' he
writes in his journal on Christmas Day, ' to finish my
exploration before next Christmas ; ' and his prayer on
New Year's Day, 1870, is to be enabled ' to finish the
work in hand and retire before the year is out.'

More than half that year went by and again he was in
Bambarré and again he had failed utterly, defeated this
time by the weather and the Manyema mud. The first
day out he had a touch of fever, and then for days the
rain came down, drenching him to the skin, and, combined
with bad drinking water, inducing ' choleraic symptoms.'
And now his journal, which in his earlier days in
Africa had rarely mentioned health, becomes something
like a hospital-record. ' Greatly reduced in flesh.' ' Choleraic purging again.' ' Laid up by sheer weakness.' ' Weakness and illness goes on because we get wet so often.'
' Rest from sickness in camp.' ' Excessive weakness from
purging.' These distressing entries are spread over the
first five weeks of the march, during which the indomitable man staggered on, not merely in constant rain, but
often through liquid mud waist-deep, and sometimes
through floods and streams up to the neck. Could any one
but Livingstone have done it ? Or, at least, could any one
else, so ill and in such discomfort, have written down in
his journal, at a weary day's end, a passage like the
following : ' Caught in a drenching rain which made me
fain to sit, exhausted as I was, under an umbrella, trying
to keep the trunk dry. As I sat in the rain, a little tree-
frog, about half an inch long, leaped on to a grassy leaf,
and began a tune as loud as that of many birds and very
sweet ; it was surprising to hear so much music out of so
small a musician. I drank some rain-water as I felt faint
—in the paths it is now calf deep. I crossed a hundred
yards of slush waist deep in mid-channel, and full of holes
made by elephants' feet, the path hedged in by reedy grass,
often intertwined and very tripping. I stripped off my

clothes on reaching my hut in a village, and a fire during the night nearly dried them. At the same time I rubbed my legs with palm oil, and in the morning had a delicious breakfast of sour goat's milk and porridge.'

A few days later, arrived at Mamohela, he is positively cheerful. 'Rest, shelter, and boiling all the water I used, and above all the new species of potato called *nyumbo*, much famed among the natives as a restorative, put me all to rights.' But even Livingstone could get no farther ; and week after week he was held up at Mamohela, about sixty miles north-west of Bambarré. On May 1, the entry runs : 'Rains continued ; and mud and mire from the clayey soil of Manyema too awful to be attempted.' And now, yet again, the Arabs were on his tracks. A party of them passed his way, and were hired by a local chief for ten goats and a tusk to help him prosecute a blood feud. Result : forty natives killed, thirty-one enslaved, sixty goats appropriated. A second party came in from the north boasting of the slaughter of another forty Manyema and the burning of nine villages. And then, as if this was not enough to prejudice Livingstone's chances of further progress, yet another of his earlier misfortunes was repeated. When, towards the end of June, the rains, after a fall of 58 inches, having ceased at last, he prepared to march once more, his porters deserted. Nevertheless he marched. 'Now my people failed me '—that is all he says—'so, with my three attendants, Susi, Chuma and Gardner, I started off to the north-west for the Lualaba.'

He was soon involved again with the Arabs. 'We passed through the nine villages burned for a single string of beads,' he reports on June 30 ; and next day, 'While I was sleeping quietly here, some trading Arabs camped at Nasangwa's, and at dead of night one was pinned to the earth by a spear : no doubt this was in revenge for relations slain. . . . The survivors now wished to run amuck in all directions. . . . Death to all Manyemas glared from the eyes of half-castes and slaves.' And a massacre would doubtless have occurred but for the fortunate arrival of one of Livingstone's 'gentlemen slavers,' none other, indeed, that his particular friend, Mohamad Bogharib. Mohamad had been quick to scent the new ivory-field and had been on his way to Bambarré when Livingstone, soon after leaving Ujiji, had overtaken him. So the old comradeship had been renewed and the old kindnesses on Mohamad's part—the gift of a goat for Livingstone's Christmas dinner and of opium to ease his 'choleraic' pains. At this time he had gone off trading by himself, and it was chance that had brought him to Nasangwa's at so critical a moment. He at once joined with Livingstone, and with more authority than Livingstone's, in 'enforcing peace.' 'The traders went off, but let my three people know, what I knew long before, that they hated having a spy in me on their deeds.'

Meantime Livingstone had begun to doubt the possibility of reaching the Lualaba by the north-westerly route. The country, though widely populated, was almost impassable. 'Trees fallen across the path formed a breast-high wall which had to be climbed over : flooded rivers, breast and neck-deep, had to be crossed ; the mud was awful, and nothing but villages eight or ten miles apart. In the clearances around those villages alone could the sun be seen.' And when he heard from Mohamad's party not only that the going ahead of him was just as bad ('exceedingly difficult from forest and water'), but also that it was not the shortest way to the Lualaba which in that direction made a deep westward bend, he was driven again—and how he hated it !—to contemplate another failure and another retreat. Then came another ailment to decide the matter. 'For the first time in my life my feet failed me, and now having but three attendants, it would have been unwise to go further in that direction. Instead of healing quickly as heretofore when torn by hard travel, irritable eating ulcers festered on both feet ; and I limped back to Bambarré.' He arrived there on July 22, and there he remained eight months !

13

Eight dreary months of pain and illness and inactivity and dejection. For nearly three of them Livingstone was immobilised and tormented by those ulcers—at times intensely irritating, at times so painful that he could not sleep at night. They were at once a symptom and an aggravation of his general debility : and now—for the first time again—he began to doubt his powers of recovery and to wonder whether indeed he had strength enough left to finish his task. The following sentence appears abruptly in his journal during August. ' The severe pneumonia in Marunga, the choleraic complaint in Manyema, and now irritable ulcers warn me to retire while life lasts.' That is the one and only occasion from beginning to end, on which the bare thought of giving up, of retiring before his work is done, creeps into Livingstone's journal. And then it is only a thought, and he dismissed it at once. ' Patience,' he had said a little earlier ; ' all will be for the best, for it is in Providence and not in me.' He certainly needed patience, for it was not till the end of September, after another attack of fever ' which reduced my strength, taking away my voice and purging me,' that at last his health improved. By then the rainy season had set in, cleansing the germ-laden dust of Bambarré ; and, whether for that reason or because he had tried, on Arab advice, an application of malachite, the ulcers healed and disappeared. ' I am thankful to feel myself well,' he notes on October 10. But that did not mean that he could start at once for the Lualaba. The rain may have helped to heal him, but it had made the countryside almost impassable. And this time Livingstone hesitated to plunge into the morass with only his three ' faithfuls ' and no drugs at all. ' I feel the want of medicine strongly, almost as much as the want of men.' And there now seemed little hope of men or medicine coming from the coast. It had always been doubtful if his letters had got through, doubtful if his friends at Zanzibar had any idea where he was ; and now a new and dreadful obstacle was barring the inland roads. It was the time of the great epidemic of cholera, which (as will be related presently) decimated Zanzibar from November 1869 to July 1870, and thence spread fast and far along the trade-routes into the interior. In a relatively mild form it reached Bambarré and took its toll of victims. Livingstone ascribed his own ' purging fever ' to it. It was reported to be ' terribly severe on the way to the coast.' Would any motive, except perhaps the lust for ivory, keep any caravan afoot when death was on its track and in such ghastly shape ?

So, week after week, Livingstone sat idle at Bambarré, turning over and over in his mind the possibilities of the discovery, the great crowning discovery, which lay, it seemed, only just beyond his grasp—it was only some sixty miles to the Lualaba and then he would take to the water and go easy—and yet remained, week after week, quite unattainable. What could he do ? It was no use writing letters and dispatches home. There was little to record in the journal. He could only read ; and between his leaving and returning to Ujiji he read the whole of the Bible through four times. And, as he read, the idea of the work that lay ahead of him, of the great discovery, assumed a new and almost mystical shape. Like another constant reader of the Bible who was soon to work and die in Africa, he had been disquieted by the attacks of Victorian scientists on the historical validity of the Old Testament. But Livingstone had a far steadier and more sober mind than Gordon. He never bemused himself with metaphysical fantasies. And it was not with symbolism but with the concrete business of exploration and archæology that his thoughts and hopes were now concerned. Suppose in lands no Christian had yet trod some solid evidence were found to confirm, even on one small point, the truth of the sacred book which Christianity had made its own, would not that provide a more effective refutation

of the disbelievers than any amount of historical or philo-
sophic argument ? And, as he read and re-read Exodus,
he fell, as he puts it, into a ' waking dream.' . . . ' Moreover the man Moses was very great in the land of Egypt,
in the sight of Pharaoh's servants and in the sight of the
people.' How had he attained such greatness ? Not by
killing one Egyptian, nor by his long sojourn in the land
of Midian. How, then ? Might there not be 'a sub-
stratum of fact ' in the legend of Moses going up into
Inner Ethiopia with Merr, Pharaoh's daughter and his
foster-mother, and founding there a city which he called
' Meroe ' in her honour ? If so, the puzzle would be solved.
Such an exploit would well account for his prestige. . . .
Inner Ethiopia—somewhere far up the Nile—near its
actual source, maybe—in the very district he was going
to explore—why not ? . . . ' I dream,' he confesses to the
journal, ' of discovering some monumental relics of Meroe.'
' If anything confirmatory of sacred history does remain,'
he goes on, ' I pray to be guided thereunto. If the sacred
chronology would thereby be confirmed, I would not
grudge the toil and hardships, hunger and pain, I have
endured. The irritable ulcers would only be discipline.'
Once conceived, this new idea fastened on Livingstone's
mind. Two months after the last-quoted entry in the
journal occurs the following : ' In this journey I have
endeavoured to follow with unswerving fidelity the line of
duty. . . . All the hardship, hunger and toil were met
with the full conviction that I was right in persevering to
make a complete work of the exploration of the sources of
the Nile. . . . The prospect of death in pursuing what I
knew to be right did not make me steer to one side or the
other. I had a strong presentiment during the first three
years that I should never live through the enterprise, but
it weakened as I came near to the end of the journey and
an eager desire to discover any evidence of the great Moses
having visited those parts bound me, spell-bound me, I
may say ; for if I could bring to light anything to confirm
the Sacred Oracles, I should not grudge one whit all the

labour expended.' And again, ten days later : ' I long
with intense desire to move on and finish my work. I
have also an excessive wish to find anything that may exist
proving the visit of the great Moses and the ancient King-
dom of Tirhaka. But I pray give me just what pleases
Thee, my Lord, and make me submissive to Thy will in
all things.'

There was another ancient book which wove itself into
Livingstone's dreams during those long empty days at
Bambarré. About the time at which the Pentateuch was
being shaped into its final form, Herodotus visited Egypt,
and he devoted several chapters of his immortal History
to a discussion of the problem of the sources of the Nile, a
problem as mysterious and intriguing to keen and curious
Greeks in the dawn of modern science as it was to the
geographers of the nineteenth century. The discussion
begins with the following passage. ' As to the sources of
the Nile, not one writer of the Egyptians or of the Libyans
or of the Hellenes, who came to speech with me, professed
to know anything, except the scribe of the sacred treasury
of Athene at the city of Sais in Egypt. To me however
this man seemed not to be speaking seriously when he said
that he had certain knowledge of it ; and he said as
follows, namely that there were two mountains of which
the tops ran up to a sharp point, situated between the
city of Syene, which is in the district of Thebes, and
Elephantine, and the names of the mountains were of the
one Crophi and of the other Mophi. From the middle
between these mountains flowed (he said) the sources of
the Nile, which were fathomless in depth, and half of the
water flowed to Egypt, towards the North Wind, the other
half to Ethiopia and the South Wind.'*

A fantastic story, and geographers had hitherto paid it
no more serious attention than had Herodotus himself.
But when two traders arrived one day at Bambarré from
Katanga and told Livingstone that, three or four days'

* Herodotus, book ii, chap. 28 (G. C. Macaulay's translation). The locality of
Thebes and Elephantine was near that of the modern Luxor and Assouan. Sais was
in the delta about 65 miles east-south-east of Alexandria.

march southward of the copper-mines, four rivers rose from ' fountains ' within a space of ten miles and ' a mound rises between them, the most remarkable in Africa,' he instantly recalled the scribe of Sais and began to wonder whether, after all, his story might not have been founded on a distorted version of the truth. Again the idea lodged itself in his mind. Those pagan mountains could not inspire the same intense emotion as Meroe, but the tradition of them added one more exciting element to the dream that might, that surely would, come true as soon as he could take the road again. Feature by feature —the clustered palms, the black shadows, a gleam of water—the mirage was taking shape before the thirsty traveller's eyes.

14

MEANWHILE the intervening belt of country was becoming, month by month, more difficult to traverse. Neither the cholera nor the mud had checked the Arab rush for ivory. In the size and speed of its profits the ivory-trade, as Livingstone observed, was ' like gold-digging ' ; and indeed this Asiatic invasion of Manyema in 1869-71 was not unlike the European invasion of Victoria in 1851-52 or of the Transvaal in 1886-87. But happily the ' diggers ' at Bendigo or Johannesburg were not confronted with a thickly-settled native population, and there is nothing in their story to compare with the ruthless cruelty of the Arabs. The Manyema were by no means submissive or unwarlike folk. ' They fear no one,' it was said, ' though he has many spears.' But their own spears, it seemed, were useless against the weapons of civilisation. ' They tell us truly,' noted Livingstone, classing himself as an ' invader ' with the Arabs, ' that, " were it not for our guns, not one of us would return to our own country." ' And so—for a time—the Arabs did as they liked in the villages of

Manyema. 'Huts are appropriated,' says the journal, 'and no leave asked :. firewood, pots, baskets and food are used without scruple, and anything that pleases is taken away ; usually the women flee into the forest, and return to find the whole place a litter of broken food.' And that was not the worst of it. The Arabs and their slaves were never shy of letting off their terrifying guns. Three of them, for instance, at Katongo's village, 'fired into a mass of men who collected, one killed two, another three, and so on ; so now that place is shut up from traders.' Nor did the women always escape into the bush. 'These Swahili,' Livingstone angrily observes, ' are the most cruel and bloodthirsty missionaries in existence, and withal so impure in talk and acts, spreading disease everywhere. The Lord sees it.'

The other evil, moreover, the Slave Trade, had by no means disappeared. Though ivory was now their first objective, the Arabs took such chances as came their way of buying or kidnapping slaves. And, familiar as the whole brutal business was to him by now, Livingstone was still as sensitive, still as quickly stirred to pity and wrath, as when he first fell foul of it in 1861. The following moving passage was written at Bambarré. ' The strangest disease I have seen in this country seems really to be broken-heartedness, and it attacks free men who have been captured and made slaves. My attention was drawn to it when the elder brother of Syde bin Habib was killed in Rua by a night attack, from a spear being pitched through his tent into his side. Syde then vowed vengeance for the blood of his brother, and assaulted all he could find, killing the elders and making the young men captives. He had secured a very large number, and they endured the chains until they saw the broad River Lualaba roll between them and their free homes; they then lost heart. Twenty-one were unchained as being now safe ; however, all ran away at once, but eight, with many others still in chains, died in three days after crossing. They ascribed their only pain to the heart, and placed the hand correctly on the spot. . . . Some slavers expressed surprise to me that they should die, seeing they had plenty to eat and no work.'

And in another passage Livingstone recalls what Africa has suffered in the west from Europe and in the east from Asia. ' The education of the world is a terrible one, and it has come down with relentless vigour on Africa from the most remote times. What the African will become after his awfully hard lesson is learned is among the future developments of Providence. When He who is higher than the highest accomplishes His purposes, this will be a wonderful country, and again something like it was of old, when Zirah and Tirhaka flourished and were great.'

But already in this year there were signs that Africa was beginning to rebel against the Arab ' missionaries ' and their ' education.' Reprisals were attempted by injured villagers. Traders' camps were attacked by night, sometimes not unsuccessfully. The death of one leading Arab has just been recorded. Another had his camp set on fire several times. And presently the natives ventured to stand their ground and fight by day. At one place, nor far north-west of Bambarré, they stole four guns from a trading camp, and, when the traders came in force to recover them, they ' fought very fiercely with arrows and not till many were killed and others mutilated would they give up the guns.' Another raiding party ' were completely overpowered and compelled by the Manyema to lay down their guns and powder-horns on pain of being instantly despatched by bow-shot : they were mostly slaves who could only draw the trigger and make a noise.' Such conflicts not only meant loss of life among the traders—at one time every trading party lost three or four men—but they taught the Manyema that guns did not always kill and that the Arabs were better shots than their slaves. ' The next thing they will learn,' notes Livingstone, ' will be to grapple at close quarters in the forest when their spears will outmatch the guns in the hands of slaves.' ' It will follow, too,' he adds, ' that no one will be able to pass through this country.'

Livingstone, indeed, was in a dilemma. His porters, if
ever they arrived, would not be numerous nor armed. To
venture alone with them into the west country, as he had
a year ago with only three, would now be simple suicide.
And it was not a pleasant alternative to accompany an
Arab caravan, hoping that, if the natives should venture
to attack it, they would be repelled. Should the order of
events in Nyasaland be reversed? The explorer follow the
path opened by the slaver? Yet how else could he discover the sources of the Nile? What other choice could
Livingstone make since he was no longer, as in the old
days, master of circumstances? And there was this much
to reassure him. The Arabs themselves had begun to
realise that bloodshed, or at any rate indiscriminate bloodshed, was bad business. They were coming to the conclusion 'that the Manyema are not to be shot down
without reasonable cause.' It meant trouble and no ivory.
So, with good fortune, Livingstone might not be involved
by his dubious companions in any fighting; and sooner
or later he would get beyond the danger-zone and no
longer need their escort. 'When Syde and Dugumbé
come,' says the journal, 'I hope to get men and a canoe
to finish my work among those who have not been abused
by Ujijians and still retain their natural kindliness of disposition. None of the people are ferocious without cause.'

And at last, as autumn drew on, news came to Bambarré that those two acquisitive 'Ujijians' and others
were on their way, 'with 700 muskets and an immense
store of beads, copper, etc.' But still the dreary weeks
went by. 'I am grievously tired of living here,' says
Livingstone in November. 'Mohamad [Bogharib] is as
kind as he can be, but to sit idle or give up before I finish
my work are both intolerable; I cannot bear either, yet
I am forced to remain by want of people.' 'O for
Dugumbé or Syde to come,' he cries on December 6;
and on the 10th: 'I am sorely let and hindered in this
Manyema. . . . This is the sorest delay I ever had.' And
on New Year's Day, 1871, comes the usual prayer—'O

Father, help me to finish this work to Thy honour.' Never before, in fact, had Livingstone been so depressed as at this time. It was not only the interminable delay, the cumulative effect of his enforced inaction, month after month, while the prize and recompense of all his life seemed waiting for him just over the horizon. He was feeling again his utter loneliness, and longing for home or at least news of home. Great things had happened and were happening in the world he had left behind him in 1866—Königgratz and the Peace of Prague and the formation of the North German Bund, Garibaldi's march on Rome, the French withdrawal from Mexico and the death of the Emperor Maximilian, the federation of British North America, Gladstone's accession to power and the disestablishment of the Irish Church, the opening of the Suez Canal, and, to crown all, the Franco-Prussian War. These were thrilling and fateful events, but for all he knew of them Livingstone might have been living on another planet. And there was a more personal side to his loneliness. Isolation from the great world, ignorance of its doings, might be endurable if he could keep in touch with his family and friends. But this was equally denied him. Only one scrap of news, it appears, penetrated to Bambarré. He heard in February (1870)—from whom or by what agency is not recorded —of Young's search-expedition (1867). That was something indeed—he was deeply moved by the thought that his friends had been so gravely concerned about him—but that was all. 'I am in agony for news from home,' he confesses in October : 'all I feel sure of now is that my friends will all wish me to complete my task.' And when he mentions the rumour that Dugumbé and his associates are coming, his first thought is of the letters they may bring.

Winter was nearly over before the broken link with Zanzibar, if not with England, was at length restored. On January 27, ' Caravan reported to be near, and my men and goods at Ujiji.' So Kirk *had* received his letter and acted on it ! Next day an Arab caravan arrived. It

brought dreadful news of the cholera at Zanzibar. Early
in November the infection had crossed the narrow waters
from the mainland and found an ideal field for its ravages
in the insanitary old town. The first reports of such
disasters nearly always go beyond the facts ; and, bad as
the truth was, the account which the leaders of the caravan
gave to Livingstone was a good deal worse. ' Great
mortality . . . 70,000 victims in Zanzibar alone . . . my
" brother," whom I conjecture to be Dr. Kirk, has fallen.'
Was this true ? Had he really lost his old comrade of the
Zambesi, his new ally in the war against the Slave Trade ?
He was not kept long in suspense. His whereabouts had
been discovered sooner than he anticipated, and on
February 4 ten of his men arrived from Ujiji. They, too,
made the most of the cholera, though in fact, as will be
seen, they had got clear of Zanzibar before it reached
there. ' Great havoc was made by cholera,' says the
journal, ' and in the midst of it my friend exerted himself
greatly to get men off to me with goods.' Again in a letter
to Waller at this time : ' Ten men have come from Kirk,
who, like the good fellow that he is, worked unweariedly
to get them and the goods off in the midst of disease and
death.'[1] The men also told him that ' the first gang of
porters *all* died,' but they could not indulge their romantic
propensities so far as to confirm the most painful item of
the previous news. For they brought a letter from Kirk
himself. From it Livingstone learned that the request for
goods and men was the only one of his letters from Ujiji
that had reached Zanzibar. So all those forty and more
had been lost or destroyed. And what of the longed-for
letters from home ? They had not come with Kirk's. Were
they waiting at Ujiji ? Had they even got as far ? . . .
But it was easier to endure his isolation now. He had his
men. He could escape at last from his prison at Bambarré
and follow his ' dream.' In a few months' time, perhaps,
he would have made it come true and be on his way home.
' I propose to leave on the 12th.'

15

THE START was actually made on February 16; but already by then Livingstone's exaltation had lost its edge. Those ten men at once proved unsatisfactory. They had come, they said, to bring Livingstone back to Zanzibar, not to follow him farther into the wilderness; and they struck for higher wages. It was not surprising. If Livingstone had been aware of all the circumstances, he would have realised that the really surprising thing was that the men had ever arrived at Bambarré.

When Kirk received that one letter from Ujiji which managed somehow to slip through to Zanzibar, he had been a little more than three years at his post. And already it was proving almost as severe a test of endurance as the Zambesi Expedition. For his new chief, Churchill, was not strong enough to stand the hot malarious climate. He had a great deal to do in his double office—in one year there were more than one hundred cases in his consular and vice-admiralty courts—and he only succeeded in getting it done by asking his agency surgeon to share the burden. In June 1869, he was forced to take sick-leave, and Kirk, appointed to act for him, had to shoulder the whole of the work 'without a bit of assistance,' as he wrote home, ' except that of my wife who is as good as any two clerks.' When Churchill returned to duty in August, 1870, he soon had a relapse, and by the end of the year Kirk was alone again. ' I could not leave the agency in better hands,' wrote Churchill to the Bombay Government; and, since his own return to Zanzibar was now impossible, he suggested that Kirk should be appointed to succeed him.[1]

It was during Churchill's first long absence, on the evening of October 2, 1869, that Kirk received that letter of May 30 from Ujiji,[2] and that same night he wrote to Lord Clarendon, who had long been anxious for news of Livingstone, enclosing a copy of it. He would ' lose no time,' he said, in complying with Livingstone's request. 'There will, however, be some difficulty in getting faithful men as the Arabs of Unyanyembe, being of the El Harthi tribe, are by no means loyal subjects of Seyyid Majid, and are, as Dr. Livingstone tells us, still engaged in the Slave Trade.'[1] That warning note was justified. It is clear, indeed, from what has already been related that Livingstone had unwittingly chosen for his headquarters in the interior what was probably the worst possible place for keeping in touch with his base at Zanzibar and obtaining reinforcements and supplies. Ujiji itself, it has been seen, was a nest of Arab slavers. The leading Arabs of Unyanyembe, which barred the road to the coast, were more considerable and respectable folk, but they too were implicated in the Trade. So were their friends and agents at Zanzibar. So, also, indirectly—since all the financial strings led back to them—were the Indian firms. And all these people, whatever their outward professions, were necessarily bound together in defence of the great vested interest which spread its net from Bambarré to Zanzibar and in antagonism to the man they knew to be its most relentless and influential foe. Nor were they incapable of giving effect to their sentiments. Without any open show of hostility, scarcely even of discourtesy, they had almost completely cut off Livingstone's communications. What chance, then, was there of Kirk being able to restore them ? If he himself or indeed any other white man could have led the caravan to Ujiji, it would have been quite another story. As it was, he was powerless to control its members from the moment they got beyond his reach. If the prestige of a British Consul actually on the spot had proved quite ineffectual at Ujiji, it was not likely that his colleague at Zanzibar could make his distant influence felt all up the long road from the coast. The only authority that could be exercised from a distance in East Africa was the Sultan's ; and whereas, as has been seen, the Sultan's ' passport ' had been used with some effect by Livingstone in the area south of Lake Tanganyika, it had been accorded no more respect at Ujiji than his own consular cap. The only guarantee, apart from their personal honesty, for the good behaviour of the rank and file of a caravan dispatched from Zanzibar was fear of the Sultan's punishment on their return ; and its effectiveness depended on the ' loyalty ' of the ruling Arabs in the interior and their readiness to deal with offences on the Sultan's behalf and report them to Zanzibar.

But was the effectiveness of the Sultan's authority—it might be asked—so very important? Could not honest men be found at Zanzibar who would be faithful to their contracts for other reasons than fear of the Sultan's unsavoury jail? Not easily. The ' unemployed ' in that dirty and decaying outpost of Arab rule in Africa were not endowed with the simple virtues either of Arabs in their desert homes or of Africans in a village in the bush. Most of those who were domiciled in Zanzibar had grown up in the debasing atmosphere of slavery until the ' liberation ' of 1860.* Those who had drifted in from other islands or the coast were mostly vagrant and shiftless folk with no roots, no traditions, no morals. It is significant that, when Livingstone spent those seven weeks at Zanzibar in 1866 preparing for his expedition, ten of the twelve best men he could find were Musa and his companions from Johanna. How could Kirk hope to do better ?

There was another factor in the situation which must have made it difficult not merely to get trustworthy porters but to get any porters at all. Rumours were abroad that the cholera was coming—that dreadful scourge of backward peoples unprotected by modern sanitation or preventive medicine, no less destructive than bubonic plague itself and even more terrifying with its threat of swift, inescapable, agonising death. Twice before in this generation, in 1836 and 1858, a cholera epidemic, radiating from its source in the crowded congregation of Moslem pilgrims at Mecca, had spread along all the contiguous trade-routes of Asia and Africa. In 1858 many of the

* See *The Exploitation of East Africa*, 172-3.

East African coast-towns were ' almost depopulated.'
About 20,000 people died in Zanzibar. And now, starting
from the same focus, the irresistible enemy was again
marching steadily southwards, not along the coast this
time, but overland from the Red Sea through Ethiopia
and the Kenya highlands. As long as it was only a rumour,
Kirk refrained from raising a scare in Whitehall or
Bombay ; but in this same October, a week or two after
he had written to Clarendon, the grim truth was known.
The news had come, Kirk reported to Bombay, that ' the
Masai were dying of some malady that the Arabs at
once named cholera.' Soon after that it reached the sea
at Pangani. In November the first deaths occurred at
Zanzibar.

The first result of such an epidemic was to immobilise
the urban populations. Though a town might seem
doomed, it was no escape to fly into the country. All up
the routes inland the same agony and death were waiting.
It seemed better to stay in the town, to be certain of some
shelter and care and perhaps even medical attention, to
die, if it must be, at home and not among the vultures in
the wilderness. It is a safe assumption, therefore, that
Kirk would have failed to find even so few as fifteen men
willing to take the Ujiji road if they had known for certain
how close the cholera was coming. As it was, he found
them just before it was too late. He applied as a matter of
course to Ludha Damji. It was this old-established Indian
firm, it will be remembered, that had supplied Speke with
porters, and it was its manager, Koorji, whom Livingstone
himself had commissioned to dispatch a caravan to Ujiji.
Since the letter of May 30 spoke only of the goods being
pilfered and said nothing of their poor quality or the dishonest packing, Kirk had no reason to trust the firm less
than Livingstone had trusted it. In both cases it was a
risk, and Kirk, for his part, did what he could to reduce
it. He summoned the fifteen men produced by Ludha
Damji to the Consulate and questioned them. They
' declared themselves freed men, and part of those set free

when the great liberation of slaves took place in Colonel
Rigby's time' (1860), but they had remained in the
service of the ' banyans ' who had previously owned them.
That, at least, was reassuring : for, as Kirk afterwards
remarked, there was ' no better recommendation of a
native than when after many years the freed man continued to attach himself to the house of a former master.'
So, after carefully making sure that ' each man fully
understood every word written in the contract,' he sent
them on their way. The party sailed from Zanzibar before
the end of October.[1]

They had got away just in time. Early in November
the cholera reached the town and spread with dreadful
rapidity through its narrow filthy streets. For weeks it
raged unchecked. It died down in February only to
revive in March. It was not till July that the townsfolk
could draw clean breath again. Between 12,000 and
15,000 of them had died—a literal decimation. There
were several fatal cases among the crews of European and
American ships in the harbour, but of the sixty or so
white residents in the town only Kirk's infant daughter
was attacked and she survived. When the scourge was at
its worst, the life of the town was paralysed. The sultry
streets were deserted, their customary noises hushed. It
was like a besieged city, wrote an observer. Among the
people of Zanzibar island as a whole there were between
25,000 and 30,000 deaths, again roughly one in ten ; and
the infection spread fast and far along the trade-routes on
the mainland. The total mortality must have run well
into six figures.*

The caravan had got away, but the invisible foe was
soon in hot pursuit of it. And perhaps that little gang
of men did not altogether deserve to escape the doom
of those they had left behind. For, quite unknown, of
course, to Kirk, they had concocted a pretty piece of
rascality before they left Zanzibar.

On the recommendation of Ali bin Salem Buraschid, an

* *The Exploitation of East Africa*, 54-5.

Arab of the town, Ludha Damji had appointed a certain
Sherif as leader of the caravan ; and this Sherif had at
once determined to use his commission as a means of
making money for himself. He obtained twenty-five boxes
of soap and eight cases of brandy with a view to trading
on his own account in the villages on the way to Ujiji and
took them to Bagamoyo where he purchased also a quantity of opium and gunpowder. He then packed the soap
inside the bales of goods consigned to Livingstone—thus
obtaining ' freight ' for nothing. For the carriage of the
brandy, opium, and gunpowder he hired additional
porters and paid them out of Livingstone's cloth and beads !
' The Banyan [Ludha Damji?] and Sherif,' as Livingstone
afterwards put it, ' had interposed their own trade specu-
lation between two Government officers, and thenceforward all the expenses of the journey were defrayed out
of my supplies.' Therein, it is clear, lay the extra induce-
ment which had outweighed the rumoured risk of cholera.
It was the chance of making far more money than their
wages that had tempted those fifteen gamblers to take the
road. And some of them soon paid for their daring. Before
the caravan reached Koota, not many miles from the
coast, the cholera gripped it. For several weeks they
camped where they were, immobilised by sickness and
terror. Five died. The survivors meandered on with no
thought whatever of making up for lost time, but stopping
as they felt inclined, at this village or that, to do a little
business. At three places trade seems to have been specially
brisk : at any rate they settled down at each of them for
a month or so, retailing their brandy, opium, gunpowder
and soap. At last, in December, they reached Ujiji. They
had taken fourteen months on a journey which Livingstone
declared could easily have been done in three. But it was
his time they had wasted, not their own. Their venture
had been a great success. Sherif had sent back from
Unyanyembe to his accomplices at Zanzibar a consignment of ivory worth £60, ' carriage-paid,' of course, out
of Livingstone's goods. By the time they got to Ujiji, they

had sold out all their stock ; and for that very good reason Sherif declined to go farther. Having fulfilled the only real purpose which had brought him from Zanzibar, he preferred to make himself comfortable where he was and await events. The means to comfort were at hand—in the white man's unexhausted bales—and he made use of them with due method and precision. He issued eight yards of calico per month to each of the men and to his concubine, twenty-four yards to himself. He also appropriated some of Livingstone's finest beads wherewith to purchase the local drinks—*pombe* and palm toddy. Long afterwards it was the talk of Ujiji that ' he lay drunk for a month at a time.' He was much too happy, in fact, to worry about Livingstone ; and even when trading-parties returned to Ujiji with orders from Livingstone that if his men had arrived they were to join him with the goods at Bambarré, Sherif would not go himself. But he did do something. He dispatched seven of the men to Bambarré, keeping three for his own service at Ujiji. And he sent with them a small quantity of the coarsest and cheapest beads, a few pieces of calico, and—' in great mercy,' wrote Livingstone in the bitterness of his heart—half of the coffee and sugar. One other little packet, which Sherif did not want but which was more valuable to Livingstone than all the rest put together, seems to have been included in this consignment. Its cover bore the word ' quinine ' and Kirk's initials.* Having thus satisfied his conscience, Sherif shortly afterwards parted with all that remained of Livingstone's ill-fated property (except the other half of the coffee and sugar, a bundle of poor unsaleable beads, and a few pieces of calico) in exchange for ivory and slaves. This last proceeding seems to have startled, if not shocked, even the Arabs of Ujiji or at least those few of them who were not unkindly disposed towards Livingstone. But when they ventured to expostulate, the hardy scoundrel had his answer or answers ready. ' You know nothing about the matter. I alone know that the Consul ordered me to

* See p. 114 below.

remain one month at Ujiji and then sell off and return.'
Or alternatively, when no further news came from Bambarré, he had ' divined on the Koran,' he said, and found
that Livingstone was dead. Or again, as he wrote to the
Arab Governor of Unyanyembe, he had sent slaves to
Manyema who had returned and reported the white man's
decease. Was it not, then, permissible to sell the goods ?
. . . Finally, alarmed at news of warfare near Unyanyembe, he took the further store of ivory he had collected
and deposited it in a neighbouring village, and then
returned to his pleasant life at Ujiji. He had still those
few pieces of calico.[1]

16

MEANWHILE the seven men, together with three others
who for some unknown reason had thrown in their lot
with them, had arrived at Bambarré. What they learned
there was not calculated to mend their ways or manners.
They were met by the two ringleaders of the party which
had deserted Livingstone in the course of the previous
year ; and they heard from them of his futile wanderings,
of his broken health, of his helplessness and dependence
on the Arabs, and also, no doubt, of his gentle and for-
giving disposition. Clearly this was not the sort of white
man to be afraid of, and from the first the newcomers'
attitude to Livingstone was truculent. They asserted, to
begin with, that they were still slaves, and named their
banyan masters—in two cases, Ludha Damji himself. The
three recruits, on the other hand, said they were free men.
Why the seven did not say the same, as they had said it to
Kirk, is probably to be explained by their wish to make
Livingstone realise that they were not free to obey *his*
orders. At any rate they told him at once that their
masters' orders were not to go with him farther into the
interior but to bring him back to the coast. Those likewise,

they declared, were Consul Kirk's orders. And they spread it round Bambarré that Kirk had written to Livingstone bidding him return forthwith. ' They swore so positively,' records Livingstone himself, ' that I actually looked again at Dr. Kirk's letter to see if his orders had been rightly understood by me.' Of course he had not been mistaken. Of course the letter stated that the men had been engaged to follow Livingstone ' as porters, boatmen, woodmen, or in any other capacity ' wherever he chose to go. But even the production of that letter did not quell the mutineers. They changed their ground. ' They could not follow me, because I had not fifty or sixty guns, because I had not enough percussion-caps for their flint guns, because I wished to go where there were no Moslems, etc. etc.' Nor even when Livingstone yielded—not very wisely perhaps— to their demand for higher wages, even when he offered them twice as much as free labour could earn at Zanzibar, would they surrender. They were stronger than Livingstone and knew it. Alone he could do nothing. So once more he was obliged to ask for help from others, from the Arabs. Faithful Mohamad Bogharib was at Bambarré and also the formidable Dugumbé ; they and their associates, however much their opinions of Livingstone and his work in Africa may have varied, seem all to have wanted to aid him in his present plight. ' Dugumbé and his friends,' says Livingstone, ' offered to supply everything I needed and told the banyan slaves so ; and I begged them not to force me back and thereby frustrate the object for which great expense had been incurred and forfeit all pay. They answered him, too, in a sneering way and departed muttering. In fact, as most of the Arabs are in debt to the banyans, the slaves think they can assume airs over them and, as it appears to me, over the English too. . . .' It was Mohamad Bogharib who cut the knot at last. Something rougher, he saw, was needed than Livingstone's appeals, backed though they were by Dugumbé. He drew his pistol—and the ' slaves ' gave in. On February 16 the little caravan set out in pursuit of Livingstone's dream.[1]

And then at once, though the auspices for his success could scarcely have been less favourable, the mere movement and change of scene wrought their usual spell on Livingstone. The tone of the journal changes in a page from despondency to cheerfulness. 'The country is beautiful and undulating,' he writes on February 23 : 'light green grass covers it all, save at the brooks, where the eye is relieved by the dark green lines of trees.' Next day, at Mamohela, 'we were welcomed by all the Arabs, and I got a letter from Dr. Kirk and another from the Sultan . . . all anxious to be kind.' Even the information that the Lualaba made a great bend to the west-south-west did not daunt him. 'I had to suspend my judgment,' he notes, coolly enough, 'so as to be prepared to find it after all perhaps the Congo.' And a few days later comes a rare passage of description which even Livingstone could hardly have written in those days of illness and misery at Bambarré. 'Our path lay through dense forest, and again, on 5th, our march was in the same dense jungle of lofty trees and vegetation that touch our arms on each side. We came to some villages among beautiful tree-covered hills, called Basilangé or Mobasilangé. The villages are very pretty, standing on slopes. The main street generally lies east and west, to allow the bright sun to stream his clear hot rays from one end to the other, and lick up quickly the moisture from the frequent showers which is not drained off by the slopes. A little verandah is often made in front of the door, and here at dawn the family gathers round a fire, and, while enjoying the heat needed in the cold that always accompanies the first darting of the light or sun's rays across the atmosphere, inhale the delicious air, and talk over their little domestic affairs. The various shaped leaves of the forest all around their village and near their nestlings are bespangled with myriads of dewdrops. The cocks crow vigorously, and strut and ogle ; the kids gambol and leap on the backs of their dams quietly chewing the cud ; other goats make believe fighting. Thrifty wives often bake their new clay

pots in a fire, made by lighting a heap of grass roots : the
next morning they extract salt from the ashes, and so two
birds are killed with one stone. The beauty of this morning
scene of peaceful enjoyment is indescribable.'

It was not always so. ' In some cases we found the
villages deserted ; the people had fled at our approach in
dread of repetitions of the outrages of Arab slaves. The
doors were all shut.' But even when he crossed the slavers'
tracks, it was a consolation, a reminiscence of earlier
journeys in happier parts of Africa, to find the people
friendly at least to him. ' Many have found out', he says,
' that I am not one of their number. . . . They stand up
and call out loudly, " Bolongo, Bolongo ! " " Friendship,
friendship ! " . . . I overhear the Manyema telling each
other than I am the " good one " : I have no slaves.'
And, to cap all, he soon had reassuring news of the Lualaba.
' This great river,' he was told, ' makes a second great
sweep to the west, and there are at least 30° of southing ;
but now it comes rolling majestically to the north, and
again makes even easting. It is a mighty stream, with
many islands in it, and is not wadeable at any point or
at any time of the year.' Surely it was the Nile ! . . . That
entry was made when Livingstone was only six miles
from the river. He was getting very near the end of his
journey and of his happiness.

Next day (March 10) a report came in of fighting in
the north. A powerful chief, Luapanya, had collected ' an
immense body of archers ' and forced a battle on Mohamad
Bogharib's trading-party. ' The consequence was they
killed Luapanya and many of his people.' Later on he
heard that Mohamad, his friend Mohamad, had allowed
or incited his followers to trick the natives of another
district into a quarrel : they had then shot down the men
and carried off many of the women and children as slaves.
From the south, too, came bad news. Arabs had attacked
a village, killed three men, and taken women and children
for slaves. So again the shadow of the Slave Trade darkens
the pages of the journal. ' The traders from Ujiji are

simply marauders . . . they thirst for blood more than
for ivory, and the Manyema are an easy prey.' 'I am
heartsore and sick of human blood' is the single entry for
March 20. And that was not the only sign that the balance
of Livingstone's fortunes was swinging back again. Cold
rain set in. Some of his men fell sick. The march was held
up till they recovered. And on the very last day there was
another crackle of mutiny. The men again demanded
higher wages and flung back the beads which Livingstone
gave them for 'rations.' 'The banyan slaves,' laments the
journal, 'are again trying compulsion—I don't know what
for. . . . It is excessively trying, and so many difficulties
have been put in my way I doubt whether the Divine
favour and will is on my side.' Dejection could go no
deeper. What was he doing in Africa, what use was all
his life and work, if not in accordance with God's will?
But the mainspring of Livingstone's fortitude had not yet
snapped. That doubt could not be harboured long; and
when he reached Nyangwé (March 29) and gazed on the
river of his dream, it was gone. 'I went down to take a
good look at the Lualaba here. It is narrower than it is
higher up, but still a mighty river, at least 3000 yards
broad, and always deep. . . . The current is about two
miles an hour *away to the north.*'

And now there only remained the last and easy stage
of Livingstone's journey—six days down the Lualaba to
the influx of the Lueki, then up the latter to the country
of Katanga and the conical hills and the fountains of the
Nile. But for this, of course, canoes were needed or at
least a canoe; and Livingstone soon found that it was
quite as difficult to obtain one now as it had been on the
banks of the Luamo in 1869. The natives were not, it
seemed, unfriendly: several of them promised to get him
canoes; but nothing happened. And the reason was soon
clear—the same old reason. 'They all think,' Livingstone
records after a fortnight at Nyangwé, 'that my buying a
canoe means carrying war to the left bank; and now my

banyan slaves encourage the idea : " He does not wish slaves nor ivory," say they, " but a canoe in order to kill Manyema." Need it be wondered at that people who had never heard of strangers or white men before I popped down among them believed the slander ? ' Another fortnight passed and it was still the same story. ' Waiting wearily and anxiously. . . . Even the owners of canoes say, "Yes, yes ; we shall bring them," but do not stir. They doubt us, and my slaves increase the distrust.' On May 3 he was told by a friendly trader named Abed that ' a canoe will come in five days.' It did not come. And presently his impotence was made the more galling by the fact that a party of Arab traders arriving at Nyangwé and desiring like Livingstone to go down the river had no difficulty at all about getting canoes. ' Hassani,' says the journal, and it is now June 14, ' got nine canoes and put sixty-three persons in three ; I cannot get one.'

As it happened, the sequel to this incident was consoling. Hassani had never explored the Lualaba before, and after four days' journey his party came to a point where the river suddenly narrowed to cut its way through a mountainous ridge of rock so that its mighty waters, penned in on either side, were thrown in surging whirlpools against one wall and then back against the other. No canoe could live there ; and the first of Hassani's flotilla was instantly upset and five lives lost. The rest at once turned back to Nyangwé, without troubling to test the possibilities of carrying the canoes beyond the narrows. Now, if Livingstone and not Hassani had obtained those canoes, his own canoe would certainly have led the way ; exactly the same disaster might have befallen him as he had seen befalling Kirk on the Zambesi in 1860 ; and he might not have had Kirk's luck in getting out alive.* All that wearisome delay, indeed, now seemed to Livingstone directly providential. ' In answer to my prayers for preservation I was prevented going down to the narrows. . . . We don't always know the dangers we are guided past.'

* See *Kirk on the Zambesi*, 178-9.

It was a sign, too, that he must change his plan. He must avoid the narrows on the Lualaba which might also, he conjectured, occur on the Lueki owing to the extension of the same rocky ridge to westward. In fact he must march overland to the Lueki. But for that he still needed or thought he needed a canoe—to cross those three thousand yards of water flowing at his feet. Other folk were crossing all the time. Nyangwé was the most important centre in that part of Manyema and natives flocked from all sides to its market. Livingstone's own men could cross ; for he sent them over, he says, ' to the other side to cut wood to build a house.' He only could not cross, it seems, except in his own canoe. And so again he sat and waited. In the middle of July he was still waiting.

This was one more symptom, surely, of the failing of Livingstone's old powers. Ten years earlier he would probably have got his canoe. In any case he would have crossed the Lualaba. It was not a dangerous voyage. The current was not fast nor turbulent. There was wood available. Why did he use it to build a house in which to sit inactive instead of a raft in which he could have paddled across the river ? Was it his queer fatalism ? Did he per-suade himself that, if canoes were not available, he was not meant to cross in some less customary craft ? Or was it lethargy ? He complains once or twice of intestinal trouble and headache, relieved by discharges of blood which he regarded, casually enough, as ' safety-valves to the system.' Whatever the reason, there at Nyangwé he chose to stop, sitting in his new-built house—' a great comfort, for the other was foul and full of vermin '— watching the busy native life, counting the people that passed his door—there were seven hundred, he notes, one market-day—reading his Bible through again and brooding over the sacred oracles—watching the river, his mighty river flowing by, sounding its depth, marking its every rise and fall, eagerly noting the report that every year it overflows its banks ' as the Nile does *further down*,' buying each species of the fish that were caught in it in order to

make sketches of them and compare them ' with those of
the Nile *lower down*, and observing, when the flood rises,
that ' the water is a little darker in colour than *at Cairo.*'
His only real recreation or diversion—it is clear from the
journal—was a visit to the frequent markets where, fas-
cinated by the colour and the movement of the crowd, he
could forget for a time the weariness of waiting.

April 10. Chitoka or market to-day . . . With market
women it seems to be a pleasure of life to haggle and joke
and laugh and cheat : many come eagerly and retire with
careworn faces ; many are beautiful, and many old ; all
carry very heavy loads of dried cassava and earthen pots
which they dispose of very cheaply for palm-oil, fish, salt,
pepper, and relishes for their food.

May 16. At least 3000 people at market to-day, and my
going among them has taken away the fear engendered by
the slanders of slaves and traders, for all are pleased to
tell me the names of fishes and other things. . . . There is
quite a roar of voices in the multitude, haggling. It was
pleasant to be among them compared to being with the
slaves who were all eager to go back to Zanzibar.

May 24. The market is a busy scene—every one is in
dead earnest—little time is lost in friendly greetings. . . .
Each is intensely eager to barter food for relishes, and makes
strong assertions as to the goodness or badness of everything : the sweat stands in beads on their faces : cocks
crow briskly even when slung over the shoulder with their
heads hanging down, and pigs squeal. . . . The men
flaunt about in gaudy-coloured *lambas* of many folded
kilts—the women work hardest—the potters slap and ring
their earthenware all round to show that there is not a
single flaw in them. I bought two finely shaped earthern
bottles of porous earthenware, to hold a gallon each, for
one string of beads. . . . It is a scene of the finest natural
acting imaginable. The eagerness with which all sorts of
assertions are made—the eager earnestness with which
apparently all creation, above, around, and beneath, is

called on to attest the truth of what they allege—and then
the intense surprise and withering scorn cast on those who
despise their goods. Little girls run about selling cups of
water for a few small fishes to the half-exhausted wordy
combatants. To me it was an amusing scene. I could not
understand the words that flowed off their glib tongues,
but the gestures were too expressive to need interpretation.
May 27. A stranger in the market had ten human under
jaw-bones hung by a string over his shoulder : on inquiry
he professed to have killed and eaten the owners and
showed with his knife how he cut up his victim. When I
expressed disgust, he and others laughed. . . . I see new
faces every market day. Two nice girls were trying to sell
their venture which was roasted white ants, called
" Gumbe."

These pages are reminiscent of Livingstone's journals
on earlier expeditions : those hours spent at the market
were his happiest. Back in his house, there was little to do
but think, especially in the long dark hours that follow the
early tropical sunset. And his thoughts were mostly bitter
thoughts about the ever-repeated, intolerable frustration
of his purpose, of his dream ; and, as sick and tired men
will, he began to brood over his misfortunes, reiterating
and dissecting his grievances and raking over and over in
every detail the misconduct of the wretched creatures who
had deserted and betrayed him. He wrote at this period,
for example, an account of Musa's cowardice—of exactly
what he said in his terror of the Mazitu—and that affair
was now five years old.[1] But the more recent scandal, the
conduct of Sherif and his men, was naturally his chief
obsession, and it was aggravated every day by the behaviour at Nyangwé of the ' banyan slaves.' Aware once
more that Livingstone was both helpless and harmless, they
became as undisciplined as at Bambarré. Their master's
inactivity meant little work for them, but that little was
not done without murmurings of mutiny and demands for
higher pay. On one occasion, so Livingstone was told,

they dissuaded some friendly natives from selling him a
canoe. On another, they were overheard, 'plotting my
destruction.' ., 'If forced to go on, they would watch till the
first difficulty arose with the Manyema, then fire off their
guns, run away, and, as I could not run as fast as they,
leave me to perish.' And that was not the worst. A party
of them, whom Livingstone had sent to a village a few
miles distant to try to arrange the purchase of a canoe, went
off marauding on their own account and slew three natives.
At last Livingstone determined to disarm and dismiss them;
but, when it came to the point, 'they relented and professed to be willing to go anywhere,' and feeling, no doubt,
that he would be even more helpless, if that indeed were
possible, without them, he changed his mind. But they
were still a constant trial. 'I cannot state,' says the journal,
and no wonder, 'how much I am worried by those
wretched slaves.' Fortunately they were not Livingstone's
only servants and companions. Susi, Chuma, and three
other 'faithfuls' were with their master all through those
dark days and afterwards to the end. But there is no
mention of them in the journal of these months. Its pages,
save only for those descriptions of the market, seem reserved
exclusively for record of misfortunes and misconduct. It is
always that rascal Sherif and those 'banyan slaves.' One
further manifestation should be recorded of Livingstone's
distempered mood. He often thought of England, of his
family and friends and the honour he had won and had
yet to win, but he must needs think also of his 'enemies,'
of the critics and sceptics who had minimised his earlier
achievements and questioned his results, even of the
ridiculous Mr. Cooley,* and of others less respectable who
had dishonestly made profit from his name. It was absurd,
of course, that Livingstone of all men should vex himself
with the sayings and doings of such little folk; absurd, but
also symptomatic and pathetic.

* W. D. Cooley was an academic geographer of some repute in British scientific
circles. In 1852 he published *Inner Africa Laid Open* in which he declared that there
was only one great lake in Central Africa and that the snow-mountains, Kilimanjaro
and Kenya, recently discovered by Rebmann and Krapf, were a myth. As late as
1864 he still insisted that Lakes Nyasa and Tanganyika were one lake.

17

THERE was one source of consolation for Livingstone during those bad months. Reports had reached him of the fight which his old lieutenant had begun against the Slave Trade at Zanzibar. Writing to his daughter Agnes of the ' perfectly indescribable ' bestiality of the Trade, ' Kirk,' he says, ' has been working hard to get this murderous system put a stop to. Heaven prosper his noble efforts.'[1] To Waller he writes that he has heard of pressure being brought on the Sultan with good prospects of success. ' I believe a great deal is owing to the exertions of our friend. Kirk, on whom for my share may heaven's rich blessings descend.'[2] And at this time he wrote three letters to Kirk, the first long intimate letters written since his wanderings began that reached Kirk's hands ; and since, informal and discursive as they are, they not only supplement the journal but improve on it as a reflection of their writer's mind, harassed and weary and yet able now and again to turn out sparks of its old vigour and even its old fun, they may be printed here in full.[3]

The first is written, for lack of writing-paper, on a proof-sheet of the *Proceedings* of the Royal Geographical Society, recording a meeting on November 8, 1869, at which, as it happened, a letter of Livingstone's from ' near Lake Bangweolo ' had been read. Crowded though it is over every inch of the paper, the fine writing is scarcely ever difficult to read, even when, the margins exhausted, it crosses the letterpress itself.

(i)

WEBB'S LUALABA OR LACUSTRINE RIVER,
25 *March*, 1871.

MY DEAR KIRK,

I very thankfully received your letter of 28th Feb. 69, sent by Sheikh bir Nassib at Mamohela about 7 days N.W. of

Bambarré, containing a welcome one from Agnes to you. By it I first learned that you had taken unto yourself a wife who has presented you with a daughter. Blessings on them both. H.C. * people think each has an angel. I only know that the little ones are angels themselves and come as ministering spirits of peace and love. I have but one regret in looking back on my stationary missionary life and that is that I did not play more with my children, but I worked so hard physically and mentally that in the evening there was seldom any fun left in me. I thankfully accept your invitation to lodge with you at Zanzibar, but I feel so woefully far away and am going still farther in order to make a complete work of the exploration of the sources of the Nile. I have been sorely let and hindered in Manyema, and, reaction against the bloody Ujijian slaving having set in, I went off not without apprehension, and until I get beyond the region of bloodshed I cannot feel safe. It is not slave trade, it is slaking thirst for blood and catching free people very many of whom die before reaching the coast. I shall give you an episode which happened about a fortnight ago close by the spot where I write.

My spirits are beyond measure depressed in writing on such matters for the public and I can only give half-statements for fear of letting heartless dawdlers drawl from their club sofas " exaggeration," " overdrawing," etc. The restrained exposure of the vile Portuguese deeds on the Shiré in my last book made me oblivious to anything else. My own and family interests were unheeded. Lord Palmerston sent a Queen's Counsel to ask me " what he could do to aid me as he was most anxious to serve me." I could only think of the work in Africa and asked the East African ports to be opened to lawful commerce for all nations. It never occurred to me that he meant ought for myself or children till I was out here and Lord Palmerston dead.

The episode I mention was by Mohammed Bogharib's people and he being the best man of all who have come to trade in Manyema you may, if you can, imagine the conduct of the people of the worst. Ben Hassani, Ben Mbegu, and Ben Omad, the heads of the party sent to trade, gave the Manyema near to Moené Lualaba 25 copper bracelets, worth at Ujiji about 2½ dollars—this was the trap—they went down the river and sold all the rest of their copper for ivory. Coming

* High Church?

back they demanded ivory for the 25 rings and began to shoot the men in cold blood and capture women and children and grass-cloth, goats and fowls. They continued the murdering for three days in a densely populated district and carried off an immense number of women and children because Muhamad does not intend to trade here again. With all his goodness I have no doubt that he knew the plan and will receive his full share of the captives. They will come into Zanzibar as traders and the people are *bought* slaves, but there is not one slave among them and to make the matter the more atrocious the very men who murdered and captured repeatedly declared to me that the people now victimised were remarkably civil and kind. Thousands come over the river every market day to hold markets at various points for flour, cassava, beans, ground nuts, fish, salt, oil, bananas, plantains, sweet potatoes, sugar cane, grass cloth, earthenware, ironware as knives, spears, needles, fowls, sheep, goats, pigs, slaves, ivory ; and it was particularly noticed that, when the men of two districts were engaged in actual hostilities, the women go from market to market with their wares unmolested. Women were never touched until now by these Muhamadans. As a rule not a slave is sold in Manyema except by the ruffian strangers. It would be only justice if the Sultan would set free all captives from Manyema as soon as they arrive. They were not traded for but murdered for. In talking with these Ujijians I always protest against shedding human blood. They think that by rhyming out " God is great " etc., all sin is forgiven. A slave of Thani ben Suelim of Ujiji, named Yahoo, boasted in my hearing of having with his comrades killed one hundred people and burned 9 villages, all for a single string of red beads which a Manyema man tried in vain to steal. I said to him, " You were sent to trade, not to murder." He replied, " We *are* sent to kill people ; that is our work." One of my people was killed, I suppose in blind revenge. A man was pinned to the ground with a spear near the 9 villages and I was sleeping in another [tent ?] close by. Three were killed at another village and we don't know who are friends and who have just cause to seek revenge of all strangers. I find great difficulty in getting a canoe after the Bogharib feat of arms. All flee from us. Your men seem as eager for bloodshed as others. All long to be able to brag of bloodshed. That Shereef Bosher* has put me to great

* So spelt in MS.

inconvenience by refusing to send me my own beads and other things while he stops to feast at my expense. He thinks that he and his three slaves are earning salary. I have sent orders to take the goods and give them to Msengeghere, a trustworthy man. Awaha, the other headman, has enlarged scrotum, had it at Zanzibar and onwards, says now it pains him ! ! and wants pay without work.

I feel extremely thankful for all you did for me in the most trying circumstances a man could be placed in. I send a cheque for Rs. 4000 by Muhamad Bogharib.

Lualaba torrents smaller down here than stated in my despatch—' 2 to 4 miles '—but it is still a mighty river from 1½ to 2 miles. Please to detain the despatch and letters if you hear of any being on the way down and near. I should like to rewrite all the hearsay written only in apprehension of never coming out.

Not a single line from Sir Paraffin Young since I left England and I have written him by every opportunity. The money I sent for was to be lifted from £1000 in Coutts' hands —mine, not his. Letters may be in the box which Muhamad bin Saleh had my note to open and take out medicine and letters, but Mr. Shereef refused to allow him.

If you write to Seward, remember me kindly to him and to his wife. Take good care of your better half and child. Move about as often as you can. Good people are scarce. I am thankful to hear you say that my words have had some little effect at home. I have often said with a sore heart, I have laboured in vain and spent my strength for nought and in vain. Yet surely my work is with the Lord and my judgement with my God. The cheery prospect of stopping the East Coast slave trade belongs to you, and therein I do greatly rejoice. The Sultan must get troops which will scour the mainland and catch the bloody thieves inland. By the counsel of an old man near him he is said to have parted with his Belooches* to save expense. He must not trust the Arabs. They are such liars. Their prophet lied to reform his country-men who now lie because it is ingrained in their constitutions.

In the event of detaining the despatch and letters you might give the substance of my letter to you to the Government. I am rather anxious to give but little to the public. Four spurious publications were concocted from my letters on my journey across the continent. One, a five-shilling book,

* Mercenary soldiers.

was sold in America and all over the world extensively as
" *the book*." It was by a schoolmaster named Adams. Rout-
ledge sold a shilling book as mine at all the railways in
England and America, and offered me £20 to hold my peace
about it. A secretary of the London Missionary Society
issued a pamphlet, " Dr. L.'s life and travels, with a map by
the author," and again advertised it with " revised by
himself " ! Another secretary performed a like piece of
villainy, but palmed it off as from the " Society," knowing
that I would not injure a great institution doing work of
priceless value in the world. Another secretary of the same
Society indulged in a tirade in a London church against me
as " morally guilty of the death of Mr. Helmore."* Cooley
regularly proved me all wrong in the ' Athenaeum ' as soon
as my letters reached home. The Liambai, which we found
to be a mile broad, was " an undeveloped river " that ran
under the Kalahari desert and was lost and I was a fool to
say that it was a river at all. Give Waller a hint not to answer
him by name. It is the breath of life to him to be named.
When I was silent he *entreated* me to argue the point of the
Liambai with him and ' Athenaeum ' shut out his letters
when I only joked at him without naming him, ' the great
apostle of hearsay geography.' Waller does not seem to know
James Russell Lowell's poems. He is a Northerner and lashed
the slaveocracy of the South when they uttered the same
trash as the anthropologists till they were red-hot with rage.
" The mass ought to labour and we lie on sofies," etc.

A friend at Mamohela gave me a young Soko or gorilla
lately. She sits 18 inches high and is the most intelligent and
least mischievous of all the monkeys I have seen. I could not
take her with me as I am mobbed enough already : two
Sokos, she and I, would not get a breath of air. She is to be
kept for me at Ujiji. She walks on the backs of four fingers,
the space between the first joint and second touching the
ground. The nails and thumbs do not touch it. It is like the
daft minister you know. The legs are hitched forward as if
the arms were crutches.

Moosa Kamaals was detained many months and was sent

---

* Livingstone's account of the friendliness of the Makololo encouraged the L. M. S.
to send a missionary party, headed by the Rev. H. Helmore to Linyanti. It arrived
there early in 1860, but within a few months Helmore and his wife and four of the other
seven white members of the party died of malaria, and the survivors abandoned the
enterprise. R. Lovett, *History of the L. M. S.* (London, 1899), vol. i, chap. 4 ; W. G.
Blaikie, *David Livingstone* (6th ed., London, 1910), 231-2.

back to Ujiji. He hid his letter as his wages depended on it. The 40 letters went off same date as Moosa Kamaals. I suspect the Governor is guilty not to allow evidence of the plunder of my goods by his man Musa bin Salum going to the coast. Giving off my goods to his own creature, who stopped the porters ten days while he plundered, was villainy —the porters needed no one [?], they had come so far honestly —and then Salum went off to buy ivory in Karangwe. I fear my two guns are abstracted from the box which Shereef nurses. You packed it and it is now re-packed with, I suspect Shereef's connivance, but I may be mistaken. It is suspicious that Shereef persisted in keeping it close[d] in spite of my written order to Muhamad bin Saleh to open it and send it entire. The men came without loads. A party went from us to Ujiji, told Shereef that I was near and waiting for him, [and] invited him to come with them. So he is inexcusable.

There is no signature to this letter. Indeed there is scarcely room for it. But the following postscript is squeezed in along one edge. 'The Governor is very liberal with presents of foolscap paper, London maker's name Millington, same as yours. Suspicious. I got a sheet of my own paper.'

The second and third letters, though their dates are more than a month apart, are written on the two sides of one half-sheet of blue-grey foolscap. It was the paper, as it chanced, marked with Kirk's initials, in which he had dispatched that precious packet of quinine in 1869.[1] Since Livingstone's supply of ink was now exhausted, he had written these letters with a red fluid which, as the journal records, he had made for himself from the seeds of a plant, called by the Arabs *zugifaré*. The colour is faded now, but the characters are still legible except at one place where the paper has been folded. Guesses have been inserted here between brackets. There is no form of address to Kirk at the head of this letter.

(ii)

14th May, 1871. Chakanja Ludha's slave and Juma, slave of Mumea, ringleaders of mutiny and the loudest in asserting that the Consul told him not to [go] forward [but to bring me] back and not to follow me if I went to " a bad country," demanded leave for 15 days to go and buy [?] of lambas where cheap on our West, and on my refusing went and told Abed what ample rations they got at the coast and now would leave me. I refused because Abed has got a canoe for me—price not settled as owner is sick—and I sent a party about six miles off to examine another, see the owner, measure it, and come back with him if willing for the price next day. They remained away six days. I could not trust more of my leaders out of sight, so sent other two of the slaves with guides to order the party back. These went on with them to kill Manyema and they did kill three men. I told them I would never let them go anywhere unless I could go myself. A party is going to buy copper as it is smelted near us. They killed a great number who stood in mute amazement at the guns and their effects. These ringleading worthies in everything that is bad hope to repeat this blood-shed because they incur no danger and would get slaves. I never imagined that human or Mohammedan nature rather could be so atrociously vile. By the back of this I give them a dismissal. Twice refused to go North at Bambarré, then in the way threw back their rations of beads, demanded double though what I gave was three times more than the Arabs give their slaves. I am glad to get rid of them by their own desire. They got two to follow them by loud talking of what they get at the coast and they know that my beads are nearly all at Ujiji. As to wages you will know best. They compelled me to an advance of six dollars at Bambarré—a distinct breach of their engagement with you.

I am far West. Loeki or Lomamé is at least 60° further— very broad—a true Lake Lincoln above. When on its west bank we shall be some six miles only from the mouth of the Congo. The people swarming and friendly till abused by bloodhounds. They drink a cup of coffee after each meal. The trees are abundant ; I am to get some ; it is well dried in the fruit rind. If Waller likes to set a trap for Cooley he might publish about my great Westing and draw the author of " Inner Africa LAID open " out on my stupidity in thinking Lualaba ought else but the Congo. Then publish this addendum. You will naturally, if very pig-headed like the great apostle of hearsay geography, swear I have been following the Congo instead of the Nile ; but here the mighty river takes a sweep towards the East, takes in the Lomamé, and becomes more grand than ever, 6 or 8 miles broad with many very great inhabited islands in it before it joins or receives the *Kisiwa* which must be Lake Albert. Ivory is like grass— this is great news for Suahili—and at 2 rings of copper a tusk. I wish that licence were refused to all the Sultan's subjects for interior trade who are guilty of bloodshed causelessly.

DAVID LIVINGSTONE.

The men were not dismissed, as has been seen : so the back of the sheet was available for the third letter, written six weeks later.

(iii)

TO DR. KIRK from DR. LIVINGSTONE. 26th June, 1871.

On this page I intended to put an Arabic dismissal to the ringleaders. I use it now to say please do not be offended with palavers. I am really reduced to beggary notwithstanding all the bountiful provision you with immense difficulty made for me and that too almost entirely by the villainy of the unmitigated drunken blackguard Shereef. His Banian [owner?], a British subject, is in part to blame ; for he must have known his habits and his brandy when he imposed them on us. He is reported to have bought ivory with my goods, and this ivory ought to be stopped at the custom house as is done in case of Arabs till he refunds. If Seyed bin Majid sends the list of goods left by Shereef you will judge of the extent of loss. If not, then the case had better wait till I return. Remember that the list containing 12 Frasilahs samsam and the watch is that destroyed by Shereef. I have that of samsam 6 Frasilahs, Langio 3 Do., and Pink 3 etc. All Dugumbé's people saw the packet and think, as he refused it to Dugumbé, it is hidden. I feel sore most of all about the watch, though it is hard too to be living from hand to mouth in beggary while my Banian slaves lived sixteen months in clover and idleness earning, they supposed, from five to seven dollars per month. They are independent of the Arabs but so they are of us and of honesty.

I go west of this to Lomame—60°, then buy a canoe, if Dugumbé will advance the price, and go south to the watershed and four fountains. Dugumbé is very friendly and a gentleman with more exploring enterprise in him than any other. He is going to sow and be here at Nyangwe for three years, sending every now and then to Ujiji. Letters sent to him will be safe. His people will bring some goods for me from Ujiji and I shall share liberally with him.

I ought [to] have mentioned that a dyke of basalt or other igneous rock cuts across the river 4 days of the canoe below this, and the immense body of water is jammed rushing through the jutting ends which are not parallel [?] and form whirlpools in which canoes whirl round and round helplessly. I am thankful I was not there or I would have been foremost in this and a cataract below—and no Makololo to help me.* I thought next of going up river to Kamolondo, the broad part of Webb's Lake river, but another cataract intervenes, so I go due west on foot on the 2nd day of New Moon, about 9th July.

In this jumble of odds and ends you will see how my mind is confused. I should have added up there that I don't go down river at present because in turning up Lomame from Lualaba I should probably meet the same basaltic dyke in the ascent, for such dykes run a long way across country. Here I have a chance of cutting Lomame above it.

DAVID LIVINGSTONE.

I had to pay the carriers of Shereef's brandy. From first to last his own trade for ivory was what he followed shamelessly.

* An allusion to Kirk's accident ; see p. 104 above.

18

LIVINGSTONE'S prospects had changed for the better when
he wrote the last of those three letters. By the middle of
June he seems to have almost abandoned hope of getting
a canoe and to have felt—again it was not the old Livingstone—that he would never get away from Nyangwé without the help of the Arabs who had got him away from
Bambarré. Mohamad Bogharib was not available : he
had done all the trade he wanted in the Lualaba country
and was returning westwards ; but it was reported on
June 14 that Dugumbé was approaching and on the 18th
he arrived. ' He has a large party and 500 guns. He is
determined to go into new fields of trade, and has all his
family with him, and intends to remain six or seven years,
sending regularly to Ujiji for supplies of goods.' Here was
a sharp contrast with Livingstone's lot. Here were strength
and self-confidence and the means of action. Who could
play the part of friend-in-need better than this bold and
prosperous Arab ? And Dugumbé, it seemed, was quite
ready to play it. He sent Livingstone a generous gift of
beads, which Livingstone reciprocated with some of the
fine calico he still possessed. He promised at once to solve
his immediate problem. ' I will buy you a canoe,' were
nearly the first words he said to him. But he also pointed
out the difficulties, obvious enough to Livingstone, that
obstructed the success of his westward journey. ' Your own
slaves are your greatest enemies,' he told him ; for their
' slanders have put all the Manyema against you.' Ten
days later (July 1), Livingstone suggested a definite plan.
Might he go overland with Dugumbé's caravan to the
Lomamé and then with his help obtain a canoe in which
he could proceed alone up the river, examine the Katanga
country, and return to Nyangwé ? And meantime could
Dugumbé have his remaining goods brought from Ujiji to
Nyangwé ? To these proposals Dugumbé gave no firm

reply. ' He again referred to all the people being poisoned
in mind against me, but was ready to do everything in his
power for my success.' Four days later Livingstone tried
again. He offered Dugumbé 2000 dollars for ten men to
replace the ' banyan slaves ' and accompany him to
Katanga and thence back *via* Lake Tanganyika to Ujiji.
' I added that I would give all the goods I had at Ujiji
besides.' Still no clear answer. ' He took a few days to
consult with his associates.' What was passing in the
Arab's mind can only be guessed at. He was not the loyal
Mohamad Bogharib, but there is no reason to doubt that
he was really ' very friendly,' that he wanted to help the
helpless white man to fulfil his queer desires. At the same
time he may well have disliked that white man poking his
nose too deeply into those virgin fields he meant to exploit
himself ; he may well have shared in some degree the
Ujijians' belief that Livingstone was not as harmless as
he looked. At any rate he temporised. He advised Livingstone to try to persuade his own men to go on with him
by explaining his exact intentions. ' I did explain,' says
Livingstone, ' all the exploration I intended to do ; for
instance, the fountains of Herodotus beyond Katanga,
Katanga itself and the underground dwellings, and then
return. They made no remarks, for they are evidently
pleased to have me knuckling down to them.' When
pressed they would only consent to march if Dugumbé's
party accompanied them, and then only to the Lomamé
and back. A few days later they took the same stand in
Dugumbé's presence—to the Lomamé and no farther.
Dugumbé harangued them at length but in vain. He told
them they would lose their pay. ' Yes,' they said, ' but
not our lives.' And so they ' walked off from him muttering, which is insulting to one of his rank.' At this point
Livingstone became well-nigh desperate. He almost fell
on his knees to Dugumbé. ' I have goods at Ujiji,' he
pleaded, ' I don't know how many, but they are considerable. Take them all and give me men to finish my work !
If not enough, I will add to them ; only do not let me

be forced to return, now I am so near the end of my undertaking ! ' But Dugumbé's only answer was the answer
he had given a week before. ' He said he would make
a plan in conjunction with his associates and report to
me.'

One can imagine the mental tension with which Livingstone recorded the details of that discussion in his journal.
Was Dugumbé, after all, a broken reed ? Was the only
chance of getting to Katanga flickering out ? ' I am dis-
tressed and perplexed what to do,' he confesses, ' so as not
to be foiled. . . . All seems against me.' . . . His fears
were quickly justified. Next day (July 15) the shocking
tragedy occurred which wiped out every hope he had
cherished, every plan he had made at Nyangwé, and,
almost with the force of a physical blow, sent him staggering
back along the path to Ujiji.

It was market-day ; and in the course of the morning
Livingstone paid his customary visit to the market to forget
his troubles for an hour or two amid the chatter and
laughter of the Manyema crowd. It was unusually hot
and sultry, but the attendance was fairly good—over 1500
people, he reckoned, mostly women. He saw three of
Dugumbé's followers there and observed with surprise that
they were carrying guns in violation of the rules of the
market : but, ascribing it to their ignorance, he said
nothing. Presently, finding the heat oppressive, he began
to walk back towards his house. As he left the market, he
noticed that one of the three armed men was quarrelling
over the purchase of a fowl and had seized hold of it. A
minute later—he had not walked thirty yards—he heard
two guns go off. At once the whole market was in confusion. Sellers and buyers threw down their wares and
ran. The flight took two main routes. One body made
for the upper end of the market-place, and into this
thronging mass the three gunmen began steadily firing.
The second group rushed down towards a narrow inlet from
the river where some fifty canoes lay beached. At this creek,

by manifest design, was stationed another party of armed
men who at once opened fire on the fugitives. It was here
that the worst sights were seen. The crowd of panic-
stricken men and women dashed for the canoes and strove
to launch them and escape by the river. But they had
forgotten in their terror to bring their paddles with them,
and the creek was soon jammed with overladen and un-
manageable canoes, unable to get free, jostling, overturn-
ing, sinking, while more fugitives came dashing down the
beach, leaping into the shallows, and forcing their way into
the mêlée. Meantime the gunmen kept up a steady fire.
Many fell dead on the shore. The wounded, shrieking with
pain and fear, jumped or scrambled or crawled into the
water. But escape that way was barred, and there was
more chance, it seemed, for those who ran along the bank
and, plunging into the river, struck out into mid-stream.
Soon Livingstone could see a long line of heads making for
an island about a mile from shore. Unhappily the terrified
survivors had made no allowance for the current which
soon carried them out of their course and away downstream
till they could swim no more. One by one they disappeared, some quietly, some throwing up their arms to
heaven as they sank. A number of them were picked up
by the three canoes which alone had succeeded in getting
out, and at once began to paddle frantically with hands
and arms. But it was only a temporary reprieve. Other
survivors in desperation clung to the unstable craft and
tried to clamber in, till soon they were all three capsized
or swamped and their human freight thrown back into the
river to drown. Almost the only survivors were those who
kept their heads and, turning back towards the shore, got
to land again downstream. The creek and the river, in
fact, were death-traps, and those were more fortunate who
tried to escape by land. Most of them saved their lives
but nothing else. The traders' slaves rushed after them or
intercepted them and robbed them of all they had. For
hours afterwards women were going about the market-
place, collecting and carrying off the packages and per-

sonal possessions which the fugitives had thrown away in panic.

The devilry was not confined to Nyangwé. Before the trouble began in the market Livingstone had heard the sound of desultory firing on the other side of the river ; and, as the day wore on, columns of smoke, rising straight into the still air, showed that several villages were in flames. The followers of Tagamoio, an associate or partner of Dugumbé, were carrying out—so it afterwards appeared —a thorough and deliberate plan of murder and arson ; and, long after the tragedy by the waterside at Nyangwé was over, men and women were still being shot down and their huts burnt beyond the river. When Livingstone sat down in the evening to review the terrible events of the day, he could hear, across nearly two miles of water, the wailing of the women on the farther bank. And next day, when all was quiet at Nyangwé, the killing and enslaving continued over there till in the early afternoon Tagamoio's people, glutted with destruction, withdrew at last to their canoes and crossed the river, beating drums, firing off guns, and emitting yells of triumph which were answered, as they drew near, from Dugumbé's camp with a ragged fusillade from the men and joyful ' lullilooing ' from the women. At that time Livingstone counted seventeen columns of smoke. It was reckoned later that the total of villages burnt was twenty-seven. The estimate of natives killed varied from 330 to 400. On the aggressors' side there were three casualties : the firing-party by the creek killed two of their own folk in their reckless shooting ; and one of their native followers, getting into a canoe with a view to plunder, was overset and drowned.

Throughout those two ghastly days Livingstone was suffering an agony of mind such as he had never known. The scene in the market-place and at the creek was enacted under his eyes. Scores of natives, mainly women, amongst whom he had spent so many happy mornings, were slaughtered a few yards from where he stood, quite powerless to save them. His first thought, he recorded that night, had been to draw his pistol and shoot the three nearer murderers. ⦿ But Dugumbé had restrained him. For Dugumbé had taken his stand near Livingstone at an early stage of the proceedings—was it to prevent his interfering or was it, perhaps, to protect him ?—and now he strongly urged him not to implicate himself in the endless difficulties and dangers of a blood-feud. ' I was thankful afterwards.' Livingstone confesses, ' that I took his advice.' Meantime, a few of the terrified natives had thrown themselves at Livingstone's feet, and Dugumbé, it seems, made no objection when he promised to protect them. But, though he was unquestionably the most powerful Arab in Nyangwé and though his own followers were involved in the massacre on the right bank, he did nothing to stop it. All he did —and this may have been due to Livingstone's presence— was to save a few of the fugitives from the river. He ordered a canoe to put out and help the swimmers, and twenty-one were picked up. One woman refused her chance of life, thinking that rescue meant enslavement. Livingstone declares, moreover, that at his urgent request Dugumbé tried to stop the butchery and destruction on the other side of the river, sending a party across to give orders to that effect to Tagamoio's people. If these were his orders, it is significant that his men were not afraid to disobey them. They joined the marauders, feasted all night with them on stolen goats and fowls, and helped them next morning to burn a few more villages. At a later stage Dugumbé certainly behaved better than he need have done. He allowed Livingstone to restore the twenty-one survivors from the river and a dozen other captives to their friends, and this ' of his own free-will,' says Livingstone, as if clinging to any shred of evidence that might palliate the conduct of this Arab ' gentleman.' Dugumbé promised, too, that the thirty-three canoes, which still lay, when all was over, in the muddy blood-streaked creek, should be returned to their owners. That and no more was what Dugumbé did that day. And Livingstone for his part could do nothing. He stood and watched, half-numb with horror, while the hideous scene bit itself indelibly into his soul. He felt, he says, as if he were in Hell. The burning heat of the sun, the crackle and flash of the firing —it was like a vision of Gehenna and the bottomless pit.

One feature of the massacre seemed to Livingstone a refinement of atrocity. The great majority of the victims had been not only women but marketing-women ; and it happened that, while the men of Manyema were doubtless used to the risk of death at any time or place, local custom strictly forbade interference with women going to market and back. No instance of attack or robbery was known. Even during open inter-tribal warfare, ' the women,' so the Manyema proudly asserted, ' pass among us to market unmolested.' But it was no use dwelling on the peculiar horrors of the tragedy. More practical or more personal questions for Livingstone were who had been responsible and what had been their motive. There could be no doubt about the answer to the first ; and it was given by Dugumbé himself when Livingstone asked him ' to catch the murderers and hang them up in the market-place.' He would have done it, said Dugumbé, if the crime had been committed by people of Manilla—a slave-adventurer of whom more anon—but ' it was done by Tagamoio's people and others of *his party*,' which, as Livingstone explains, was the party ' headed by Dugumbé ' or in other words Dugumbé's people or in one word Dugumbé. He might and he did deny that he had ' sent ' Tagamoio on his foray over the river, though the two attacks were manifestly concerted ; but he would not and did not deny his own responsibility for the massacre in the market. The motive was a trifle less obvious but by no means obscure. The reply given to Livingstone's repeated appeals to Dugumbé and others —' For what is all this murder ? '—was always the same. The slave Manilla had presumed to go about the country not only trading on his own account, but killing and burning which things ' could only be done by free men,' and for the furtherance of these pursuits had bound the village-headmen of the Nyangwé district on both sides of the river in formal ties of ' friendship.' The massacre was intended to punish Manilla through his ' friends.' But this did not satisfy Livingstone. He saw, he could hardly fail to see, that the real motive was wider—to strike terror into the hearts of the Manyema, ' to make an impression in the country as to the importance and greatness of the new-comers,' and incidentally, maybe, to teach them whom to make ' friends ' with, and whom only, for purposes of trade.

These questions as to the authorship and motive of the crime were, as has been said, personal questions for Living-stone, because the Arabs at Nyangwé and especially Dugumbé had been his close associates during the past month. And was it not in Dugumbé's company and with his help and protection that he had been hoping to start on his journey to Katanga ? The very thought of it now sickened him. The sight of the massacre had filled him with ' unspeakable horror.' He could not bear to remain in contact with its perpetrators. He prepared for instant flight from Nyangwé. ' Many of the headmen who have been burned out by the foray,' says the journal for July 16, ' came over to me and begged me to come back with them, and appoint new localities for them to settle in again.' But even to this appeal he would not listen. ' I cannot remain,' he told them, ' among bloody companions and I shall flee away.' He was able, however, before he left, to reassure himself in some measure as to the future of those headmen. For Dugumbé had quickly realised that mas-sacre was a two-edged instrument for the promotion of trade. ' Dugumbé saw that by killing the market-people he had committed a great error, and speedily got the chiefs who had come over to me to meet him at his house and forthwith mix blood. They were in bad case. I could not remain to see to their protection, and, Dugumbé being the best of the whole horde, I advised them to make friends and then appeal to him as able to restrain to some extent his infamous underlings. One chief asked to have his wife and daughter restored to him first, but generally they were cowed and the fear of death was on them. Dugumbé said to me, " I shall do my best to get all the captives, but he must make friends now in order that the market may not be given up." Blood was mixed, and an essential condition was " You must give us *chitoka* (market) ".'

Next day Livingstone fell ill with what had now become a recurrent symptom of his internal disease—fever and violent headache, relieved (as he puts it) by ' a copious discharge of blood.' It was brought on, he says, by the shock of the massacre ; and, as he lay sick, the thought of it and of the havoc it had made of his plans and hopes tormented him. ' " Don't go away," say the Manyema chiefs to me ; but I cannot stay here in agony.' Yet a return to Ujiji was the only possible alternative, and that meant to turn his back on his goal when it had never seemed so near, to postpone for yet another weary age of weeks and months the finish of his last task, the blessed sense of a life-work done, the withdrawal from the field in deep content and with honour, the happy homecoming. What a waste of time and travel—' at least forty-five days in a straight line, equal to 300 miles or, by the turnings and windings, 600 . . . and all after feeding and clothing the banyan slaves for twenty-one months ! '

Nor, of course, could Livingstone take counsel or comfort now from his old Arab associates. Their friendliness, indeed, during those last few days was as embarrassing as it was ostentatious. ' Dugumbé sent me a fine goat, a *maneh* of gunpowder, a *maneh* of fine blue beads, and 230 cowrie to buy provisions on the way.' And when Livingstone proposed to leave them some of his cloth in return, ' he sent me two very fine large Manyema swords and two equally fine spears. . . . He is very friendly. . . . All the rest of Dugumbé's party offered me a share of any kind of goods they had, and pressed me not to be ashamed to tell them what I needed. I declined everything save a little gunpowder.'

So the last day at Nyangwé came, and, as it happened, it was a market-day again. ' A few market people appear to-day, formerly they came in crowds. A very few from the west bank bring salt and buy back the baskets from the camp slaves which they threw away in panic : others carried a little food for sale. About 200 in all, chiefly those who have not lost relatives. One very beautiful woman had a gunshot wound in her upper arm tied round with leaves. Seven canoes came instead of fifty ; but they have great tenacity and hopefulness, an old-established custom has great charms for them, and the market will again be attended if no fresh outrage is committed. No canoes now come into the creek of death.'

Next morning (July 20) Livingstone started for Ujiji. ' All Dugumbé's people came to say good-bye and convoy me a little way.'

19

IT will be remembered that in the previous autumn Livingstone had felt obliged to wait at Bambarré not only for his own porters but also for Dugumbé and his large and well-armed escort before venturing on the risky journey to Nyangwé. And certainly the danger to which any small party of strangers was exposed in the intervening country was no less now than it had been then. There had been no pause during the past six months in the Arab exploitation of that area ; and every fresh outrage had added its fuel to the flame of rage and hate and the longing for revenge among the Manyema. But this time the journal says nothing of the risk ; and it may well be doubted if Livingstone gave a thought to it as he trudged along, sick at heart, with his face to hateful Ujiji and his back to all his hopes. Before long, however, it was forced back into his mind by what he saw. On the sixth day of the march, after traversing a beautiful and well-cultivated district— ' the path runs along the top of a ridge, and we see the fine country below all spread out with different shades of

green as on a map '—he passed through a long string of
villages which had been burned since he had come that
way in March. The damage had been done, he learned,
by the Arabs' ' people ' in ' sheer wantonness . . . as a
sort of horrid Moslem Nigger joke. . . . Men are worse
than beasts of prey, if indeed it is lawful to call Zanzibar
slaves men.' Soon after that comes the first note of anxiety.
At Kasongo's, about a third of the way to Bambarré,
Livingstone found a large gathering of Arabs who asked
if a body of their men with goods might accompany his
little party to Ujiji. He at once agreed. ' This will increase
our numbers and perhaps safety too among the justly
irritated people between this and Bambarré.' A week later
the trouble began. On August 4 the joint caravan had
marched ' through miles of villages all burned because the
people refused a certain Abdullah lodging ' ; and on the
6th they came to a stockaded village where they slept
somewhat uneasily. ' The people were evidently suspicious
and unfriendly.' Next day, though Livingstone had been
taken ill again—so ill that he took ' almost every step in
pain '—they hurried on to another village where they
found the conduct of the natives still more disquieting.
' The people all ran away and appeared in the distance
armed and refused to come near ; they came and threw
stones at us, and afterwards tried to kill those who went
for water.' ' We sleep uncomfortably,' notes Livingstone
that night, ' the natives watching us all round.' Next
morning the suspense at last was ended. Soon after leaving
the village, where Livingstone had tried in vain to parley
with the natives, they came to a place where the forest
closed in upon their path so narrowly that the walls of
dense vegetation brushed their shoulders as they walked ;
and at one of the thickest and darkest points they found
their way barred with trunks of trees. Clearly this was the
chosen spot for an attack. Yet nothing happened. They
peered about them, but in the half-light of that dense
jungle they could detect no enemies in ambush. Only
when he bent to the earth and looked upwards towards

the distant sunlight could Livingstone make out a dark
form here and there. Still nothing happened. The caravan continued on its way, climbing round the obstacle
and winding off in single file through the forest till Livingstone, who was walking last, was left alone. Then he
heard a rustle in the thicket, and a spear flashed across his
back, almost grazing it, and stuck quivering in the ground.
He darted forward, and another spear missed him by a
foot's breadth in front. Farther ahead two men were
killed. And that was all. For some reason the attack
was not pressed home. Closing the gaps in the file, the
little column hurried on. From time to time a shot was
fired at random into the darkness. But there was no
response save jeers and curses, uttered quite close to them
by enemies they could not see. Thus, for five long hours,
they ran the gauntlet. ' I became weary with the constant
strain of danger,' noted Livingstone afterwards with
characteristic simplicity : ' and—as, I suppose, happens
with soldiers on the field of battle—not courageous, but
perfectly indifferent whether I were killed or not.' At
length they reached a cultivated clearing in the forest.
And there Livingstone had the last of his three miraculous
escapes from death in that one day. He noticed a gigantic
tree which had been burnt about the roots to bring it
down ; and, as he looked, there was a sudden crack and
the tree came falling straight in his direction. ' I ran a few
paces back and down it came to the ground one yard
behind me and, breaking into several lengths, it covered me
with a cloud of dust. Had the branches not previously
been rotted off, I could scarcely have escaped.'

By evening they had left the forest and their enemies
behind them and reached some cleared lands round the
village of a chief named Muanampunda, who came to meet
them ' in a stately manner ' and unarmed. He had heard,
he said, the sound of firing in the bush and had come to
ask what was the matter. Livingstone explained that he
had been mistaken for Mohamad Bogharib or some other
marauding Arab and persuaded the friendly chief not to

start another blood-feud by trying to punish his assailants. And then at last they could sit down and rest in peace. But, before he slept, Livingstone wrote out an unadorned account of the day's adventures. ' I lost all my remaining calico,' he complains, ' a telescope, umbrella, and five spears, by one of the slaves throwing down the load.' Of his more alarming experiences he speaks briefly but gravely. The first spear-cast was the narrowest shave of the three. ' As they are expert with the spear, I don't know how it missed, except that he was too sure of his aim and the good hand of God was upon me.' And in that last thought he found the moral of his triple deliverance. ' I took it as an omen of good success to crown me yet, thanks to the " Almighty Preserver of men." '

On August 11 the caravan arrived without further incident at Mamohela which they found deserted by the Arabs and the camp ' all burned off.' News was obtained here of more fighting in the neighbourhood—news which confirmed Livingstone in his belief that the tide had begun to turn against the Arab invaders. ' During the last foray, the people learned that every shot does not kill, and they came up to a party with bows and arrows and compelled the slaves to throw down their guns and powder-horns. . . . This is the beginning of the end which will exclude Arab traders from the country.'

' I rested half a day,' the journal continues, ' as I am still ill.' And it is soon evident that Livingstone was quite unfit for travel. The entries become short and intermittent : a whole month of them fills little more than one printed page. On August 16, he is ' very ill ' again with dysentery. On the 19th and 20th he is obliged by sheer weakness to rest all day. On the 22nd he creeps into Bambarré—where he found Mohamad Bogharib's party and another, homeward bound with huge stores of ivory —and after five days' silence he declares he is ' better and thankful.' But the entry on the 29th is ' Ill all night and remain,' and on the 30th ' Ditto, ditto.' The next day, however, he was ' up and half over the mountain range,' and so, forcing himself onwards, resting only when his legs refused to bear him, he reached Lake Tanganyika at the end of September. It was yet another proof of his amazing power of endurance. ' Almost every step was in pain,' he says again. His appetite failed. The least bit of solid food at once excited a return of dysentery. The dust from the track got in his eyes and set up ophthalmia, ' like that which afflicted Speke . . . my first touch of it in Africa.' And to make matters worse he was ill-shod in tight badly-made French shoes and for the last part of the way the path was strewn with sharp and painful fragments of quartz. When he reached Ujiji, Livingstone summed up his sufferings during those last few weeks of the journey in a memorable phrase. ' I felt,' he said, ' *as if dying on my feet.*' Nor was it only physical pain and exhaustion. ' The mind, sorely depressed, reacted on the body. All the traders were returning successful : I alone had failed and experienced worry, thwarting, baffling, when almost in sight of the end towards which I strained.' Thus wretched in body and soul, after another fortnight spent in obtaining a canoe and crossing the lake, at last on October 16 he arrived once again at Ujiji.

And once again his hopes of what he would find there were disappointed. Not that he had set them high. He knew, of course, that Sherif had been making free with his goods ; but he did expect that something would be left, a little calico, a few beads, just enough to keep him alive till the new and better porters came from Zanzibar. And there was nothing left, not a yard of calico, not a string of beads. Livingstone in other words was almost penniless. He would have been quite penniless if he had not taken the unusual precaution, when he set out for Manyema earlier, of leaving a small quantity of ' barter-goods ' in the charge of Mohamad bin Saleh ' in case of returning in extreme need.' This little store was happily intact, but Livingstone reckoned that the daily purchase of food would exhaust it in about a month. And what then ? Could he bear to live on Arab charity ? ' I had made up my mind,' he wrote in the journal, ' to wait till men should come from the coast, but to wait in beggary was what I never contemplated, and I now felt miserable.' And the misery was not made easier to endure by the sight of Sherif's slaves strutting home from market with ' all the good things' they had purchased with Livingstone's cloth and beads or by the conduct of the unspeakable Sherif himself. ' He came without shame to shake hands with me, and, when I refused, assumed an air of displeasure as having been badly treated ; and afterwards came with his *balghere* (good-luck salutation) twice a day, and on leaving said, " I am going to pray." ' With his customary charity Livingstone set him down as a ' moral idiot ' ; but presently the sight of him and his play-acting was more than he could bear. ' If I were an Arab,' he told him, ' I would have your hand and both ears cut off for thieving.' He did not come again.

The gloom was deepened by news of events on the westward road. During Livingstone's absence in Manyema the friction between Arabs and Africans west of Unyany-embé had developed into open warfare on a bigger scale than had been known in those parts for many years. What chance, then, was there of the porters and goods Livingstone had already asked for coming safely through to Ujiji or of his being able to communicate his present plight to Zanzibar ?

So, day after day, he sat in his house at Ujiji, with his back to the wall, in something like despair. The only ray of comfort came, as it had come before, from the better-minded Arabs who at least were unwilling to let Livingstone die of hunger. ' One morning Seyd bin Majid said to me, " Now this is the first time we have been alone together : I have no goods, but I have ivory ; let me, I pray you, sell some ivory and give the goods to you." . . . I said, " Not yet, but bye-and-bye." ' For there was still something left of his little store, and not till all of it was gone, not till the month was up, would he accept the beggar's fate. But would it ever come to that ? How long could his wasted strength hold out ? He could get no proper nourishing food, still less the stimulants and delicacies he needed. And utter depression was leagued with physical disease to drag him steadily downwards. Without relief alike for failing body and failing spirit he could not live much longer.

As everybody knows, relief did come, just at the end of the month, quite suddenly and in an utterly unexpected form. On the morning of November 10, the faithful Susi came rushing to his master, crying ' An Englishman ! ' It was too good to be true, and Livingstone, incredulous, sent Susi darting back to ask the white man's name. But something clearly was afoot. All the inhabitants of Ujiji seemed to be pouring into the street in front of Livingstone's house, and among them came Mohammad bin Saleh, Seyd bin Majid and the other leading Arabs. It *was* true, they assured Livingstone. A large well-laden caravan was coming in, bearing countless bales of goods, tin baths, huge kettles, cooking-pots, tents, and what not. ' This must be a luxurious traveller,' thought Livingstone, ' and not one at his wits' end like me.' And it *was* a white man, though not English ; for the big flag carried at the head of the column was the Stars and Stripes. A moment more, and Stanley himself was making his way through the excited crowd to where Livingstone stood, the Arabs in a semicircle round him. And then the world-famous allocution— ' Dr. Livingstone, I presume.'[1]

20

THE remarkable man who has broken so unexpectedly on to our African stage was a very different sort of person from those who have so far played their parts on it— different in origin and upbringing, in experience of life, in character. But in one respect he was akin to the leading actor. He had something like Livingstone's strength of purpose and the self-reliance and physical courage that went with it. The story of his life is a story of the triumph of will-power over circumstance. No other famous man of his time got so high from a start so low. No one can understand him who forgets that. He never forgot it himself.[1]

Henry Morton Stanley was born in 1841 at Denbigh in North Wales, the son of a cottager, John Rowlands, with whose name he was christened. The father died when he was two years old, and soon afterwards his mother went to take service in London. She left the child in the care of his two uncles who boarded him out with a couple of old folk for half a crown a week. When he was five, the uncles, who were now married and disinclined to bear the growing cost of his maintenance, consigned him to the workhouse at St. Asaph. There he spent nine years, an almost daily victim to the savage cruelty of the half-lunatic master of the workhouse school. For the rest of his life he was haunted by memories of that grim time and by one memory above all others. He had heard that his favourite schoolmate, a delicate, comely and seemingly well-bred lad of about his own age, had suddenly died. Spurred by a mixture of affection and curiosity, he crept with one or two companions into the mortuary and, turning back the covering sheet, beheld the waxen body scarred by livid bruises. But the barbarities of those formative years did not break his spirit, they hardened and toughened it ; and, when he was fifteen, a more than usually ferocious assault

drove him at last to desperate resistance. He struck out
with his foot, caught the madman in the face, smashed his
spectacles, and sent him reeling to the ground. Seizing the
blackthorn which had dropped from his hand, he heartily
belaboured him until he realised that the fall on the stone
floor had stunned him. He had incurred unimaginable
penalties, but he did not wait for them. Before his victim
had fully recovered, he scaled the workhouse wall and ran
away.

He sought a refuge with his relatives. His paternal
grandfather, a prosperous farmer, showed him the door.
His uncles, one now a butcher, the other an innkeeper,
were kindlier, but they made it clear that he was not
wanted. For a time he lodged with a schoolmaster cousin,
paying for his keep by helping with the teaching. The
prospect of a better job took him to Liverpool where
he lived with a married aunt and got work first at a
draper's shop and then at a butcher's. But here, as elsewhere, he presently began to feel that his appetite was
putting a strain on the household resources, and in 1859,
now a slender youth of eighteen, he obtained the post of
cabin-boy on an American ship bound for New Orleans.
Cheated of his wages at the end of the voyage, he slipped
ashore and wandered penniless about the town. And there
at length his courage and independence were rewarded.
A benevolent cotton-broker, named Henry Stanley, took
pity on him, found him work, and presently adopted and
renamed him as his son. Young Stanley spent the next two
years, probably the happiest of his life, in visiting the towns
of the Mississippi valley with his new father, reading all
the books he could get, and preparing himself for a business
career. But in 1861 old Stanley suddenly died without
having made any legal provision for young Henry, who
was thus left alone and adrift again. Not for long, however. On the outbreak of the Civil War, he was induced by
his love of his father's 'South' and the moral compulsion
of his associates in Arkansas to enrol himself as a volunteer
in the Confederate army. After ten months of service, not

without hardship and danger, he was taken prisoner at the battle of Shiloh and confined at a camp at Chicago under shockingly harsh and insanitary conditions. At the end of two miserable months he took the only available means of release from the disease and death surrounding him by enlisting in the Federal artillery. He can scarcely be charged with treachery on this account. He was a new-comer to the States, and it was for personal not political or patriotic reasons that he had fought for the South. As to the rights and wrongs of the conflict he was frankly indifferent. ' I had a secret scorn,' he wrote long after-wards, ' for people who could kill one another for the sake of African slaves. There were no blackies in Wales, and why a sooty-faced nigger from a distant land should be an element of disturbance between white brothers was a puzzle to me.'[1]

A few days after his enlistment he fell ill, and on re-covery was discharged from service a free man but still very weak and with no money and no work. Food and shelter provided by a charitable farmer enabled him to regain his strength, and in the autumn of 1862 he joined a ship bound for Liverpool and made his way to his mother's house at Denbigh, only to be denounced as a disgrace to the family and once again shown the door. With another indelible scar on his soul he returned to his sea-life, worked a passage back to America, and made several voyages to the Caribbean and the Mediterranean. Once he was shipwrecked at night off Barcelona and swam ashore, the sole survivor. In the autumn of 1864 he enlisted in the Federal navy as a ship's writer, and took part in the two expeditions against Fort Fisher. The accounts of the fighting which he ventured to send to the press were welcomed by the editors for their fluent and forcible style ; and on his discharge at the end of the war in the spring of 1865 he at once decided to adopt the journalist's career. His success was rapid. Adventure was what he and the more popular newspapers wanted, and he and they got plenty of it in the course of the next few years. In 1866 he invaded Anatolia from Smyrna with one companion, was caught, robbed, beaten, and threatened with death by brigands, and only escaped with difficulty to Constantinople. In 1867 he attached himself to General Hancock's column in the course of its operations against the Red Indians. In 1868 he joined the staff of the *New York Herald*, a highly enterprising if somewhat sensational journal, and was commissioned to accompany Sir Robert Napier on his march into Abyssinia. His reputation was established by his dispatches on this campaign and confirmed by a brilliant ' scoop ' at its close. On his way out, with notable foresight, he had promised the chief of the telegraph station at Suez to make it well worth his while if his dispatches were forwarded without delay. His final dispatch was thus the first to be cabled on from Suez, and immediately afterwards the cable broke. For a considerable time, therefore, the only news of the fall of Magdala and the death of King Theodore that reached New York or London was Stanley's account in the *Herald*. It was a triumph all the more striking in the end because it was at first widely regarded as a daring imposture; and it brought Stanley at a bound to a front place among the newspaper-correspondents of the world—a long journey to have made in twelve years from the workhouse wall at St. Asaph.

It was at this moment that the fates began to interweave the threads of Stanley's life and Livingstone's. Anti-climax is the bane of such newspapers as the *Herald*, and Mr. James Gordon Bennett, its young manager and the son of its proprietor, was anxious to repeat as soon as possible the ' scoop ' of Magdala. But there was nothing doing in the world. Europe was taking breath between two wars. Asia seemed more than usually lethargic except for some civil strife in Japan. And from Africa, despite the *cliché*, came nothing new, nothing at any rate on the Abyssinian scale, nothing but a rumour that the lost Livingstone had found the source of the Nile and was on his way down the river. Something, perhaps, might be made of that. Livingstone was certainly 'good copy' in America as well as in England. If the representative of the *Herald* were the first journalist to meet him, it would provide a striking head-line. So in November 1868, Stanley, who had been on a roving commission through the Mediterranean islands to Spain, was instructed to proceed to Aden and investigate. The rumour, of course, was false. At that time, as has been recorded above, Livingstone was still in the neighbourhood of Lake Bangweolo : he did not reach Ujiji till March 1869. So Stanley obtained no news at all of him at Aden, nor from the American consul at Zanzibar, to whom he wrote. After a useless wait of more than two months at Aden, he was recalled to London and sent thence to Spain, where he witnessed at close quarters and at considerable risk the revolutionary fighting at Saragossa and Valencia. It was an exciting, exhilarating life. It gave full scope to Stanley's restless energy. It earned him all the money he needed. It had already brought him to the head of his profession. But he was determined to do better than that, to work in a higher field and to win a greater name than journalism could offer. 'So long as my life lasts,' he noted in his diary during those days in Spain, ' I feel so much master of my own future that I can well understand Cæsar's saying to the sailors, "Nay, be not afraid, for you carry Cæsar and his fortunes ! " I could say the same : " My body carries Stanley and his fortunes." With God's help I shall succeed.'[1] Soon after he wrote those words he was sum-moned by telegram to meet Mr. J. G. Bennett himself in Paris and received the commission which was to prove the first step in his becoming one of the famous men of his time.

The manager of the *Herald* had decided on another attempt to 'feature' Livingstone. Since Stanley's return from Aden the mystery of his whereabouts had deepened. In England men were wondering, as they had wondered in 1867 before the Young Search Expedition, whether he was really still alive. Now and again, in the course of 1869, statements and counter-statements as to his fate had been appearing in the columns of *The Times*. 'Those who know Livingstone,' wrote Waller in January, ' will feel the least alarm. . . . Africa is a large place.' In April came news from the Cape that Livingstone had returned to Zanzibar and left again to make his way home by way of the Great Lakes and the Nile—a report which Murchison promptly discredited. He had lately heard from Kirk, he said, and there was still no news of Livingstone at Zanzibar on March 5. In July Consul Churchill came home on leave and spoke confidently of Livingstone's safety. Equally confident was a communication from Murchison in September. In view of Livingstone's well-known tenacity of purpose and ' herculean ' physique, he wrote, ' I hold stoutly to the opinion that he will overcome every obstacle.' He had probably followed a river-system flowing west from the Tanganyika area and might be expected to emerge on the Atlantic coast. This provoked the egregious Mr. Cooley to an angry attack on the Royal Geographical Society for sending Livingstone on a dangerous expedition and then resting ' in unbounded hopefulness ' as to his fate. In all probability he was being held prisoner by Chief Casembe. To this Mr. Bates effectively retorted that Livingstone had written cheerful letters from Casembe's, announcing his intention of proceeding to Ujiji. There was cause for anxiety, Bates admitted, in the lack of news of his arrival at Ujiji ; but, perhaps, as Murchison had suggested, he had been diverted to the west. Finally, on October 1, a letter from Sir Samuel Baker appeared, dated from Alexandria in the previous month, saying that the writer was about to start up the Nile and expected to get news of Livingstone when he approached the southern end of Lake Tanganyika.[1] That was all very well, no doubt. Livingstone's friends were probably right. Letters might come any day to say that he was safe and well. But nobody knew for certain where he was, and Mr. Bennett was quite justified in thinking that the English-speaking world would like to know and that it was the *Herald's* business to supply the knowledge. Hence the telegram to Spain.

The sequel is recorded in Stanley's brisk reporter's style in the introduction to *How I Found Livingstone*. Reaching Paris late on October 17, he went at once to the Grand Hotel and found his chief in bed. ' After throwing over his shoulders his *robe de chambre*, Mr. Bennett asked " Where do you think Livingstone is ? " " I really do not know, sir." " Do you think he is alive ? " " He may be or he may not be," I answered. " Well, I think he is alive, and that he can be found, and I am going to send you to find him." ' The proposition took even Stanley aback. He knew nothing of Central Africa and he believed, he says, ' in common with almost all other men,' that Livingstone was dead. He ventured to suggest that the search would be very costly ; it would need at least £2500. But cost, it appeared, mattered nothing to Mr. Bennett. ' Draw a thousand pounds now,' he said, ' and when you have gone through that, draw another thousand, and when that is spent, draw another thousand, and when you have finished that, draw another thousand, and so on ; but FIND LIVING-STONE.' The *Herald*, Mr. Bennett explained, was prepared to pay any price for news that would interest the world. But the finding of Livingstone, he went on, was not a desperately urgent matter, and it was not to be Stanley's immediate objective. It was to be the climax of an extensive journalistic programme.

' I wish you to go to the inauguration of the Suez Canal first and then proceed up the Nile. I hear Baker is about starting for Upper Egypt. Find out what you can about his expedition, and, as you go up, describe as well as possible whatever is interesting for tourists ; and then write up a guide—a practical one—for Lower Egypt : tell us about whatever is worth seeing and how to see it. Then you might as well go to Jerusalem ; I hear Captain Warren is making some interesting discoveries there. Then visit Constantinople, and find out about that trouble between the Khedive and the Sultan. Then—let me see—you might as well visit the Crimea and those old battlegrounds. Then go across the Caucasus to the Caspian Sea : I hear

there is a Russian expedition bound for Khiva. From
thence you may get through Persia to India ; you could
write an interesting letter from Persepolis. Bagdad will be
close on your way to India : suppose you go there and
write up something about the Euphrates Valley Railway.
Then, when you have come to India, you can go after
Livingstone. Probably you will hear by that time that
Livingstone is on his way to Zanzibar ; but, if not, go
into the interior and find him if alive. Get what news of
his discoveries you can ; and, if you find he is dead, bring
all possible proofs of his being dead. That is all. Good-
night, and God be with you.' ' Good-night, sir,' I said :
' what it is in the power of nature to do I will do ; and
on such an errand as I go upon, God will be with me.'[1]

Clearly Mr. Bennett was not over much concerned for
Livingstone's safety. He was in no hurry about finding
him. Why should he be ? He probably shared the general
opinion that, if he were alive, he knew how to look after
himself ; and in any case it was not the business of a
newspaper to fit out a rescue-party for a strayed explorer.
Its only business was to get news of him if he had ' news-
value.' But in justice to Mr. Bennett it must be said that
the thought of helping Livingstone did occur to him. Find
him, he had said, and ' get all the news you can of him ' ;
and then—so Stanley relates—he had added, thoughtfully
and deliberately, ' The old man may be in want : take
enough with you to help him, should he require it.'

The programme was duly executed. A month after the
Paris interview Stanley attended the opening of the Suez
Canal. He then went up the Nile with a party of the
Khedive's guests and interviewed the chief engineer of
Baker's expedition. Then, turning his back on Central
Africa and Livingstone, he proceeded to Jerusalem, inter-
viewed Captain Warren, and climbed down the excavation
pits to the foundations of Solomon's Temple. He went
next to Constantinople and the Crimean battlefields ' with
Kinglake's glorious books ' in hand : and thence to
Trebizond where he met the Arabian traveller, Palgrave,

and to Tiflis where he interviewed Baron Nicolay, Governor of the Caucasus. And so over the mountains to Persia. At Teheran he stayed with the Russian Ambassador. At Persepolis he wrote his name on one of the monuments. Thence he rode by way of Shiraz to Bushire where he took ship and, visiting Bunder-Abbas, Muscat and Karachi *en route*, arrived at Bombay on August 1, 1870. He had now carried out the whole of his preliminary programme ; the columns of the *Herald* had been enriched with a long series of vivid dispatches ; the last and principal objective alone remained ; and on January 6 1871, over fourteen months since leaving Paris, he landed at Zanzibar.

21

IT so happened that those months of procrastination had given Stanley's quest more reality than it would otherwise have had. When Mr. Bennett told him to find Livingstone, Livingstone was not lost. On October 14, 1869, three days before the historic conversation in the Paris bedroom, a telegram from Bombay had appeared in *The Times*, summarising a report from Kirk to the effect that a party of Arab traders had arrived at Zanzibar with the news that Livingstone was or had been recently at Ujiji. It was true. Livingstone, it will be remembered, was at Ujiji from March 14 to July 12, 1869. But Mr. Bennett may not have seen this item in *The Times* or, if he saw it, he may have regarded it as only one more unsubstantial rumour. So Stanley was sent off on his circuitous route to Central Africa. But he had not got far before the report was confirmed. Early in November Murchison communicated to *The Times* a further statement from Kirk that Livingstone had arrived safely at Ujiji ; and a few weeks later—when Stanley was in Egypt—it was known that letters had been received from Livingstone headed ' Ujiji, May 13.' After

another month a letter from Bishop Tozer was published
saying he had talked to an Arab at Zanzibar who had
seen Livingstone at Ujiji in July.[1] But then the curtain
had fallen again. Was he still at Ujiji ? If so, why had no
more letters arrived at the coast ? At a meeting of the
Royal Geographical Society in mid-December, Murchison
once more aired his view that Livingstone might be
marching west : that would explain, he said, the long
silence.[2] But it certainly seemed as if Livingstone was lost
again, and another crop of rumours was the inevitable
result. In February, 1870, a gentleman wrote to *The Times*
from Donegal, enclosing a letter from his son-in-law, in
command of H.M.S. *Peterel* on the West African coast. A
Portuguese trader, said the captain, had brought news that
Livingstone, when on his way to the Congo and the coast,
had been killed and burnt at a distance of ninety days'
march from the river by natives who believed that he had
caused the death of their king by witchcraft. The captain
confessed that he thought the story true : but it was
instantly blown to pieces by Murchison and Waller. They
both pointed out that the rumours implied a time-table
which could not possibly be fitted in with the last date at
which Livingstone was known to have been at Ujiji. And
Waller reminded the public that the Portuguese had been
responsible for similar *canards* during the Zambesi Expedition : they ' have long since used up the nine lives of our
noble traveller.' In another letter he declared that Kirk
could be counted on not to relax his efforts to communicate
with Livingstone. ' In the meantime I would ask your
readers to await quietly and patiently further news from
Ujiji whither Livingstone will assuredly repair if all be
well.' But still the idle talk went on. Later in the year it
was reported from the Cape that Livingstone was at
Mozambique waiting for a ship to take him home.[3] ' As
I see so many false tales regarding Dr. Livingstone reach
you,' wrote Kirk to Murchison in June, ' I only write this
letter to say that there is nothing authentic known of him
here and not even a rumour of his having been heard of.

I have sent assistance to the porters and men who have delayed through deaths among their number by cholera, and urged the Arabs at Unyamwezi* to push the stores on without delay.' At the moment of writing the rains had stopped transport. 'No caravan sets out for yet another month, and then I shall send on the letters which have come to the doctor's address.'[1] Kirk, in fact, was taking the common-sense view. He was assuming confidently—and quite correctly—that Livingstone would return to his base at Ujiji, sooner or later, as he had said he would. On that assumption he had dispatched Sherif's caravan in October 1869, and had followed it up with reinforcements a few months later. His chief had taken the same view in 1870. In order to make more certain that Livingstone received the men and stores he had asked for, Churchill, before going on leave to England, enrolled a second caravan to carry a duplicate set of stores to Ujiji. He engaged the men in Kirk's presence, and the latter was prepared to vouch for it that each of them understood every word of his contract. This caravan left for Bagamoyo on November 1.[2]

So, when Stanley arrived at Zanzibar, Livingstone was lost in one sense but not in another. He was lost in the sense that no one knew at that moment exactly where he was. But it was known where he had recently been and whither, if he carried out his expressed intentions, he would shortly return. If he should change his plan and go wandering away towards the Atlantic, then indeed in a fuller sense of the word he would be 'lost.' But there was no reason to expect that ; and to Kirk Livingstone was no more lost in Manyema in the winter of 1870 than he had been lost in Nyasaland in the spring of 1859 when he and Kirk had left their base at Tete to explore the Shiré Highlands. And when, as it turned out, Livingstone did keep to his plan, and did return to Ujiji, and Stanley, ten days later, met him there, could it strictly be said that Stanley had found him ? What Livingstone really and desperately

* The Country of the Unyamwezi round about Unyanyembe.

needed was not so much to be found as to be relieved—to be provided with the food and drugs and barter-goods which he had failed to obtain from Zanzibar. What happened to Sherif's caravan has been related. Arab obstruction and the dread of cholera had stopped the next one or two consignments at Unyanyembe. And for the same reasons the last caravan, the one dispatched by Churchill with Kirk's aid in November 1870, had come to a halt at the very first stage of its journey. In the middle of February Kirk was dismayed to learn from a servant at the consulate that some of the men who were supposed to be three months on their way had been seen at Zanzibar. He promptly sent one of his *peons* (office messengers) to Bagamoyo to obtain reliable information. He reported ' that, although some of the party set out, there still remained at Bagamoyo a number of loads for which bearers had not been found.'[1] Kirk acted promptly. H.M.S. *Columbine* happened to be at Zanzibar on Slave Trade patrol, and its commander readily granted Kirk's request to take him over to the mainland, all the more readily perhaps because it offered a chance of some good shooting. On arrival at Bagamoyo —so Kirk reported to the Foreign Office in a dispatch of February 18—he found that the bad news was true. The men of the caravan were still living in the village. But they had some excuse. They had expected, as usual, to complete their complement of porters at Bagamoyo from Nyamwezi who had been employed on coastward caravans from Unyanyembe and were waiting to return home. But at this time few such men had come down ' in consequence of deaths last year from cholera among their friends.' However, ' by using my influence with the Arabs,' Kirk was able to secure enough porters to take all but four loads of the goods, and before night fell on the day he landed he had seen them off along the Unyanyembe road. Next morning he followed them up himself a day's march inland beyond the Kingani River to Kikoka, and satisfied himself by inquiry on the spot that the party had actually passed through the village on their westward way. ' Once fairly off on the road,' he told Granville, ' there is little to induce these people to delay, whereas at Bagamoyo, living in good huts among their own people . . . had I not gone in person they might have loitered several months.' Back at the coast Kirk arranged for the remaining four loads to be taken as far as Unyanyembe by an Arab caravan with a request to the Governor, Said bin Salim, to forward them on to Ujiji. He also visited, in the company of the French Consul, the French mission to whose care a number of rescued slaves had been entrusted. Last but not least, he enjoyed some sport at which he proved himself a better shot or at least the owner of a better rifle than the officers of the *Columbine*.[1]

22

STANLEY, meantime, had received a friendly welcome from the little international community at Zanzibar. ' Taken as a body,' he says in the first chapter of his book, ' it would be hard to find a more generous or hospitable colony of white men in any part of the world.' And he records his special gratitude to the American consul, Mr. F. R. Webb, who put him up in his house for the month he spent on the island. But he was shocked to find most of these white folk lacking in ' the indomitable energy which characterises Europeans and Americans.' They seemed to him to have yielded too easily to the climate, to have become inert and apathetic, to have allowed themselves ' to dwindle into pallid phantoms of their kind . . . with hardly a trace of that daring and invincible spirit which rules the world.' Of the few individuals he mentions, one was Bishop Tozer, and Livingstone would have chuckled over his ribald description of ' this High Church (very High Church indeed) prelate in his crimson robe of office and in the queerest of all head-dresses, stalking through the streets of Zanzibar.' More important and far more unfortunate in its consequences was the unfavourable impression Stanley formed of Kirk.

To some extent, perhaps, there was a natural antipathy between the sober, reserved Scottish official and the exuberant, self-confident American journalist. But Stanley seems to have felt it so quickly and so strongly as to suggest that he was prejudiced against Kirk before they met. Conceivably Consul Webb may have spoken not too warmly of his colleague ; for Stanley had arrived, as it happened, at a moment when the sense of international rivalry among the foreign residents at Zanzibar was more than usually acute. The British enjoyed no special privileges. The French, the Germans and the Americans possessed the same rights of residence and trade under similar commercial treaties. Their business interests were greater. There were four German, three American and two French firms, and only one British—Fraser & Co. But, though the British Government was notoriously indifferent to British enterprise in this little backwater of the commercial world, its agent at Zanzibar had always held a higher place and maintained more intimate and influential relations with the Sultan than those of the other Powers. There were several reasons for this. The British connexion, to begin with, was much the oldest. The Sultan's predecessors had been in close diplomatic contact with the British authorities in India long before the great Seyyid Said shifted his capital from Muscat to Zanzibar in 1840.[1] Secondly, if there was little direct trade with Britain, there was a great deal with India ; and, since the Indian traders were British subjects or ' protected persons,' the British Consul had far more work to do on their account than the other Consuls on account of their little groups of resident compatriots. Thirdly, Seyyid Majid had inherited from Seyyid Said the conviction that the best chance of maintaining the independence of his ' dominions ' in an unstable and acquisitive international society lay in the friendship of the British Government and the protection of British sea-power. And, lastly, the price which each successive Sultan had to pay for that friendship and protection involved them all in constant and intricate negotiations with the British Consul. Any one who has had the patience to peruse the dusty files of official correspondence is aware that the one subject in which the British Government was really interested—the subject which occupies nine-tenths of those innumerable dispatches—was the abolition of the Arab Slave Trade. By successive stages it had secured the limitation of the Trade. The last treaty, that of 1846, had bound the Sultan to prohibit his subjects from trading in slaves outside Zanzibar and his ' dominions ' on the mainland. But Palmerston and his successors had made no secret of their intention sooner or later to bring about the complete abolition of the Trade, and it was the opportunity of taking a hand in that task which, as has been recorded above, attracted Kirk to Zanzibar. To any one who had seen, as he had seen, what the Slave Trade meant in the Shiré valley or had watched, as he had watched, the tight-packed slave-dhows sailing into harbour almost under the Consulate windows and their living cargoes being bundled out on the beach, cramped, staggering, sometimes falling in their tracks and left inanimate to the rising tide or the hungry pariah dogs*— to any one of ordinary human feeling who had come to close quarters with the ghastly business the chance of being able to do something to destroy it was more than enough to compensate for a tedious and rather lonely life in dirty, steamy, pestiferous Zanzibar.

It could only be destroyed by persuading the Sultan to outlaw it and to permit the British Navy to see that his laws were obeyed—no easy task since most of his wealthiest and most powerful subjects were directly engaged in the Trade and he himself derived the bulk of his revenue from it. Said had conceded and Majid had maintained the restrictions of 1846 only under unrelaxing pressure from the British Government ; and by 1870 the British Govern-

---

* The methods of the Arab Slave Trade are described in *The Exploitation of East Africa,* chap. vi.

ment had become convinced that that pressure had not only to be continued but increased, that the restrictions of 1846 were quite inadequate, and that the Sultan must somehow be induced to acquiesce in more drastic measures. It was now that the practical value of the Livingstone-Kirk combination became apparent. It was Livingstone, on the one hand, whose description of the horrors of the Trade in the Nyasa country, backed by his personal appeals during his last stay at home, had roused British public opinion to demand that Britain should do her duty on the east coast of Africa as she had done it on the west. It was Kirk, on the other hand, who, in a series of long, detailed, unemotional dispatches, informed the Foreign Office of the facts about the Trade—its volume, its range, its methods—and proved beyond dispute the need for a new and more rigorous policy. The Select Committee of the House of Commons appointed to consider the question in 1871 were so much impressed by the service Kirk had rendered that, though a matter of administrative personnel would normally have been regarded as beyond their terms of reference, they recommended at the close of their report that, ' having in mind his long and tried experience of Africa, its climate, its slave-trade difficulties, and his knowledge of the Sultan,' Kirk's position at Zanzibar should be strengthened and confirmed.[1]

Kirk, therefore, was certain of the backing of his superiors in Whitehall when, in the course of 1870, he began to intimate to Majid that something more was needed than the Treaty of 1846. Sooner or later, no doubt, he would have got his way, but with Majid's death in October the whole situation changed. To all appearance his arrogant, impulsive, hot-tempered successor, Barghash, intended to have no more of the old humiliating interference with the Sultan's sovereign authority, to set his British mentors at defiance, even to repudiate the Treaty of 1846. It was a first-rate diplomatic crisis, and it was aggravated by the fact that Churchill had recently returned from a spell of sick-leave with neither health nor temper

much improved. He adopted an impatient and over-
bearing attitude which only served to stiffen Barghash's
obstinacy into frank hostility. But Churchill was then at
the end of his tether, and in December his physical condition forced him to abandon his post for good. Thus Kirk
was left to face the crisis alone, and by the manner of his
dealing with it he revealed the gifts of mind and character
that made him a great diplomatist. Churchill had talked
of deposing Barghash by *force majeure*. Kirk ruled out a
course so violent and so certain to provoke not only civil
war among the Arabs but a sharp and uncomfortable
international reaction. He did not browbeat Barghash.
He treated him with studied courtesy. He said nothing
about the Treaty of 1846, as if he took its execution for
granted. He was offering Barghash, in fact, a chance to
recover his temper and change his attitude without loss of
face. Given time for reflection, Barghash, he knew, was
bound to realise that, if only to maintain his authority
over the more fanatical and rebellious elements among his
Arab subjects, he needed the prestige which only British
backing could afford him. And that is what happened.
Barghash had been rude to Churchill : he was polite to
Kirk. It was the beginning, indeed, of a genuine friendship between the two men which lasted till the unhappy
days of 1885 when a pacific British Government overrode
Kirk's policy and betrayed Barghash in order to enable
Bismarck to carve a German colony out of his ' dominions '
on the mainland.* By the end of the year Kirk could tell
the Foreign Office that the crisis was over. ' So far from
keeping at a distance,' he wrote in March, 1871, ' nothing
is done by him [Burghash] without informing me or asking
my advice. . . . With the French, American and German
Consulates I find that His Highness has greatly lost favour
since he has treated this Agency with proper respect and
as taking precedence in everything without question.'[1]

Kirk's success, which was duly noted and commended
by the Foreign Office, must have excited a little jealousy

* *The Exploitation of East Africa*, chaps. xvii.-xix.

among his colleagues, and possibly Consul Webb felt sore
and talked about ' swelled heads.' But it seems much
more probable that Stanley's prejudice, if prejudice there
were, was derived from another quarter. Among all the
residents at Zanzibar Stanley picked out one for special
praise. He describes him as ' one of the sturdiest of Scots-
men, a most pleasant-mannered and unaffected man,
sincere and unaffected in whatever he did.' More, he was
energetic : he defied the climate. ' No man can charge
Capt. H. C. Fraser, formerly of the Indian Navy, with being
apathetic, whatever else malice may suggest.'[1] But there
was something else that could without malice be suggested.
For Fraser was one of those Europeans who were to be
found often enough in the nineteenth century pursuing a
dubious livelihood in out-of-the-way corners of the tropical
world. Five years before Stanley came to Zanzibar he had
made himself into a company for the cultivation of sugar-
cane on large estates which had been bought or leased in
the island.[2] It was a highly speculative venture. Money,
no doubt, could be made out of sugar. Arab landowners
made plenty of it out of cloves. But everything depended
on the labour supply ; and, while the Arabs worked their
plantations with the slaves they bought in the market at
Zanzibar, British subjects, though the law still allowed
them to own slaves, were prohibited, wherever they
might be, from buying them by the Act of 1843. Free
labour was exceedingly scarce at Zanzibar, and Fraser
would have been quite unable to launch his enterprise if
he had not conceived an ingenious device for getting
round the law. He obtained the slaves he wanted—there
were over 700 of them in 1867—not by purchase but on
hire. For the payment of £5 in the first year and smaller
sums thereafter the Arab owners put the slaves at the ' sole
disposal ' of Fraser & Co. for five years. At the end of
that time they were to be freed. Consul Seward reported
these proceedings to the Foreign Office and asked for
instructions. In his own opinion, he wrote, the transaction
was tantamount to a purchase of the slaves and the promise

of their ultimate freedom was merely an attempt to cover
its illegality with a ' veil of philanthropy.' If allowed to
stand, the arrangement would at once increase the demand
for slaves at Zanzibar and undermine Arab faith in the
sincerity of British hostility to the Slave Trade. ' Is this
man an Englishman,' they would say, ' that slaves are
bought for him?' Lord Stanley consulted the Law Officers
and obtained a firm opinion. Fraser & Co., he told
Seward, had broken the law and should be asked if they
have anything to say before proceedings are taken
against them. Seward, meantime, to whom the scandal
of a public trial was probably unwelcome, suggested a
way out. He asked Majid to use his influence to set the
slaves free. Majid assented. The slaves were freed. The
proceedings were dropped. Fraser carried on with paid
free labour as if nothing had happened. But, before long,
he was in grave financial difficulties. He had incurred
heavy debts, and he broke or evaded the undertakings he
had made to discharge them. At the end of 1874 he was
declared bankrupt. When he suddenly left Zanzibar for
Natal, it was discovered that he had taken with him, and
also shipped by the previous mail-boat, large quantities of
sugar which rightly belonged to his creditors. ' Captain
Fraser's career at Zanzibar during the past few years,'
wrote acting-Consul Prideaux to the Foreign Office, ' has
been of the most doubtful nature, and the English name
has been seriously compromised in consequence.' The
explorer Cameron made a similar report in 1875 ; but
the ' high character of the British Consul [Kirk],' he added,
' has prevented any real harm being done.'[1]

Such was Stanley's sturdy Scot. It may be taken for
granted that he bore a grudge against all the occupants of
the British Consulate he had had to do with. He certainly
hated Kirk, as the sequel will show. And it may well be
that he twisted Stanley's mind against him. It is difficult,
at any rate, to understand Stanley's account of his meetings
and talks with Kirk unless he had been somehow prejudiced
against him beforehand.

He felt ' quite a curiosity,' he says at the outset, to see ' this much befamed man ' who was always described in the newspapers as Livingstone's ' former companion ' and who, if any one, would be able to inform him as to Livingstone's whereabouts. On the second day after his arrival he was taken by Webb to the British Consulate and introduced to ' a man of rather slim figure, dressed plainly, slightly round-shouldered, hair black, face thin, cheeks rather sunk and bearded ' as the representative of the *New York Herald.* ' I fancied at the moment that he lifted his eyelids perceptibly, disclosing the full circle of his eyes. If I were to define such a look, I should call it a broad stare. During the conversation, which ranged over several subjects, though watching his face intently, I never saw it kindle or become animated but once and that was while relating some of his hunting feats to us.' It does not seem to have occurred to Stanley that Kirk, who, since Churchill's departure, had had to cope with all the duties of the Consulate single-handed, may have been none too pleased with the interruption of the morning's work ; and it was a pity, perhaps, that he had not seen him a few years earlier on the Zambesi or the Shiré, at grips with disease and hardship and danger, the only member of the Expedition on whose strength and energy Livingstone could unfailingly rely. As it was, he seems to have jumped to the conclusion that Kirk was a victim of the lassitude and *ennui* which he found so deplorably prevalent among the Europeans at Zanzibar.

A few days later he was at the Consulate again. Every Tuesday evening Kirk and his wife were ' at home ' to their fellow-residents, and the newcomer had doubtless received an invitation. The account of what passed which he gave in his book was a striking example of the new journalism. A guest at a small private party, he felt himself as much entitled to tell his readers what he saw and heard as if it had been a great public function. To start with, he says, he was sadly bored. There was nothing but the smallest of small talk, nor any more stimulating refresh-

ment than ' a kind of mild wine and cigars.' ' It was all
very fine, I dare say, but I thought it was the dreariest
evening I had ever passed, until Dr. Kirk, pitying the
wearisomeness under which I was labouring, called me
aside to submit to my inspection a magnificent rifle.' Talk
of sport led on to talk of travel, and presently Kirk was
telling a story of his adventures with Livingstone. That
was the cue for which Stanley had been waiting. ' " Ah
yes, Dr. Kirk," I asked carelessly, " about Livingstone,
where is he, do you think, now ? " ' But Kirk evaded a
direct reply. No doubt he was alive, he said ; caravans,
indeed, were frequently being dispatched to him. But it
was time he came home. ' " He is growing old, you know,
and, if he died, the world would lose the benefit of his
discoveries." ' But Stanley, too, was evasive. He regarded
it as essential for the success of his ' scoop ' that nobody
should know he was looking for Livingstone until he had
found him ; and he had put it about that his purpose was
to explore the River Rufigi. ' Suppose I met Livingstone
in the course of my travels,' was all he dared say, ' how
would he like it ? ' ' " To tell you the truth, I do not think
he would like it very well. I know if Burton or Grant or
Baker or any of those fellows were going after him and he
heard of their coming, Livingstone would put a hundred
mils of swamp in a very short time between himself and
them." '[1]

Kirk, it is clear, had taken alarm. He knew how
Livingstone hated the more blatant kind of publicity, how
deeply he would resent being ferreted out in order to make
copy for the *New York Herald*, how often and sharply he
had been annoyed by the publication of unauthorised
accounts of his travels and discoveries. He knew, too, how
resolutely he was bent on exploring alone.* Naturally,
therefore, he did his best to discourage this self-assured
young American journalist from trying to make contact
with him. It would have been better for every one concerned if Stanley could have brought himself to take Kirk

* See pp. 19, 26 above.

into his confidence and tell him frankly that he had come
not only to find Livingstone but to load a caravan, regard-
less of expense, with such supplies as he might be in need
of. For, if Kirk had known that that was Stanley's intention, he must have welcomed it. For several years now
he and his colleagues at the Consulate had been trying from
time to time to get ·goods up to Ujiji. He had felt his
responsibility and done his best to discharge it. But he
had always known that, without a white man to lead and
control it, there could be no certainty of a caravan, at any
rate with all its bales intact, attaining its destination.
Stanley, in fact, was the solution of his problem ; and, if
only he had been aware of his real purpose, he would
surely have put those other considerations aside and done
all he could to help him on his way. As it was, there
seemed to be no particular reason why he should take
much interest in Stanley's plans. He was rather puzzled,
one suspects, by his arrival at Zanzibar. He knew little
about the new journalism. He had probably never seen
the *New York Herald*. Whether he liked or disliked the
newcomer, he doubtless hoped he would not get into
trouble on the mainland. But that was Webb's affair, not
his. His only duty was to protect Livingstone from an
intrusion he was sure he would resent.

If Kirk was at cross-purposes, so was Stanley. And this
was stranger. For Stanley was delighted with the success
of his ruse about the Rufigi. ' Very few, I believe, ever
coupled the words *New York Herald* with a search after
Dr. Livingstone. It was not my fault, was it ? ' Evidently
not ; nor, surely, was it Kirk's. Yet Stanley seems to have
thought that Kirk ought to have guessed his secret. He
mocks at him for believing his Rufigi story. ' What newspaper could dispatch a " special " to discover the sources
of an insignificant river ? ' But that was not the worst of
it. As he brooded over that unfortunate conversation he
seems to have come to the strange conclusion that Kirk
had guessed his secret, but that, for some extraordinary
reason, he did not *want* Livingstone to be ' relieved.' That,

at any rate, is what he plainly hinted when he came to write his book. ' Dr. Kirk,' so he sums the matter up, ' very kindly promised to give me all the assistance in his power, and whatever experience he possessed he was willing, he said, to give me its full benefit. But I cannot recollect, neither do I find a trace of it in my journal, that he assisted me in any way. Of course, he was not aware that my instructions were to hunt up Livingstone ; otherwise Dr. Kirk, I have no doubt, would have made good his word.' The irony is obvious enough.

23

No comment by Kirk on his meeting with Stanley is on record. Stanley is our sole authority. And the story of his forthcoming venture into Africa, except for Livingstone's brief account of the four months he spent in Stanley's company, is likewise told by him alone. From *How I Found Livingstone in Central Africa*, therefore, the ensuing narrative must be almost wholly drawn ; its text will be frequently quoted ; and it may be useful at this point to say something about that celebrated book.

It is a peculiar book, utterly different from those in which the other great African explorers of that time described their expeditions, from Livingstone's *Zambesi and its Tributaries*, from Burton's *Lake Regions of Central Africa*, from Speke's *Discovery of the Sources of the Nile*, from Baker's *Albert Nyanza*. It is not merely or mainly a difference in style between books that rank as literature and a book which in its vividness and vigour, its strong colours and racy language, its forced dramatisation, exemplified the best sensational journalism of the day. The main difference may be detected in the titles. To some extent all travel-books must be personal, but Stanley's is intensely so. He describes at length not only what he does but what he thinks and feels ; and these disclosures are often highly emotional. Stanley in fact is revealing, and consciously revealing, his own character. Maybe there is nothing surprising in that ; but what is surprising is Stanley's apparent ignorance or disregard of the effect his personal revelations might have on his readers. For the primary test of a white man's character in the tropics lies in his behaviour towards the weak and backward people who inhabit them ; and Stanley relates how harshly on occasion he behaved in Africa towards Africans with a startling, almost a disarming candour. It is puzzling. Was Stanley being deliberately ' realistic ' about himself ? Was he saying in effect : ' I was a workhouse brat ; I was not brought up, I was whipped up, and I have had a hard time since. I am tough and proud of it. Would you expect anything else ? ' Or was he quite indifferent to other people's opinion of him ? Or was he so insensitive or so unacquainted with the normal moral standards of civilised society as not to realise what impression some of his pages would make on many of those who read them ? Perhaps the last alternative is indicated by the fact that, when one or two of the more lurid passages were criticised by English reviewers, Stanley excised them from later editions of his book.* But the present reader will doubtless form his own opinion. If he is an expert psycho-analyst, he will probably find it easy.

To return to Zanzibar and to Stanley who had got no help, he says, from Kirk. Nor did he get much from the narratives of those two Englishmen who had already made the journey to Ujiji where, as must long have been widely known at Zanzibar, Livingstone had fixed his inland base of operations. He carefully read Burton's and Speke's books ; but they told him little about the organisation of a caravan or its cost, about the kind of goods he must take for paying wages or for *hongo*, about the sort of supplies that Livingstone might want. All such information, however, was easily obtainable from the Arabs who knew the road and the Indians who fitted out their caravans. Of

* See p. 212 below.

the Indian firms Stanley did not deal with the old-established Hindu house with which the British Consulate and British explorers had always dealt but with a younger and possibly more efficient Moslem firm, the head of which was the American Consul's broker.[1] Having cashed drafts on Bennett for several thousand dollars, Stanley was soon crowding the storeroom Webb had put at his disposal with his mounting purchases. It contained in the end 22 sacks of beads, 350 pounds of brass-wire, 42 bales of cloth, coils of rope, saddles, some collapsible canvas boats, guns and ammunition, axes, tools, kitchen utensils and much else. Stanley confesses that the amount of it all took him aback. It weighed at least six tons. 'How will it ever be possible, I thought, to move all this inert mass across the wilderness?'[1]

That, of course, raised the old question of man-power. Porters were now virtually unobtainable in Zanzibar, and Stanley depended on hiring most of them at Bagamoyo. But he was fortunate enough to find six of the men who had served with Speke—'Speke's faithfuls' they were called —and were willing to serve with him. Stanley also engaged eighteen *askari*—the mercenary soldiers of the East African coast, mostly hailing from Beluchistan—and, in an ill-starred hour, two Europeans. One of them was a Scot, W. L. Farquhar, who had been first mate on the ship in which Stanley had sailed from Bombay, 'a capital navigator and excellent mathematician, strong, energetic and clever, but a hard drinker.' The other was J. W. Shaw, a Cockney, previously third mate on an American merchantman. An intimation of the trouble Stanley was to have with this couple was given him at the moment of his departure from Zanzibar on February 4. Everything was ready; four dhows were loaded up with all those goods and chattels and two horses and twenty donkeys; and Stanley was about to give the order to sail when he noticed that the two white men were missing. They were hunted down in a liquor-shop, where, it would seem, they had been trying to drown their misgivings about the

formidable adventure to which they had committed themselves. ' Have I done quite right,' Shaw asked Stanley in
a dolorous voice, ' to promise to go with you ? ' ' Get into
the boat, man, at once. We are all in for it now, sink or
swim, live or die—none can desert his duty.' So all three
white men sailed. Only one of them saw Zanzibar
again.

The hiring of porters at Bagamoyo was, as it had always
been since the cholera, a difficult and tedious job. It took
Stanley, champing with impatience, over six weeks before
he could get all the men he wanted. It was during this
time, as it happened, that Kirk crossed from Zanzibar to
see about Livingstone's goods. Stanley met him ; but, if
this was a last chance of clearing up the misunderstanding
between them, it was not taken. On the contrary, while
Kirk remained as ignorant as ever of Stanley's real intentions, Stanley was apparently confirmed in his strange
belief that Kirk was quite indifferent to Livingstone's fate.
At any rate he makes it plain to his readers that sport was
Kirk's main object in coming to Bagamoyo. They are
given to understand that his journey to Kikoka and back
was nothing but a ' hunt,' and that he devoted a couple
of hours at most to Livingstone's business just before
re-embarking for Zanzibar.

Stanley had decided to march his caravan in five
sections. The first set out on February 18. The third with
Farquhar in command, on February 25. The fifth, with
Stanley and Shaw, on March 21. The personnel of the
whole caravan made an imposing total—157 porters with
4 headmen, 23 soldiers, 5 cooks and odd men, and 3
whites—192 in all.

Livingstone, it will be remembered, started inland from
Mikindani with 60 men. But the size and wealth of the
two caravans were not the only points of contrast. There
was a difference in speed. Livingstone trudged across
Africa : Stanley strode. He reached Unyanyembe in four
months. Burton and Speke took five, and, whereas they
had taken the road in the dry season, Stanley marched

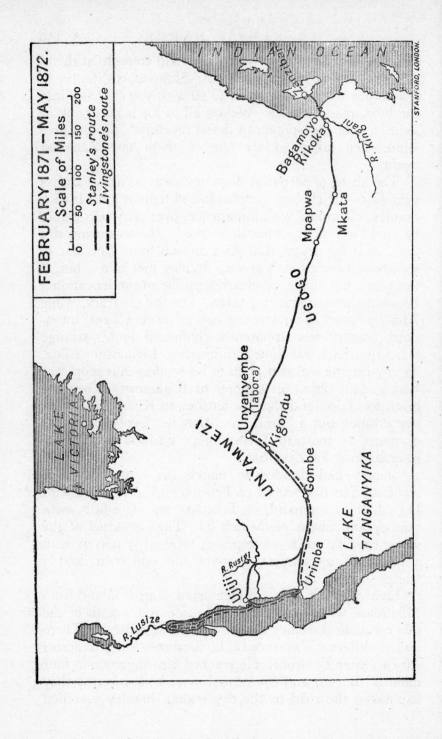

FEBRUARY 1871 — MAY 1872.

Scale of Miles

0   50   100   150   200

——— Stanley's route
- - - Livingstone's route

INDIAN OCEAN

Zanzibar

Bagamoyo
Kikoka
R. Kingani

Mpapwa
Mkata

UGOGO

Unyanyembe
(Tabora)

Kigondu

UNYAMWEZI

Gombe

LAKE VICTORIA

LAKE TANGANYIKA

Urimba

Ujiji
R. Rusizi

R. Lusize

STANFORD, LONDON.

through the ' rains ' which, though unusually light this
year, fell steadily for a fortnight, swelling the rivers, filling
the swamps, and bogging the track. Nor was he less
delayed than other travellers by long haggling over *hongo*
and by frequent bouts of malaria and dysentery. He could
not, indeed, with all his own indomitable vigour, have
made the pace if he had not driven his men along with a
stern discipline such as Livingstone, as has been seen, was
incapable of practising. The signal for the early morning
start was the crack, ' like a pistol-shot,' of ' the Great
Master's donkey-whip.' A few weeks after leaving Bagamoyo Stanley comments on ' the virtues of a good whip.'
' I was becoming wise by experience, and I was compelled
to observe that, when mud and wet sapped the physical
energy of the lazily-inclined, a dog-whip became their
backs, restoring them to a sound, sometimes to an extrava-
gant activity.' When a crowd of Wagogo villagers pressed
round him, pointing and shouting and obstructing his
path, he seized one of them by the neck, administered ' a
sound thrashing which he little relished,' and then ' a few
vigorous and rapid slashes right and left with my service-
able thong soon cleared the track.'

But more hampering and more trying to Stanley's
temper than the slackness and stupidity of the black men
was the conduct of his two white subordinates. On May 9
he caught up the third section of the caravan and found
Farquhar in bed with a dropsical swelling of the legs,
' engendered by general debauchery.' Setting the patient
on a donkey and uniting the two sections, Stanley pressed
ahead. But Farquhar's weight and method of riding were
too much for the donkeys. He had already killed one of
them before Stanley overtook him. Now another died, and
Stanley began to fear that the drink-sodden cripple would
soon bring the Expedition to a halt. Nor was Shaw much
better. He, too, insisted on riding till Stanley made him
walk : he dawdled intolerably, and he was frequently
down with malaria. Tempers at last gave way on both
sides. On May 15, when Shaw and Farquhar came to

breakfast as usual in Stanley's tent, they gave him a surly
greeting ; and presently Shaw began to curse the Expedition and to complain in lurid terms of the way he had been
treated. Stanley relates that he patiently explained the
difficulties of the position, and added, ' " Do you realise
what you are ? Do you know you are my servant, sir, and
not my companion ? " " Servant be ——," said he. But
before Mr. Shaw could finish his sentence, he had measured
his length on the ground.' Thereupon Shaw asked for his
discharge and Stanley promptly gave it ; but it was quite
impossible, of course, for Shaw to make his way back to
Zanzibar by himself, and, before very long, he was pleading
to be pardoned and taken back. The quarrel was made
up with a handshake ; but that night, as he was falling
asleep, Stanley heard a shot, and a bullet tore through
the tent a few inches above his bed. He leapt up, and
going to Shaw's tent found him pretending to be woken
up from sleep. A gun lay near, and, inserting his little
finger in the barrel, Stanley found it warm and black with
burnt powder. Evidently Shaw had not forgotten that
blow at breakfast, but Stanley, who never lacked personal
courage, decided to ignore it. The affair, however, seems
to have decided him to cut away the incumbrance of
Farquhar. He told him that it would be better for him
if he were left behind ' in some quiet place, under the care
of a good chief who would, for a consideration, look after
him until he got well.' It cannot have been easy to be
sure about a strange chief's goodness or what he was likely
to do with a helpless white man ; but Farquhar, it seems,
agreed to the plan and remained alone in wild Africa.
Nothing more was heard of him till an Arab caravan,
which came by the same route and reached Unyanyembe
in August, brought the news that he was dead. He had
felt so well one morning, Stanley was told, that he had
declared his intention of taking the road ; but, on trying
to rise from his bed, he had fallen back and died. His body
had been dragged into the jungle and left there naked and
unburied.

Stanley reached Unyanyembe, on the heels of the other three sections of his caravan, in June. He was hospitably welcomed by the aged Said bin Salim, the Governor of the Arab trading colony, who had befriended Burton and Speke and Grant in their day. A commodious walled farmstead or *tembe* was put at his disposal, the courtyard stocked with oxen and goats and chickens, and the tables loaded with savoury food and drink.* But Stanley could not relax for long. He was now pretty sure that Livingstone was at Ujiji. On the way up from the coast he had met an Arab who had seen an old man there ' with long grey moustaches and beard, just recovered from severe illness, looking very wan ' ; and, now that he was only a few weeks' march from his goal, he was afraid lest the shy bird should hear of the stalker's approach and fly off into the wilds beyond pursuit. He was spurred on, too, by finding that Kirk's caravan had reached Unyanyembe before him and with it a sealed packet of letters addressed to Livingstone, registered on November 1, 1870. ' Poor Livingstone,' he says, noting the date ; and he promptly obtains the Governor's permission to take charge of the caravan and the letters. But at that time he could do no more to get them further on their way than Kirk could do at Zanzibar. The path was barred now by a far more serious obstacle than the fears and intrigues of Arab slavers. War had broken out across it. The people of Unyamwezi had never welcomed the Arabs' presence at Unyanyembe. They had resented their high-handed conduct and their interference with their rights and trade. In 1860 they had come to blows with them, and a long and desultory conflict had only ended when in 1865 the Arabs caught their ruling chief and cut his head off.[1] Now they had risen again under another and abler leader, Mirambo, and, encamped right athwart the Ujiji road, were threatening the colony from the west. Stanley found the Arabs preparing, against Said bin Salim's advice, to take the offensive. With their forty or fifty Arab or Afro-

* For a description of the colony, see *East Africa and its Invaders*, 305-311.

Arab gunmen, with over one thousand slaves and some hundreds of the local tribesmen, they were confident of an easy victory. Time was to show that there was a good deal to be said for Mirambo [1]; but Stanley accepted his hosts' version of his villainy, and, anxious to repay their hospitality and believing that a short campaign would be the quickest means of opening the road to Ujiji, he decided to take part in it. The preparations took more than a month —a tedious period for Stanley, during which he had his sharpest attack of fever and lay half-conscious or delirious for a week—and it was not till early in August that they sallied out. The upshot was a pitiful fiasco. An outlying party was ambushed and cut up, and on the news of it the main body broke into panic and ran for home. Stanley was left alone and in great danger, but he made his way back to Unyanyembe, filled now, as his journal shows, with the utmost contempt for the treachery and cowardice of his allies. A fortnight later, Mirambo advanced on Unyanyembe. Charging from two sides, he penetrated into the colony, set part of it on fire, and held the rest of it besieged. On the first day Stanley, whose *tembe* lay some distance from the centre of the fighting, was told that Mirambo was intending to attack him. Hoisting the Stars and Stripes and marshalling his 150 men in the courtyard, he prepared to fight to the end. ' I hope to God he will come,' says the journal : ' if he comes within range of an American rifle, I shall see what virtue lies in American lead.' But Mirambo did not come, and on the fourth night he raised the siege and withdrew his forces westwards.

So Stanley had wasted his time to no purpose. To less than none, indeed. Some of his porters had been killed, and the rest considered their engagement at an end. It might well prove impossible to fill their places. And Mirambo, stronger now than ever, still blocked the Ujiji road. In the interval between the Arab rout and the siege Stanley's journal sounds a new note of gravity. ' I am quite disappointed and almost disheartened. . . . My position is most serious. I have a good excuse for re-turning to the coast, but my conscience will not permit me to do so after so much money has been expended and so much confidence has been placed in me. In fact, I feel I must die sooner than return.' In such a mood the lethargy of tropical life seemed wellnigh unendurable. ' I almost despair of ever being able to move from here. It is such a drowsy, sleepy, slow, dreaming country. Arabs, Wangwana, Wanyamwezi are all alike—all careless how time flies. Their to-morrow means sometimes within a month. To me it is simply maddening.' And it was not only the Arabs and Africans. The unhappy Shaw was getting on Stanley's nerves. Constant attacks of malaria had reduced him to a listless wreck. ' What a change from the ready-handed bold man he was at Zanzibar ! ' At times Stanley suspected he was malingering. ' If I took a stick, I could take the nonsense out of him.'

He had made up his mind, meanwhile, that, if he could get porters, he would march south-west until he was well away from Mirambo's forces on the Ujiji road and then make a dash north-west for his goal. And, bit by bit, he did get porters, enough of them to carry a substantial part of the loads he had brought up from the coast—4000 yards of cloth, 6 bags of beads, 4 loads of ammunition together with medicine, tea, coffee, sugar, flour, canned meats, sardines and candles. On September 20, more than three months since his arrival at Unyanyembe, he began his second march with a caravan of fifty-four.

Once afoot, Stanley soon recovered his spirits. His health no longer troubled him : throughout this journey he had not one attack of fever. And he had been only a week on his way when he was freed from the burden that worried him most. Shaw had begged to be allowed to stay behind at Unyanyembe, but, though he was utterly useless, Stanley felt responsible for him. He had nursed him when he was ill, he had tried to argue him out of his lassitude and melancholia, and he still wanted to keep him under his eye. But the unhappy Englishman seemed worse on the

road than he had been at the *tembe*. He was allowed to
ride a donkey, but he frequently fell off. He seemed to
Stanley to be doing his best to compel him to let him go
back. At Kigomdu, some forty miles from Unyanyembe,
Stanley gave in. He told Shaw that his patience was
exhausted, that he was tired of trying to convince him
that his illness was imaginary, that he would let him go.
But he warned him that, if he were really ill, there would
be no one to look after him. ' Mark my words—to return
to Unyanyembe is to DIE ! ' On September 27 Shaw was
carried off by four porters on a litter. Four months later,
when Stanley was on his way back to Unyanyembe, he
met an outward-bound caravan and was told that Shaw
had got back safely to the *tembe* but had died soon afterwards.

For the next ten days the caravan made good progress
southwards into fine open country. It was like English
park-land, swarming with wild game, ' a sportsman's
paradise.' For two days Stanley halted there, and, if he
enjoyed the shooting, his men enjoyed the break in their
endless marching and the meat they got from his gun—so
much so that they were reluctant to break camp and take
the road again. Soon after the start, Stanley found the
column halted, the loads on the ground, the porters talking
angrily in groups. He realised at once that he was face to
face with mutiny—and murder. Two of the men were
lurking behind an anthill, their guns pointed towards the
track. Lifting his rifle, Stanley told them to come on.
One of them came towards him ' in a sidelong way with
a smirking smile on his face ' : the other crept round behind him. If they had had half Stanley's courage, they
could easily have shot him. But they hesitated, and Stanley,
wheeling round on the man at his back, levelled his rifle
at his face and forced him to drop his gun. That was the
other man's chance, but he lost it, and he was still fumbling
with his weapon when one of ' Speke's faithfuls ' ran up
and seized it. The danger was over. The two men were
admonished and pardoned. And then, with a swift

emotional revulsion, the whole company pledged themselves anew to follow their master, by God, to Tanganyika.

By mid-October they had completed their southward
course, and soon they were steering west and presently
north-west. On November 3 they encountered a caravan
eight days out from Ujiji. A white man, Stanley was told,
had just arrived there from Manyema. 'He has white
hair on his face and is sick.' He had been at Ujiji before,
but had gone away a long time ago. That this was Livingstone Stanley could scarcely doubt, and Ujiji was only
some 80 miles away. But he had still to surmount the
most awkward obstacle he had met since leaving Unyanyembe. He was passing now through a rich and populous
belt of country, ruled by powerful and predatory chiefs ;
and their demands for *hongo*, district after district, were
exorbitant. One claimed a whole bale of cloth ; another
nearly two bales. On November 6 Stanley had only nine
bales left. He had to pay the next chief half a bale and
was told that between him and Ujiji there were five more
chiefs who would take their toll. 'What is to be done ? '
asks Stanley. 'How am I to reach Livingstone without
being beggared ? ' The only answer seemed to be to 'run
the blockade.' Stanley questioned two of his men who
knew the country. They declared at first that it was quite
impossible to evade the *hongo*. If they were caught, they
would all be put to death. But presently they admitted
that, if suitably rewarded, they could guide the caravan
through the jungle, and that there was a chance of its
escape if strict silence were observed by night and day.
No gun must be fired, no cries raised. Soon after midnight,
accordingly, the caravan crept out of their sleeping village,
in groups of four, and stole across the grassy plain in the
light of the moon. Dawn found them approaching the
Rusugi River, and in a clump of bushes and reeds near
its bank they halted for rest and breakfast. Unluckily they
were observed by some tribesmen carrying bags of salt
along the opposite bank, who promptly dropped their
loads and ran shouting towards some villages on a hillside

a few miles off. There was no time to be lost. The men took up their loads and made for the near-by jungle, but they had scarcely reached its shelter when a woman of the party, apparently the wife of one of the porters, suddenly gave way to panic, and began uttering piercing screams. Nothing would stop her. ' In half an hour,' says Stanley, ' we should have hundreds of howling savages about us in the jungle, and probably a general massacre would ensue.' The woman's husband, ' livid with rage and fear,' asked leave to cut her head off. ' I attempted to hush her cries by putting my hand over her mouth, but she violently wrestled with me and continued her cries worse than ever. There remained nothing else for me to do but to try the virtue of my whip over her shoulders. I asked her to desist after the first blow. " No ! " She continued her insane cries with increased force and volume. Again my whip descended on her shoulders. " No, no, no ! " Another blow. " Will you hush ? " " No, no no ! " Louder and louder she cried, and faster and faster I showered the blows for the taming of this shrew. However, seeing I was as determined to flog her as she was to cry, she desisted before the tenth blow and became silent. A cloth was folded over her mouth, and her arms were tied behind her.' . . . Since Stanley carried his Winchester and 200 cartridges and he still had his armed *askari*, the danger may not have been so acute as it seemed. At any rate it did not materialise. The caravan pushed on at a quickened pace. There was no pursuit. Early in the afternoon they reached the little Lake Musunya and bivouacked. But no tent was pitched, nor fire kindled, and long before dawn next day they were on the march again. That night they reached the Rugufo River, only some forty miles from Ujiji ; and on the morrow they emerged at last from the country ruled by the blackmailing chiefs. All that day Stanley spurred his men on, and that night he bade his servant lay out a new suit and oil his boots and chalk his helmet. ' Only let one day come again, and we shall see what we shall see.' The day came. Before noon he was looking down on the little township by the lakeside. ' Unfurl the flags and load your guns. . . . . Keep close together and keep firing until we halt in the market-place or before the white man's house.' Roused by the fusillade, the Ujijians came pouring out to meet them, and Stanley was presently startled to hear Susi's ' Good-morning, sir.' A few minutes later, he was parting the crowd and walking down ' a living avenue of people ' at the end of which stood ' the white man with the grey beard.'

24

STANLEY gave Livingstone literally a new lease of life. He had brought him the tonics which his failing mind and body so desperately needed. The good food and drugs at once alleviated—it was too late for them to cure—his physical disorders. The newspapers, the letters from home, the long talks with a man who had travelled far and witnessed great events, cut through the curtain which had so long blacked-out the world and revivified the personal and public interests which had begun to fade into the background of his mind. Ten days or so after Stanley's arrival he summed it all up in his journal. ' The news he had to tell to one who had been two full years without any tidings from Europe made my whole frame thrill. The terrible fate that had befallen France, the telegraphic cables successfully laid in the Atlantic, the election of General Grant, the death of good Lord Clarendon, my constant friend, the proof that Her Majesty's Government had not forgotten me in voting 1000*l* for supplies, and many other points of interest revived emotions that had lain dormant in Manyema. Appetite returned, and, instead of the sparse tasteless two meals a day, I ate four times daily, and in a week began to feel strong. I am not of a demonstrative turn ; as cold, indeed, as we islanders are usually reported to be : but this disinterested kindness of Mr. Bennett, so nobly carried into effect by Mr. Stanley, was simply overwhelming.' There was one thing he could do to show his gratitude, and he did it at once. He wrote to Mr. Bennett to thank him for the ' extreme kindness ' which had prompted Stanley's mission. ' I had got,' he said, ' to about the lowest verge. . . . I thought of myself as the man who went down from Jerusalem to Jericho ; but neither priest, Levite, nor Samaritan could possibly pass my way. Yet the good Samaritan was close at hand. . . . It was, indeed, overwhelming, and I said in my soul, " Let the richest blessings descend from the Highest on you and yours ! " '

It would be churlish to quarrel with Livingstone's overstatement of his debt to Mr. Bennett, and Stanley could scarcely be expected to have corrected it. How could he say that the primary object of his mission was to enhance the prestige of the *New York Herald*, that the idea of helping Livingstone had been an afterthought, and that the route he had taken had been somewhat circuitous ? And after all he *had* helped him. More than likely, indeed, he had saved his life. And, as he reflected on the startling *dénouement* of the enterprise, not merely the finding of Livingstone, but the finding of him in desperate need, he began to feel that there was a mystical significance in that roundabout approach to Africa and also in the check he had suffered at Unyanyembe. He had arrived at precisely the right time. Livingstone, it might almost be said, was waiting for him, ' resting under the veranda of his house, with his face turned eastward, the direction from which I was coming. Had I gone direct from Paris on my search I might have lost him ; had I been enabled to have gone direct to Ujiji from Unyanyembe I might have lost him. . . . I began to recognise the hand of an overruling and kindly Providence.'

In further recognition of his debt to the *Herald* Livingstone drafted another letter for publication in its columns[1] —a long letter, partly about the Slave Trade, partly about

Manyema and its people. Most of it is in his own familiar
style. His description and denunciation of the Trade, his
appeal for its suppression, are highly characteristic. So is
his discourse on the Nile and the Herodotean fountains.
So, too, is his frank demand that white men should treat
black men as their equals. ' I have no prejudice against
their colour ; indeed, any one who lives long among them
forgets that they are black and feels that they are just
fellow-men.' Nor, he argues, should African physique be
judged from that of the victims of the west-coast slavers.
' If a comparison were instituted, and Manyema, taken at
random, placed opposite say the members of the Anthro-
pological Society of London, clad like them in kilts of
grass cloth, I should like to take my place alongside the
Manyema, on the principle of preferring the company of
my betters.' All that is pure Livingstonian. But there are
one or two other passages which seem a little less true to
type. There is some rather childish stuff about bogeys and
' bogiephobia,' and a rather crude portrait of a Tanganyika chief who had ' become what Nathaniel Hawthorne
called " bulbous " below the ribs.' And there is an almost
maudlin rhapsody on the beauty of Manyema women.
' Fortunately the dears could not change their charming
black eyes, beautiful foreheads, nicely rounded limbs, well-
shaped forms, and small hands and feet. But they must
adorn themselves ; and this they do—oh, the hussies !—
by filing their splendid teeth to points like cat's teeth. It
was distressing, for it made their smile, which has generally
so much power over us great he-donkeys, rather crocodile-
like.' It was this passage in particular that afforded one
or two sceptical folk in England, later on, a pretext for
questioning the letter's authenticity. But there can be no
doubt whatever that Livingstone wrote it, and the oddities
it contains are explicable enough if it be remembered that
Stanley was at the writer's elbow, suggesting, one may
reasonably suppose, the sort of thing that readers of the
Herald liked.

An early symptom of Livingstone's recovery, as Stanley

observed, was a desire to be up and doing. And as to what he should do he seems never to have been in doubt. Stanley pressed him to return with him to Zanzibar and so home if only that he might see his children and take the spell of rest he had deserved. But Livingstone would not hear of that. He must finish his work first—in other words, determine once for all whether his 'dream' were true or false. It would not take long. He only needed goods to pay his way and porters to carry them. The goods, Stanley told him, were waiting at Unyanyembe, and porters could be obtained there or sent up from the coast. It was decided, accordingly, that they should both return to Unyanyembe—but not at once. They would first make a short trip up the Lake in order to see, as no white man had yet seen, its northern end. That was an object of high geographical importance : for, if there was truth in the report that a river, the Lusizé, flowed out of that northern end, might it not conceivably continue northwards until it reached the Albert Nyanza or by some other route became the Nile ? A lake-voyage, moreover, would complete Livingstone's convalescence before he faced the rigours of the Unyanyembe road. Preparations were quickly made. A long canoe was borrowed from one of the Ujijian Arabs. Twenty of Stanley's men supplied the crew. On November 16 they started paddling up the coast.

On December 13 they were back at Ujiji. They had solved the geographical problem. The Lusizé, they found, flowed into the Lake, not out of it. Otherwise it had been an uneventful excursion. Once or twice the lakeside villagers had seemed to resent their intrusion ; but they had kept out of trouble. On one occasion Stanley observed how quietly Livingstone handled the thorny question of *hongo*—and got his way : on another how he prevented by his 'gentle patient bearing' a quarrel with a drunken chief and his excited followers from ending in a fight. There can be no doubt that those were happy days for Livingstone, passed as they were in comfort and security and in sur-

roundings of rare beauty—the calm, deep, dark-green
waters of the lake, the wooded mountains rising steeply
from the shore, the radiant African light and the deep-blue
African sky—and it was a very different Livingstone that
came back this time to Ujiji. But it would be a mistake
to suppose that he had quite recovered his old self. His
dysenteric condition was now chronic : Stanley was dis-
tressed to notice that not only a mistake in diet but any
worry or fatigue was certain to induce an attack of diar-
rhœa. And his mind was still tired. The entries in his
journal at this time are very brief. The period of four
months between Stanley's arrival and departure is covered
in fifteen printed pages or about 5000 words. And, while
Livingstone, writing to different friends about the same
events, had always, and naturally, tended to repeat himself, the repetitions of words and phrases, even of whole
sentences, are far more frequent in the many letters he
now wrote for Stanley to take home.

A fortnight was occupied with packing up. It was rainy
weather, and Stanley, who had had two attacks of fever
on the lake, was ill again a few days before Christmas.
But he was up on Christmas Eve, planning to keep ' the
blessed time-honoured day as we keep it in Anglo-Saxon
lands.' Unhappily the feast was spoiled by the cook.
' That the fat-brained rascal escaped a thrashing was due
only to my inability to lift my hands for punishment.'
' Had but a sorry Christmas yesterday ' is Livingstone's
brief entry for the 26th. Next day they started from Ujiji
by water, and on New Year's day, 1872, they were more
than half-way to Urimba, the point at which they had
decided to strike across country to Stanley's previous line
of march. Once more Livingstone's journal opens the year
with a prayer, the same prayer he had made at Bambarré
at the outset of 1871, but with a significant addition. ' May
the Almighty help me to finish my work *this year* for Christ's
sake ! ' . . . On January 7 they began the eastward
march from Urimba, and on the tenth day they struck
Stanley's old route and camped where he had camped

before. Thenceforward the track was familiar and they made steady progress, only checked by Stanley's attacks of malaria which had now become recurrent. On the first occasion they were halted for three days ; on the second Livingstone had a litter made on which the sick man was carried onward till he could ride or walk again. Livingstone himself, whose boots had been cut almost to ribbons, suffered acutely from chafed and blistered feet, and one day, towards the end of a tiring march of eighteen miles, he was attacked, as he rode on his donkey, by a swarm of wild bees which stung him all over his head. ' They gave me a sore head and face,' the journal drily records. 'The donkey,' on the other hand, ' was completely knocked up by the stings . . . and died in two days.' They reached the *tembe* at Unyanyembe on February 18. ' Doctor,' said Stanley, as they walked ' arm in arm ' into his old room, ' we are at last at home.'

They found that the war with Mirambo was still going on in a desultory fashion. There were rumours that he was dead and his people starving ; in fact he was very much alive, and, when Cameron came to Unyanyembe eighteen months later, he was still firmly planted across the Ujiji road. But he never renewed his attack on the Arab colony, and there was nothing to disturb the peace and quiet of the month which Livingstone and Stanley spent at the *tembe*. Most of their time was occupied in discussing and preparing for the future—for Livingstone's last explorations and for Stanley's return to Zanzibar. Ample supplies for both were available on the spot. The bales which had arrived for Livingstone[*] had, it is true, been pilfered by one of the headmen of the caravan who had also broken the lock of Stanley's storeroom and stolen some of his things too ; and, when Livingstone also obtained the chest of goods which he had ordered Koorji to send up to Ujiji before he left Zanzibar in 1866[†] and which had remained at Unyanyembe in the Governor's charge all those years,

* See p. 163 above.
† See p. 57 above.

he found little left of its contents. White ants had eaten most of them, even the stocks of two guns and a pistol. There was some cheese, still edible, two full and several empty bottles of brandy, and—if only Livingstone could have got it in 1867 !—a zinc case of drugs. All of which was further proof, if it were needed, that no white man's property was safe for long in the interior unless he was there himself to protect it. But there was more than enough in Stanley's stock to make good the losses and to furnish Livingstone with practically everything else he would need. Stanley kept only what he wanted for his return journey : the rest he handed over. It was sufficient, he reckoned, to keep Livingstone going for four years. Porters, however, were now quite unobtainable at Unyanyembe, mainly, no doubt, because of the war. So Stanley undertook to enlist fifty men as soon as he reached the coast, and dispatch them hot-foot inland. Those matters decided and Livingstone's letters written and his journal packed and ' sealed with five seals ' for Stanley's carriage to England, there was nothing more to be done. On March 14 Livingstone's journal briefly records : ' Mr. Stanley leaves.' Stanley describes the parting at greater length. ' We had a sad breakfast together. I could not eat, my heart was too full ; neither did my companion seem to have an appetite. We found something to do which kept us longer together.' When at last a start was made, Livingstone insisted on seeing Stanley off along the road. ' We walked side by side ; the men lifted their voices in a song. I took long looks at Livingstone to impress his features thoroughly on my memory.' They had got some distance from the *tembe* when Stanley begged Livingstone to turn back. ' You have done what few men could do,' were Livingstone's last words—the last he ever spoke to a white man : ' far better than some great travellers I know. And I am grateful to you for what you have done for me. God guide you safe home and bless you, my friend.' ' And may God bring you safely back to us all, my dear friend. Farewell.' . . . Stanley was hard put to it to repress his emotion ; and, when Susi and Chuma prolonged the parting, wringing and kissing his hands, it was too much for him. 'I betrayed myself. . . . ' " *March*! Why do you stop? Go on! Are you not going home? " And my people were driven before me. No more weakness. I shall show them such marching as will make them remember me.'[1]

25

THUS ended an episode so dramatic and of such deep human interest that it will never be forgotten. If the world remembers little else about Livingstone and Stanley, it will always remember how they met and lived together, alone of their kind in the heart of Africa, in the closest companionship day by day, sometimes sharing a hut at night. And inevitably the question will suggest itself— how did those two so different men, one already famous, the other in the act of making his fame, get on together? What did they think of one another? A full and certain answer is beyond our reach, but there is a good deal that is plain.

It is plain, to begin with, that Livingstone's sense of gratitude was genuine and profound. There is no mistaking the sincerity of his thanks to Mr. Bennett, nor of a letter he wrote home at the same time about Stanley. ' He laid all he had at my service, divided his clothes into two heaps, and pressed one heap upon me ; then his medicine chest ; then his goods and everything he had, and to coax my appetite often cooked dainty dishes with his own hand. . . . He came with true American generosity. The tears often started into my eyes on every fresh proof of kindness.'[2] As those four months went by, he was more and more touched by Stanley's manifest deference and devotion, of his constant care for his health and comfort, of his interest in every detail of his work in Africa and his anxiety to do all he could to help him finish it. Writing to Waller six months after Stanley had gone, ' He behaved,' he says, ' as a son to a father.'[1] He was certainly grateful, and he paid his debt, as best he could, by satisfying Stanley's professional needs, answering his innumerable questions, and— a ' scoop ' this for the journalist—allowing him to take down from his dictation an authentic account of his wanderings since 1866 for publication to the world.[2] Sometimes, however, his impetuous companion's curiosity must have seemed a little intrusive, and there is an amusing passage in Stanley's book in which he relates how Livingstone would often sit in silent meditation, ' his eyes gazing far away into infinite distance, brows puckered closely, face set and resolute, now and then lips moving,' and how he once ventured to break in. ' A penny for your thoughts, Doctor.' ' They are not worth it, my young friend, and let me suggest that, if I had any, possibly I should wish to keep them.' ' After which,' continues Stanley, ' I invariably let him alone when in this mood.'[3] But that was a minor point of manners, and what must have jarred far more sharply on Livingstone's feelings was Stanley's behaviour to Africans. If he ever heard from Stanley the story of his youth, he doubtless made allowances. Doubtless, too, he observed how quick was Stanley's temper and how easily he lost it altogether, especially if there was fever on him. Nevertheless those outbreaks must have pained him, and sometimes he showed what he felt by word or look. One such occasion was a quarrel with Ulimengo, the cook. When Stanley pointed out to him that the cooking-pots were poisonously dirty, he insolently answered that what was good enough for the ' big master ' was good enough for him. ' Half-mad with huge doses of quinine,' Stanley knocked him down. Ulimengo seemed to have resented this as much as Shaw, and with less deliberation. Getting up, he laid hold of Stanley who freed himself and was looking for ' some handy instrument ' when Livingstone appeared. ' I will settle this,' he said, and quietly explained to the now crestfallen Ulimengo that Stanley was tne master and must be obeyed, that he himself was only Stanley's guest, that the caravan, the food, the wages all came from Stanley's pocket. ' You are a big fool. Go and ask his pardon.'[1] . . . Another incident was or might have been more serious. It arose from that brush—to which reference has already been made—with apparently hostile natives on Lake Tanganyika. Livingstone's version is brief. One day, when they were coasting along a populous district, stones were thrown at their canoe, and they decided to keep a watch that night. In the course of it, ' a number of men came along, cowering behind rocks, which then aroused suspicion, and we slipped off quietly ; they called after us, as men baulked of their prey.' Stanley's account is more detailed. When the stones were thrown, one of them nearly hitting him, ' I suggested,' he says, ' that a bullet be sent in return in close proximity to their feet ; but Livingstone, though he said nothing, yet showed plainly enough that he did not quite approve of this.' Again, when they paddled away to safety, ' my hand was stayed from planting a couple of good shots, as a warning to them in future from molesting strangers, by the mere presence of the Doctor.'*

It is clear from Stanley's account of these incidents that he was deeply impressed by Livingstone's gentleness with Africans, whether it were a lazy servant or a mob of excited villagers. ' " You bad fellow, you very wicked fellow, you blockhead, you fool of a man " were the strongest terms he employed, where others would have clubbed or clouted or banned or blasted. His manner was that of a cool, wise old man, who felt offended and looked grave.'[2] In another passage he goes deeper. ' He can be charmed with the primitive simplicity of Ethiop's dusky children, with whom he has spent so many years of his life ; he has a sturdy faith in their capabilities ; sees virtue in them

* In a public speech at Glasgow on October 23, 1872, Stanley gave a slightly different version of this incident. ' " Doctor," I said, " do you see those two fellows behind the rock ? Just give me the word and I will settle them for ever." " No," said he ; " what is the use ? We are safe ; we have done them this time ; they are tricked, and we have done it very neatly—what is the use of shooting them ? " " Just so, Doctor," and I dropped the gun.' (*Glasgow Herald*, Oct. 24, 1872).

where others see nothing but savagery ; and wherever he has gone among them, he has sought to elevate a people that were apparently forgotten of God and Christian man.' A few years later, in the preface to his narrative of his next African journey, Stanley declared himself a ' strong disciple ' of the doctrine he had learned from Livingstone for dealing with hostile natives, the ' doctrine of forbearance.' It was a pity he forgot it on that dark day on Lake Victoria in 1875 when he set out in battle array to ' chastise ' the islanders of Bumbire.* But perhaps it was not surprising. For, while he described—and very well described—Livingstone's attitude and conduct towards Africans, he never pretended, except as regards that ' doctrine,' to be able to think and act like that himself. He seems to have believed that a Christian conception of the relationship between strong and weak races, a sense of the human rights and possibilities of black men and of the status and obligations of white men in Africa, was to be expected only of a saint, and that ordinary folk could not attain such heights. A discouraging point of view, since saints are rare ; but that Stanley genuinely held it is clear enough. Of all those curiously candid passages in which he reveals himself to his readers, none is stranger than that in which he tells how he has often overheard the servants discussing their respective masters. ' " Your master," say my servants to Livingstone's, " is a good man, a very good man ; he does not beat you, for he has a kind heart ; but ours—oh ! he is sharp—hot as fire." ' In another passage—so fast ran the ready pen—Stanley seems to have forgotten the contrast between the saint and his disciple. It occurs in his account of that same little adventure on Lake Tanganyika. After the stone-throwing, he relates, and before the night of the slip-away, they landed on a lonely beach and lit a fire and made some coffee. ' Despite the dangers which still beset us, we were quite happy, and seasoned our meal with a little moral philosophy, which lifted *us* un-

* Stanley, *Through the Dark Continent* (London, 1878), i. 270-96, and his letters to the *Daily Telegraph*, Aug. 7 and 10, 1876. Outline in *The Exploitation of East Africa*, 324-6.

consciously into infinitely superior beings to the pagans by whom we were surrounded—upon whom *we* now looked down, under the influence of Mocha coffee and moral philosophy, with calm contempt, not unmixed with a certain amount of compassion.' If Livingstone had lived to read that passage, he must, despite its half-humorous intent, have winced at it, or, more likely, blown it out of mind with a gust of laughter.

It is not only on Livingstone's gentleness with Africans that Stanley dwells. He portrays him minutely, examines his character, retails his conversation at some length. And this was not by any means only because he was ' good copy.' It is quite evident that to Stanley, at the time and ever after, his brief companionship with Livingstone was the supreme experience of his life. He had come close to moral greatness, and he was startled, captivated, subjected by it. His description of Livingstone seems instinct with wonder and devotion—real wonder and sincere devotion. Here is the gist of it.

' I defy any one to be in his society long without thoroughly fathoming him, for in him there is no guile, and what is apparent on the surface is the thing that is in him. . . . I grant he is not an angel, but he approaches to that being as near as the nature of a living man will allow. . . . You may take any point in his character, and analyse it carefully, and I would challenge any man to find a fault in it. . . . His gentleness never forsakes him ; his hopefulness never deserts him. No harassing anxieties, distraction of mind, long separation from home and kindred, can make him complain. He thinks " all will come out right at last " ; he has such faith in the goodness of Providence. . . . His religion is neither demonstrative nor loud, but manifests itself in a quiet practical way and is always at work. . . . Without it Livingstone, with his ardent temperament, his enthusiasm, his high spirit and courage, must have become uncompanionable and a hard master. Religion has tamed him and made him a Christian gentleman.' . . . Add to that the picture Stanley draws of Livingstone's personal appearance—his hair still brownish, but streaked with grey over the temples, the beard and moustache very grey : remarkably bright hazel eyes, and sight keen as a hawk's : the broken teeth alone betraying his age and the hardships he had undergone : the figure becoming stoutish under the new diet, shoulders slightly bent : the tread firm but heavy, like that of an overworked or tired man : the 'naval' consular cap, the clothes worn and patched but scrupulously clean. . . . Add, too, the scraps of Livingstone's talk and the glimpses of daily life 'under the palms of Ujiji '—the walk along the lakeside early morning and evening : the visit to the market where the villagers from all the country round brought their wares and chaffered, and the old women gossiped, and the children laughed and played : the siesta under the thatch of Livingstone's house, watching the passing townsfolk, all of them showing the respect they had learned to feel for him, even the Arab traders calling to pay their compliments and give him Allah's blessing—the service every Sunday morning at which Livingstone prayed and read a chapter of the Bible and preached a brief sermon on it in Swaheli to his 'little flock.' . . . Altogether it was a very interesting, attractive, convincing picture of Livingstone, both person and personality, that Stanley drew ; and it was all the more precious to those who knew him because it was the last that was ever drawn from life.

26

LIVINGSTONE'S older friends may have treasured Stanley's description of him and yet been hurt by the context in which it was set. For Stanley had, so to speak, appropriated Livingstone and all the credit of befriending him. Consciously or subconsciously, he exalts his own relations with him by depreciating those of others. He prefaces his tribute to the saint by recounting sundry criticisms of him—he is said to be splenetic, garrulous, demented, incapable : he is reported to have married an African princess(!) ' I respectfully beg to differ,' he solemnly declares ; and the ignorant reader is given to suppose that it was only Stanley who appreciated Livingstone's true character. It is the same with the ' finding.' The achievement is glorified by contrast. Stanley ' found ' him : the others ' lost ' him. Stanley saved him : the others were indifferent to his fate. And that, perhaps, explains what would otherwise seem inexplicable—Stanley's extraordinary treatment of Kirk. Of all Livingstone's friends Kirk was the nearest to him in point of space and the most responsible for doing what could be done to meet his needs. One might suppose that it would have been enough for Stanley's purpose to point out that he had succeeded where Kirk had tried and failed. But he was not content with that. He heightened the contrast by intimating, very plainly, that Kirk had not really tried.

The attack on him began, as has been seen, at Zanzibar. It continued at Bagamoyo. From time to time it was renewed on the road to Unyanyembe : the value of Kirk's warning about the danger of the tsetse fly to horses and the difficulties of travel in the rainy season is sarcastically impugned. At Unyanyembe the delay in getting goods to Livingstone is emphasised again ; and, when Stanley gets to Ujiji, the account he hears from Livingstone of the rascally Sherif and the misconduct of the porters in

Manyema provides him with still more evidence that Kirk had neglected his duty. That is apparently what he himself believed. Certainly he did his best to make Livingstone believe it.

That ought, of course, to have been quite impossible ; but it will be remembered how easily and strangely Livingstone yielded to his brother's mischief-making on the Zambesi Expedition ;* and Stanley was surprised to observe how obsessed his mind still was by the old grievances against Tozer and Bedingfeld and Baines. In a chapter he wrote, some ten years afterwards, for his autobiography he inserted the following excerpt from his journal. ' March 3. Livingstone reverted again to his charges against the missionaries on the Zambesi and some of his naval officers on the expedition. I have had some intrusive suspicious thoughts that he was not of such an angelic temper as I believed him to be during my first month with him ; but for the last month I have been driving them steadily from my mind. . . . When, however, he reiterated his complaints against this man and the other, I felt the faintest fear that his strong nature was opposed to forgiveness and that he was not so perfect as at the first blush of friendship I thought him. I grew shy of the recurrent theme, lest I should find my fear confirmed.'[1] It is distressing that Livingstone should have betrayed this weakness to Stanley, and still more distressing that Stanley should have been able to turn it to Kirk's hurt, to add a new and even less justifiable grievance to those old ones. His book shows clearly how he went to work. He minimised the obstacles which had cut off Livingstone from Zanzibar : ' a very little effort on the part of those entrusted with supplies to him ' would have overcome them. He told him how the last caravan had loitered at Bagamoyo and gave him his version of Kirk's visit there. Above all he encouraged Livingstone's resentment at the conduct of Sherif and the ' slaves ' ; and from their endless discussion of that wretched theme the legend took shape

* See p. 18 above.

which Stanley was presently to publish far and wide.
Livingstone, it now appeared, had repeatedly asked Kirk
not to send him slaves. If Kirk had yielded to these
'entreaties,' all Livingstone's difficulties in Manyema
would have disappeared. With trustworthy porters and
sufficient goods he would quickly have completed his
explorations and returned long ago to his home and family.*
Kirk, in fact, had let his old friend and leader down.

Up to a point Livingstone seems himself to have
accepted this version of what had happened. Forgetting
his earlier gratitude to Kirk for doing what he could to
help him in difficult circumstances, he had now become
convinced that the business of the 'slaves' had been all
Kirk's fault. Soon after Stanley's arrival at Ujiji, he wrote
a long letter to Waller.[1] It was proof in itself of his new
health and spirits—long, whimsical, intimate, full of the
affectionate banter with which he had always treated
Waller. (He sends his 'kind love' to his newly-wedded
wife : 'she must be a brave woman to take charge of one
like you.') But the tone changes when he airs, for the
first time, his grievance against Kirk. 'By some strange
hallucination,' he writes, 'our friend Kirk placed some
£500 of goods in the hands of slaves with a drunken half-
caste tailor as leader. . . . It is simply infamous to employ
slaves when any number of freemen may be hired !' Writing

---

* An illustration may be given of the technique of disparagement and detraction.
As the two travellers were nearing Unyanyembe in February, a packet of letters was
delivered to them including one from Kirk to Stanley, in which Kirk, having heard
from Webb of Stanley's arrival at Unyanyembe, asked him to take charge of the
goods, to protect them from pilfering, and to do his best to forward them to Livingstone. 'My whole reliance is in Mr. Stanley,' he had written in another letter home :
'he will do his best, I feel assured, and I have given him full power to act.'[1] Stanley
relates what he said to Livingstone on receipt of Kirk's letter. '"Well, Doctor, the
English Consul requests me to do all I can to push forward your goods to you. I am
sorry I did not get the authority sooner, for I should have attempted it."' But
Stanley, it will be remembered, had seen those goods at Unyanyembe and had
actually taken charge of them : clearly he could have taken them on to Ujiji if he
could have found porters to carry them. And how, in any case, could Kirk have
given him authority to deal with them until he knew he had gone to Unyanyembe?
. . . The last touch is the most malicious. In the same packet there were several
letters for Stanley posted in New York and forwarded by Webb from Zanzibar, but
—for the simple reason that his friends in England did not know where he was at
that time—there were only two or three for Livingstone, 'to whom, of course, they
were at once transferred, with my congratulations that he was not quite forgotten
by his friend.'

at Unyanyembe just before Stanley left, he repeats this complaint in letters to Murchison[1] and other friends, and he adds a postscript to Waller's letter which concludes : ' Tell Kirk not to believe every banyan's tale. It makes him a gape and not a disciple of David Livingstone.' That picture of Kirk as the banyan's dupe was absurd enough, but it was at any rate not so absurd as Stanley's picture. Livingstone had swallowed Stanley's estimate of Shaw and Farquhar—' depraved blackguards,' his journal harshly calls them, whose debauchery had made them ' fit provender for the grave '—but he knew Kirk too well to believe in Stanley's caricature of the faithless friend. Only once or twice in his letters can the influence of Stanley's malice be detected. There is a caustic reference to the porters ' feasting at Bagamoyo within sight of the Consulate ' and to Kirk's going there to pursue not the porters but ' the wild beasts along the Ujiji road and to show them to the captain of a man-of-war.'[2]*

Thus, if Stanley failed to break the old friendship, he succeeded in straining it. And the strain in the end was severe. When Stanley returned to Zanzibar, he took with him three unpleasant documents. The first was a letter addressed to Kirk. It began ' Sir,' and recounted in detail the misdoings of Sherif and the ' slaves.' In view of the cholera and other difficulties, it goes on, ' the call on Ludha was perhaps the easiest course, and I trust you will not consider me ungrateful if I point out that it involved a great mistake.' Why, it asks, was Sherif's conspiracy not detected ? That was written on October 30. A postscript, dated November 16, harps once again on the delay at Bagamoyo and Kirk's ' private trip ' there. It ends on a bitter note. ' I feel inclined to relinquish the hope of ever getting help from Zanzibar to finish the little work I have still to do . . . I may wait twenty years and your slaves feast and fail.'[3] The second document contained instructions which Stanley had obtained from

* There is also an apparently sarcastic allusion to a mention of Kirk, in a newspaper Stanley showed him, as ' companion of Livingstone.' (L. to Waller, Nov. 7, '71 ; ps. March 8, '72 : *Waller Papers.*)

Livingstone. ' I have been subjected to so much loss,' it ran, ' by the employment of slaves in caravans sent me by H.M. Consul that, if Mr. Stanley meets another party of the sort, I beg him to turn them back, but use his discretion in the whole matter.'[1] The third document was another letter from Livingstone to Kirk—to ' My dear Kirk ' this time—recapitulating his grievance, telling Kirk that, if he had engaged any more ' slaves ' to come up to him, he must dismiss them at once, ' no matter what expense may have been incurred,' and asking him to hand over £500 to Stanley for the equipment of the caravan he had undertaken to dispatch to Unyanyembe.[2] The meaning of all this was painfully clear. Livingstone had been persuaded to put Stanley in Kirk's place. The British Consul's duty was to be done now by an American journalist, the friend's by a stranger. As if to rub it in, Livingstone had commissioned Stanley to convey his journal and official dispatch to England without reference to the Consulate.

One can understand Livingstone's intense vexation at the complete breakdown of his plans for linking his post at Ujiji with his base at Zanzibar. It is harder to understand how he had allowed himself to be persuaded that all would have been well if only Kirk had not been gulled by Ludha Damji. He forgot, it seems, his own admission that the rupture of his communications with the coast at his end had been caused by his notorious antagonism to the Slave Trade.* As to Kirk's end, he forgot, it seems, that Ludha Damji's firm was the firm he had trusted himself† and that the men he had chosen himself at Zanzibar had proved at least as untrustworthy as the ' slaves ' : they had actually deserted him. It is easy for any one who knows what Livingstone had suffered to make allowances, but it was not so easy for Kirk who knew nothing as yet of that dreadful time in Manyema. In forwarding Livingstone's ' complaint ' to Lord Granville, he made only a brief

* See pp. 72-73 above.
† See pp. 37-38 above.

reference to its 'uncourteous tone' and 'ungenerous insinuations'—he was ready, he said, to deal with any point on which an explanation might be required—but in fact he was deeply wounded. By a happy chance Livingstone's youngest son, Oswell, had recently arrived at Zanzibar. He was staying at the Consulate, and he wrote at once to tell his father what Kirk was feeling. Happily, too, Stanley had been gone more than three months from Unyanyembe when Livingstone received the letter. His response was immediate, and this time certainly not ungenerous. 'My dear Kirk,' he wrote, ' I am sorry to hear by a note from Oswell that you had taken my formal complaint against certain banyans and Arabs as a covert attack upon yourself : this grieves me deeply, for it is a result I never intended to produce. . . . It looked to me as if a band of dishonest persons had conspired to hoodwink you and me.'[1] And he went on to talk of his plans and his final return to the coast. No grumbles about letters. Not a word of Bagamoyo. So far so good. It is better to be called a fool than a knave : better still if the critic insists on sharing your folly. And, if only the controversy had been confined to those two men whose business alone it really was, little more would have been heard of it.

Unfortunately Stanley had made it his business too, and he was now well on his way to ' tell the world ' about it.

27

His march to the coast was as rapid, for most of its course, as even he could have hoped. There was no obstruction, no serious difficulty about *hongo*. Except for one stretch through Ugogo, he returned by the route he had come ; and, since he had already described the scenery and the native people, he could compress his record of the journey into less than thirty pages of his book. He saw, and vividly described, one memorable sight—the swift reaction of a Wagogo tribe to the news that their Wahehe neighbours were raiding their cattle : the sounding of the war-horns and the speeding of the messengers to all the surrounding villages : the gathering of the tribesmen in panoply of war, the head-dresses of ostrich or eagle feathers, the knee-straps and anklets of bells, the assegais and knob-kerries and shields : all swinging off towards the forest at a steady double. ' Column after column hurried past our camp until probably there were nearly a thousand soldiers gone to the war. This scene gave me a better idea than anything else of the weakness of even the largest caravans which travelled between Zanzibar and Unyanyembe.' A little later the spectacle of another body of armed Africans provokes reflections on the danger of white travellers becoming involved in fighting. They should be so strong, he says, as to make it almost unnecessary to use their strength. ' With five hundred Europeans I could traverse Africa from north to south, by tact and the moral effect that such a force would inspire. Very little fighting would be required.'

On April 7 he reached Mpapwa where Farquhar had been left. He saw the chief and heard from him much the same account of Farquhar's death as he had heard before. The place in the jungle where the body had been laid was pointed out to him ; but he could find no bones. He had a cairn of stones erected on the bank of a stream near by.

Mpapwa is about 340 miles from Unyanyembe, and the distance had been covered in 24 days, an ' extraordinary march,' as Stanley rightly observes. But thenceforward his pace was much slower. The ' greater rains ' had set in soon after he had started ; and, while in the preceding year he had made light of their effect on travel, this year they were unusually heavy. Wide and deep the floods were out, and in mid-April the destruction they wreaked was increased beyond all living memory by a

terrific storm which at Zanzibar attained the force of a
hurricane and inflicted incalculable damage, uprooting the
clove plantations, sinking almost all the ships in the harbour, and, for one of its minor mischiefs, drenching and
gutting the British Consulate and Kirk's living-rooms with
driving spray and rain. . . .[1] Soon after leaving Mpapwa,
Stanley begins to complain of the heavy going. In the
Mukondokwa pass it is incomparably worse than it had
been on the march up. 'Close to the edge of the foaming
angry flood lay our route, dipping down frequently into
deep ditches, wherein we found ourselves sometimes up
to the waist in water and sometimes up to the throat.
. . . Every channel seemed filled to overflowing, yet down
the rain poured, beating the surface of the river into
yellowish foam, pelting us until we were almost breathless.'
Stanley even contemplates, if only for a moment, the possibility of being marooned in this wilderness of waters for a
month or more. At one river-crossing there was nearly a
catastrophe. The man who was carrying on his head the
box containing Livingstone's journal and letters stumbled
into a hole in mid-stream and was half-submerged. Stanley
instantly drew his revolver 'Drop that box, and I'll
shoot you' . . . When he reached the plain of the Makata
he found it wholly under water, and, since the rain was
now holding off, he waited for the level of the flood to
fall. He waited ten days and it fell only a few inches. So
he plunged ahead with his dogged porters, spurred on by
the thought of getting home. For two long days they
staggered and waded, often up to the neck in water, to
the Mataka river which was crossed by swimming, each
box supported on a little raft between two men. In Uzegula, some fifty miles from the coast, they came to the area
of the great storm and saw the devastation it had wrought
—the chief town virtually destroyed, dozens of villages
swept away, the whole countryside littered with debris.
On April 30 they entered the last strip of thick, thorny
jungle. Stanley had hated it in the previous year, and
now he hated it still more. 'Horrors upon horrors are in

it,' his journal exclaims—snakes in the trees, scorpions under foot, ants biting 'our legs until we dance and squirm about like madmen,' and the foul stench of decay in the malarious air. On May 4 they reached the edge of floods which stretched for four miles to the outskirts of Bagamoyo. Next day they obtained a couple of canoes, and at sunset on the 6th their journey was ended. It had taken only fifty-four days.

28

As Stanley reached the centre of the town, he was hailed by a young Englishman from the steps of a big white house. ' Won't you walk in ? ' he said. ' What will you have to drink—beer, stout, brandy? By George, I congratulate you on your splendid success ! ' It was Lieutenant Henn, who had arrived a few days earlier at Bagamoyo as a member of an expedition sent from England to attempt to do what Stanley had just so triumphantly done.

It will be remembered that at the beginning of 1871— when Stanley first arrived at Zanzibar—Livingstone's friends in England believed that he was safe ; and, as that year went on, there was nothing in the reports that came home from Churchill and Kirk to reawaken their previous anxiety.[1] Livingstone had been at Ujiji, it appeared : he had gone to Manyema : he was expected to return to Ujiji. There he would find the men and goods of the first caravan. The second, after an initial check at Bagamoyo, had been hustled on its way. In any case, if Livingstone found his difficulties in the interior to be insuperable, he could be trusted to make his way to the coast. In the course of his farewell address to the Royal Geographical Society, Murchison, optimistic to the last, declared his belief that Livingstone might be back at home by the end of the year.[2] Murchison died a few months later, and, at its meeting on November 27, Sir Henry Rawlinson, the new president, communicated to the R.G.S. the first news of the war in Unyamwezi ; and, at the next meeting on December 11, he pointed out that the whole situation was now changed. Ujiji was cut off from Unyanyembe. Livingstone might no longer be able to move seawards, nor to count on obtaining supplies. The second caravan must have been held up : it might have been destroyed. Stanley, too, was evidently blocked at Unyanyembe : so the hope, excited by the news of his inland venture, that he might make contact with Livingstone must be abandoned. There was only one thing to do. A new and fully equipped expedition, under a qualified leader, must be dispatched to Livingstone's relief without delay.[1]

The Society acted promptly on this decision. The Government was asked for a grant in aid ; but, while it expressed its sympathy with the project and gave it official backing in letters to the Sultan and to Kirk, it declined to provide further funds beyond the unexpended balance of the previous grant. The Society, therefore, appealed for help in the press and at public meetings, and in a few weeks over £4000 had been subscribed. It contributed £500 itself.[2] Nor was there any delay in choosing personnel. Lieutenant L. S. Dawson, R.N., who had recently surveyed the Upper Yangtse and the River Plate, was given the lead. Lieutenant W. Henn, R.N., was appointed second-in-command. The third member of the party was none other than Livingstone's youngest son, Oswell, now twenty years old. They left England on February 9, and, sailing to Aden by the first ship that passed through the Suez Canal, arrived at Zanzibar on March 17. There they were joined by the Rev. Charles New, a stout-hearted Methodist missionary who had been teaching and exploring in the neighbourhood of Mombasa for nine years past and was now about to retire.* Kirk lodged the quartette at the Consulate and did what he could to help them. ' But for him,' wrote Oswell Livingstone afterwards, ' the expedi-

---

* He had recently climbed to the snow-line on Mount Kilimanjaro. See *The Exploitation of East Africa*, 115.

tion would have been nowhere.'[1] Stores were steadily accumulated—no less than 190 bales—and on April 27 Dawson, Henn and New crossed to Bagamoyo, leaving young Livingstone to follow later. They had twenty *askari* and six ' Nassick boys.' They were intending to obtain porters, as usual, on the coast.

A contrast was afterwards drawn between Stanley and the R.G.S. The journalist had acted while the geographers doubted and deliberated. And Stanley himself went farther. More than once he suggested that Livingstone's friends in England, like his friend at Zanzibar, were quite indifferent to his fate. If so fantastic a libel needed refutation, it could be found in the fact that in less than five months from the time it was known in England that Livingstone might be in difficulty or danger a well-equipped rescue expedition had landed on the African coast.

But that was the end of it. On April 28, the very morrow of the landing, messengers, sent ahead by Stanley with letters for Webb and cables for the *Herald*, arrived at Bagamoyo. It was clear from what they said that Livingstone was safe and well, and had arranged with Stanley for the supply of his future needs ; and Dawson, taking the view that the objects of the expedition had been, as he said, ' forestalled,' at once returned to Zanzibar and resigned his command. On May 7 Stanley himself reached Bagamoyo and was greeted, as has been seen, by Henn, who confessed, as they sat over their drinks, that it seemed futile now for the expedition to go on. Stanley agreed. ' Livingstone doesn't want you,' he said : ' he says he has plenty of stores—enough to enable him to finish up comfortably.' All that he needed was a gang of porters and a few odds and ends, and, at his request, Stanley was going to send these off without delay. The question, however, was still undecided when both Henn and New resigned as the result of a dispute as to which of the two should take command, the older man who knew the country and had done some exploring in it or the young naval officer who

had been appointed Dawson's second. That left Oswell
Livingstone. For some time he could not make up his
mind. Having come so far, ought he not to go on and see
his father ? He crossed to Bagamoyo, took charge of the
men and stores, and began to prepare for the march. Then
he returned to Zanzibar, discussed his problem again with
Kirk, and finally decided to go home. The men were discharged, the goods sold off, and the money left with Kirk
to the credit of the R.G.S. Oswell sailed for home with
Stanley and New.

Stanley records his opinion that this decision was wrong.
It was right, he argues, to abandon the expedition, but
Oswell should have accepted his proposal that he should
accompany the caravan he was about to send to Unyanyembe. Later on, when it was known that this had been
the last chance for father and son to meet, there were many
who agreed. But that, of course, could not have been foreseen, and at the time the decision—it was ultimately Kirk's
decision—was plain common sense. In the first place the
miasma of Zanzibar had already affected Oswell's delicate
health. He had had attacks both of dysentery and of
malaria and he was suffering from a troublesome bladder
complaint as well. Secondly, though the rains were or
soon would be over, the country between Ugogo and the
sea would still be waterlogged for many weeks to come. It
would have seemed unwise for Oswell to face the hardships
of flood and swamp in any rainy season—the Arab traders
never attempted it[1]—and this season was unprecedently
bad and Oswell already ill. Livingstone himself, though
unaware of Oswell's illness or of the unusual flooding, was
uneasy at the news of the projected journey, and spoke in
a dispatch to the Foreign Office of ' the natural anxiety I
feel for the safety of my son Oswell coming through the
feverish districts between this cold highland and the coast.'[2]
New had no doubt about the danger, and not only on
grounds of youth and health. Oswell's complete ignorance
of the country and of the languages and customs of its
people was another grave handicap. ' To have attempted

such a task under such circumstances singlehanded,' he wrote, ' would probably have led to a disaster the most serious. I felt this so strongly that I ventured to express this view to Dr. Kirk.'[1] Kirk, of course, concurred. He knew from experience what African swamps and African fever meant, and he was a qualified physician. To him the risk—and it was almost worse than a risk—could not be justified on any grounds of sentiment but only by a quite imperative necessity. And there was no such necescity : for Livingstone had written that, when he had got his porters, it would only take him six or eight months to finish his work. He might be expected, therefore, to be back at Zanzibar within a year at most. With those points in mind, could any one with Kirk's responsibility have given other advice than he gave? Nor should it be forgotten that, if Oswell had gone on and got through to Unyanyembe, he could not have saved his father's life. He could never have persuaded him to leave his task unfinished and come away home with him ; and, if he had stayed at his side, he could not have warded off his fate ; he would probably have shared it.

All four members of the abortive mission made their formal reports in due course to the R.G.S. Dawson was somewhat harshly reprimanded for the precipitancy of his resignation : the personal dispute was buried in an appendix to the *Proceedings*;[2] and, though the collapse of the expedition provoked at first a sharp exchange of letters in the press, in the ordinary course the controversy would soon have died away. But Stanley did not let that happen. In his speeches in England and in his book he gave it all a thorough public airing. He dwelt at length on the discord between Dawson, Henn and New, and discussed their respective merits. Dawson was given a flattering portrait —stalwart, handsome, intelligent. Henn was commended for his pluck and honesty, but in the verbatim record of his conversation he appeared as a volatile chatterbox whose one ambition was to shoot an African elephant. New's ' little faults ' were pointed out in a lengthy passage to which the old missionary, when he wrote a book of his own, retorted with somewhat laboured self-restraint.[1] The last shaft of sarcasm, it need hardly be said, was reserved for Kirk. It was Oswell Livingstone's obvious duty to go on to his father : yet he obviously did right to adopt the advice of his father's friend.

While the R.G.S. expedition was dissolving, Stanley had crossed to Zanzibar (May 7) and was busy with his own caravan. He enlisted fifty-seven porters. All of them, it seems, were chosen from those who had already served with him : for, when he started them off, he reminded them, he writes, how rich he had made them and how good and gentle a master they knew Livingstone to be. Clothing and provisions for the march and fifty carbines were handed over by Oswell Livingstone from the stocks of the R.G.S. expedition, and £240 from the residue of the Government grant.[2] What supplies should be entrusted to the caravan had been decided by Livingstone and Stanley at Unyanyembe—tinned food, tea, needles and thread, envelopes, the current Nautical Almanac, a blank journal, a chronometer, and a ' chain for refractory people.' (To the comment afterwards made on this last item Stanley replied that, at his suggestion, Livingstone ' promised to try the moral effect of a chain.')[3] On May 27 Stanley embarked the party in a dhow for Bagamoyo. They arrived at Unyanyembe on or about August 9. That was good going, and of their subsequent conduct Livingstone made no complaint. And that was not only because they had been put on their mettle, because the behaviour of the earlier caravans was now common talk at Zanzibar, or because the Arab slavers could no longer intrigue and obstruct in the face of such publicity. It was also due to the loyalty of Stanley's men to Stanley. Stern discipline and high pay had proved effective. He, too, had his ' faithfuls,' and, when he returned to Zanzibar in 1875, he found them eager to serve with him again.

There was one last strange personal incident. Kirk had been one of the first to call on Stanley and offer his congratulations ; and, some time later, he had politely acceded to Stanley's request that he should ask the Sultan to help him (Stanley) in the choice of a leader for his caravan. Three days before the mail-boat for England was due to sail, Stanley made another request. Meeting Kirk at Webb's house, he told him that he was afraid he might be unable to dispatch his caravan before he left. Would Kirk take charge of it ? In all the circumstances that was an astonishing question: for Kirk, as Stanley well knew, had read not only Livingstone's ' complaint,' but also his instructions for the turning-back of any ' slave ' caravan Kirk might have dispatched ; and some months, of course, were to pass before he received Livingstone's explanatory and assuaging letter. At that moment, there can be no doubt, Kirk was feeling deeply wounded and resentful and he allowed himself to show it. ' I am not going,' he said, ' to expose myself to needless insult again.' Surely Stanley, who was anything but a fool, must have expected some such answer ; and his own response is more surprising. He defended Livingstone's displeasure on the least tenable of all the grounds that could be alleged for it. ' Your best friend,' he records himself as saying to Kirk, ' would have been suspected of coldness—to say nothing else—had you been told, time after time, by leaders of caravans that they had been commanded by the Consul to bring you back and on no account to go with you anywhere.'

Kirk can no more have imagined on this than on that previous occasion that the conversation would be published, but he had learned, at a price, the risks his reputation ran. At the end of his next dispatch to the Foreign Office, he reported Stanley's request and his refusal, ' as otherwise my conduct may be misrepresented ' ; and— hitting back for the first time—he intimated that Stanley's motive in making the request was ' to evade blame if his men did not reach Unyanyembe in time.'[1] Kirk, as will appear, did not escape misrepresentation on this matter, and whether Stanley's motive was what he suspected or something else may be left to conjecture. But one point is plain. There can have been no real difficulty in getting off the caravan. The conversation occurred on May 26. Stanley dispatched the caravan on the very next day. He sailed on the 29th.

29

STANLEY reached Marseilles late at night on July 23. He had been informed by cable that the European manager of the *New York Herald* would be there to meet him ; and, landing at once, he made the round of the hotels in search of him. The correspondent of the *Daily Telegraph*, who was sharing a room with the manager, relates how, at two in the morning, they were roused from their beds by a stranger who announced himself as ' Mr. Stanley.' ' All thought of further sleep for the night was abandoned ; and, having obtained some of the best wine at command in which to drink the health of the man who had so arduously and successfully explored for the explorer, we sat up till morning—listening to the recital of the marvellous adventures and discoveries of Livingstone and the not much less wonderful adventures and escapes of Mr. Stanley himself.' So Londoners at breakfast on July 25 were able to read in the columns of the *Telegraph* a far fuller version of the dramatic story than the brief outline which had hitherto been cabled home. On the 27th and 29th Livingstone's two letters to Mr. Bennett and the *Herald* were printed, by the courtesy of the latter, both in the *Telegraph* and *The Times*, having been cabled from Marseilles at a cost of nearly £2000.

The effect on public opinion was sensational. The whole country was thrilled when now at last, after years of mystery and anxiety, it knew what had happened to the man who had won so strong a hold on its heart—his long and fruitless wanderings, his sufferings in Manyema, his collapse at Ujiji, and his wellnigh miraculous rescue by the intrepid American journalist. But the news had a nasty side to it. It was not so much that the American had done what ought, it seemed, to have been done by Livingstone's compatriots. The British public as a whole betrayed no petty national jealousy : they generously acknowledged Stanley's feat : it was the kind of plucky venture that most appealed to them. The disagreeable part of the news was Stanley's declaration that the man who should have done most for Livingstone—his friend and ' companion ' and the British Government's agent on the spot—had done nothing or less than nothing. For, during that long talk at the Marseilles hotel and in further interviews when he got to Paris, Stanley poured out all his charges against Kirk—the ' slaves,' the neglect to forward letters, the shooting-trip to Bagamoyo, the refusal to help Stanley in dispatching his caravan.[1] And there was worse to come. On July 31 a banquet was given in Stanley's honour by the American residents in Paris ; and the report of his speech in the *Telegraph* contained this astonishing passage. ' He spoke in very severe terms of Dr. Kirk, whom, he said, *he had a mission from Livingstone to describe as a " traitor."* ' Later in the proceedings, a British journalist, who had made Stanley's acquaintance on the Abyssinian campaign and happened to be present, ' said, with very good taste, a few words deprecating hasty censure of Dr. Kirk ; but Mr. Stanley energetically persisted in condemning him.'[2]*

The feelings of Kirk's friends, when they read in the newspapers of this ferocious public attack, can be imagined. They at once took pen and paper to defend him. ' If there has been any neglect at Zanzibar,' wrote Churchill from his retirement, ' in communicating with Dr. Livingstone, I, as the political agent and Her Majesty's Consul there

---

* *The Times* correspondent's report of the speech contained the following : ' Mr. Stanley declared positively last night that in saying what he has said about Dr. Kirk he has been simply fulfilling a promise he made to Dr. Livingstone, who considered that he had been ill-treated by Dr. Kirk and wished to have the cause of his ill-treatment thoroughly investigated.' (Aug. 2, 1872.) In a subsequent conversation with Waller (see p. 200 below) Stanley denied that he had used the word ' traitor.'

during the last five years, must share with Dr. Kirk the
blame.' He enumerated the caravans which he and Kirk
had dispatched at intervals, and briefly explained the
difficulties that had obstructed their path to Ujiji. As to
Livingstone's letters, he pointed out that for nearly two
years not a single one had come to Zanzibar owing to
ignorance of Livingstone's whereabouts and the belief that
he was dead.[1] Oswell Livingstone, who had travelled
straight home from Marseilles, confessed his dismay at the
' erroneous opinions ' which his father had apparently
conceived of Kirk during Stanley's stay with him. ' Let
me state at once that Dr. Kirk is totally unworthy of the
accusations which are daily reaching the public, and can
have but one source. I may add that nothing could exceed
the kindness that we, the members of the Search Expedition, experienced from him and Mrs. Kirk during the
whole time we were at Zanzibar.'[2] But no one was so
shocked and alarmed as Waller : for he saw at once that
more than personal considerations were at stake. It so
happened that, talking to a correspondent of a London
evening paper in Paris, Stanley had remarked that his
opinion of Kirk's conduct was confirmed by that of a
' wealthy merchant ' at Zanzibar who had communicated
on the subject with the Indian press. The ' wealthy
merchant,' it need hardly be said, was identical with the
' sturdy Scot ' ; and it was true that the disreputable
Fraser, primed by Stanley with the contents of Livingstone's ' complaint,' had written to the *Bombay Gazette*
stating that Livingstone had brought ' very grave charges '
against Kirk and retailing the story about the ' slaves ' and
Bagamoyo.[3] The gist of this letter was cabled to London
and published in the *Standard*. That gave Waller his cue.
He wrote to inform the public of Fraser's record and to
point out that such a ' stab in the back ' was only to be
expected from a man who had suffered from the unflinching hostility to the Slave Trade maintained by the British
officials at Zanzibar and in particular by Kirk.[4] There
lay the danger of Stanley's indictment. So great was

Livingstone's prestige that, if his opinion of Kirk's conduct was indeed what Stanley said, it was sure to affect Kirk's official position. He might defend himself, he might prove that the charges against him were unfounded or unfair ; but the Foreign Office, bound in some degree to respond to public sentiment, would almost certainly find it convenient to transfer him to another post. And that would not only be a waste of Kirk's special knowledge of East Africa and a blow to his career from which he might never recover. It would seriously weaken the fight against the Arab Slave Trade. It would break up the triple alliance. It would rob it of the man who had already shown that he was wellnigh indispensable.

If Waller had been aware of Livingstone's disavowal of any intention to censure Kirk, he would, of course, have been wholly reassured. As it was, the only hope, it seemed, of saving the situation was to persuade Livingstone that he must have been mistaken ; and he wrote the longest of all his many letters to Livingstone—a letter which reveals his passionate, his almost desperate distress.[1] By then he had made Stanley's acquaintance. He had received Livingstone's letter from Unyanyembe in which he had been asked to show Stanley all possible attention and to introduce him to Murchison and Frere. He had called, accordingly, at Stanley's hotel and talked with him for five whole hours. It cannot have been a very comfortable conversation : for Stanley on his part had already told Waller in a letter from Paris of his belief that he was prejudiced against him ; and Waller, though he protests that at that time he knew no more of Stanley than of Adam, had deeply resented his public attack on Kirk. They had not been long together before a trivial, but to Waller a significant, incident occurred. Stanley had denied all knowledge of a letter which Waller had posted to him when he was in Paris, but he alluded later on to something which had been mentioned only in that letter. Waller promptly pointed out the discrepancy. ' When I saw,' he writes, ' the *sang froid* with which this man quietly shifted

his cigar to the other side of his mouth and changed the
subject without a word to something else, I confess, Doctor,
I did feel very sorry for you and very sorry for Kirk.' The
rest of the letter is mostly concerned with Kirk. Stanley
' is a plucky brave fellow enough and did you immense
service,' but, ' if he has in any way aided to unsettle your
mind respecting one of the best friends you ever had, it is
hard, very hard, to forgive him. . . . In all probability
his career is blighted by what you have said. . . . I know
what you have suffered, I know ninety-nine men out of a
hundred would have succumbed in the first six months,
I know what fever, poison, long delay, hoping against hope,
plotting and rascality can do in Africa as they can do
nowhere else in the world, and I feel for you and for the
misery you have been in as few can ; but I also feel this,
that the powers of darkness are lashed into fury at such
lives as yours and such exertions as yours and Kirk's and
our own here against the Slave Trade, and that, if they
can break us up and set us one against the other as they
have done before now, the screams of the women and children in the forests you have trodden will be more sweet
to their ears than ever.' He went on to remind Livingstone
of the immense importance of their personal alliance in the
crusade against the Slave Trade—how Kirk, ' desperately
overworked ' though he was, had regularly supplied him
[Waller] with ammunition for the campaign in England
and how ' you two have been always quoted as single in
purpose and friends in the same cause.' Yet now ' you are
reported to have said, " I don't think he will be Consul
any longer after this." ' The letter ends with a last appeal
to Livingstone's better judgment. ' You had up to a certain
point always believed him a thoroughly fine fellow. Why
not have held on tight when something came to shake you
in your belief ? . . . If, as I fear, you have done him and
his wife and children a most sad turn, I know you will
deplore it in your heart bitterly. . . . *We* in England are
to blame for not having sent an expedition to relieve you
before, not Kirk. Forgive all I have said, but the highest

service is to stand by the weaker side, and when you know, as you will some day, how strong you are and what terrible weight your words carry, I am sure you will wish you had spared your old friend.'

When this letter was dispatched to Zanzibar, Livingstone was again out of reach in the wilderness, and perhaps it was as well that he never got it. He had already admitted that his ' complaint ' might be misunderstood ; and he had not only tried to make it up with Kirk, he had written in the same terms to the Foreign Office. ' I regret very much to hear incidentally,' ran his last dispatch to Granville, ' that Dr. Kirk viewed my formal complaint against banyans as a covert attack upon himself. If I had foreseen this, I should certainly have borne my losses in silence. I never had any difference with him, though we were together for years, and I had no intention to give offence now.'[1] Could more have been expected of him ? And can any one wish that, after that, he should have received that painful letter from Waller ? For he loved and trusted Waller, those bitter remonstrances would have gone home, and the last months of his life might have been tormented by the thought that he had said more to Stanley than he meant—that, perhaps, at the end of a tiring day, in one of those interminable talks about the miseries and frustration from which he had been rescued, he had unwittingly provided Stanley with the means of wrecking Kirk's career.

30

STANLEY, meantime, was receiving a great welcome in Livingstone's homeland. As soon as those long telegrams came in from Marseilles and Paris and before he himself reached London, the leading organs of the British press acclaimed his achievement without question or reserve. ' He sets off and does it,' said *The Times*, ' while others are

idly talking or slowly planning. Africa is a very wide
target, but Mr. Stanley hit the bull's-eye at once.'[1] The
Daily Telegraph, the *Daily News*, the *Morning Post* and *Punch*
joined in the chorus. Less influential newspapers were
equally cordial. ' We could, of course, have wished,' said
the *Echo*, for example, ' that the honour of that discovery
had fallen to countrymen of our own. But it is only in
the generous sense of the word that we can be said to envy
the honour which the American press has fairly won and
well deserved.'[2] But the unison was not quite complete.
There were corners in Fleet Street in which Stanley's
achievements were accorded a great deal less than justice.
The *Standard* had ' suspicions and misgivings.' Was there
not ' something inexplicable and mysterious' in Stanley's
story?[3] Whispers were even heard that the whole affair
was a gigantic hoax. Had that meeting at Ujiji really
taken place? Might not Stanley have forged those letters
he had brought home? . . . Such imputations were, of
course, insufferable. Stanley appealed to the Foreign
Office and received prompt satisfaction from the Foreign
Secretary himself. ' I was not aware until you mentioned
it,' wrote Granville, ' that there was any doubt as to the
authenticity of Dr. Livingstone's dispatches,' and he cited
the opinion of the department charged with East African
affairs that they were unquestionably genuine.[4] But the
publication of that letter did not quite silence the in-
nuendos. No doubt, it was now admitted, the dispatches
were Livingstone's; but what about those letters to the
New York Herald, especially the second? It has been
explained on an earlier page how those letters came to be
written : how Livingstone, with Stanley at his elbow, tried
to provide good 'copy' for Bennett's paper. But the critics,
of course, were unaware of that, and they discussed the
oddities of the second letter with gusto and at length. An
article in the *Evening Standard* described ' our great traveller'
as intoxicated with ' laughing gas ' and ' getting more
yankee at every turn.'[5] ' It would seem,' said the *Saturday
Review*, ' that Livingstone has profited by his residence in

the heart of Africa to acquire a considerable familiarity
with American literature and slang and to hit off the racy
sub-erotic flavour of the *New York Herald* with considerable
success.'[1] When *How I Found Livingstone* was published in
the following November, a facetious reviewer in the
'Reviler' as the *Saturday Review* was called by some
of its gifted contributors, summed it up as the best
travel-book since Herodotus' account of his visit to
Egypt.[2] Readers of it—there were more of them in
those days than now—will remember that the Father of
History recorded, for what they were worth, several
other romantic stories besides that one about the sources
of the Nile.

Stanley's reception in British scientific circles was of a
similarly mixed character. It must be remembered once
again that Livingstone's friends and admirers in the ranks
of the R.G.S. were quite unaware of his breakdown till
Stanley brought news of it. To them he was still the
Livingstone of the march across Africa and the Zambesi
Expedition ; and that an inexperienced young journalist
could do anything to help him in the wilds of Africa must
have seemed, on the face of it, absurd. Thus on the first
report of the ' discovery ' Rawlinson had indulged in an
unfortunate witticism. ' It must be Livingstone,' he had
remarked in a letter to *The Times*, ' that has discovered
Stanley.'[3] But, when he read the cables from Marseilles
and Paris, he did not question the truth of what Stanley
said or the value of what he had done for Livingstone. On
behalf of himself and his colleagues he wrote to him to
convey ' our most cordial acknowledgment for the timely
succour rendered to him in his great need and the expression of our admiration of the energy, perseverance and
courage with which you conducted your expedition.'[4] He
went on to explain that, as the next session of the R.G.S.
would not be held till November, he had arranged for
Stanley to be invited to address the geographical section
of the British Association at its forthcoming meeting. It
met at Brighton, and the day of Stanley's appearance,

August 16, was its great day. Never, indeed, had the somewhat solemn ' British Ass ' attracted so much public attention, nor ever had its proceedings filled so many columns in the newspapers. The hall was crowded— there were over 3000 present, it was said—and among the many distinguished members of the audience was Napoleon III with the ex-Empress and the ill-fated Prince Imperial. Francis Galton, cousin of Charles Darwin and founder of the study of eugenics, who had done some exploring in his younger days in south-west Africa, was in the chair. The formal business of the meeting was Stanley's paper on the exploration of the northern end of Lake Tanganyika, and some discussion was also to be expected on the geographical results of Livingstone's recent journeys southwards and westwards of the lake. But Stanley prefaced his treatment of those scientific matters with an account of his personal adventures. It was in his liveliest style. ' The scenic, not to say dramatic, character of the narrative,' reported a not unfriendly observer, ' produced a great effect ' : while it ' carried conviction to some who were previously sceptical, the manner in which it was delivered was unfortunate in the extreme.'[1] It must have been a startling experience for the pundits and professors ; and it was not unnatural, perhaps, though again unfortunate, that Galton should have remarked, when they got down to scientific business, that it was ' facts ' they wanted rather than ' sensational stories.'[2] And certainly the paper and the discussion on it were comparatively dull. No doubts were raised as to the importance of the discovery about the flow of the Lusizé : but the belief expressed in Livingstone's dispatches as to the area in which he expected to find the source of the Nile was firmly—and rightly—questioned. The venerable explorer, Beke,* argued that the Lualaba could not be the Nile. Grant, Speke's companion on his historic march to the northern end of Lake Victoria, declared—rightly again—that it must be the Congo.[3] Finally, Rawlinson reaffirmed ' the great value attached by the Royal Geo-

* He died in 1874, aged 74.

graphical Society to Mr. Stanley's services' and their 'high opinion of his merit as a traveller'—a tribute which the meeting loudly cheered.[1]

On the evening of that day Stanley was the guest of honour at a dinner of the Brighton and Sussex Medical Society. It was a convivial occasion ; and, when Stanley gave a jocular account of some of his experiences and illustrated it with a bit of play-acting and gesticulation, the delighted doctors roared with laughter—whereupon Stanley stalked indignantly out of the room. The unhappy president, seeing what the popular newspapers made of it, had to write and explain that no sort of discourtesy had been intended and that their guest's departure had caused the greatest surprise and vexation to them all.[2]

In the course of the next few weeks Stanley was passing his book through the press, and at the end of it he inserted several pages of bitter comment on his reception. He had been told, he said, at Zanzibar and again at Aden, that his exploit was bound to excite jealousy in England. He had refused to believe it, but to his amazement it had proved to be true. And he now charged the 'gentlemen editors' of England, with only few exceptions, of giving free rein to their jealousy of an American newspaper for having done what they ought to have done themselves.[3] Then he turned on the 'gentlemen geographers.' They had 'wished men to believe' that they were anxious about the fate of their great associate. Yet how did they treat the man who had rescued him ? They had greeted him with 'a cold letter of thanks' a week after his arrival in England.[4] They had insulted him at Brighton. Worse, they had insulted Livingstone himself. They had dared to combat his ideas about the sources of the Nile. . . .[5] Later on, as will be seen, Stanley apologised for these 'rough' pages ; but he had been stung to the quick. 'All the actions of my life,' he wrote years afterwards, 'and I may say all my thoughts, have been strongly coloured by the storm of abuse and the wholly unjustifiable reports circu-

lated about me then.'[1] And he had champions in England
who gave colour to this version of what happened. ' His
provocation,' said *The Times*' reviewer of his book, ' was
more than flesh and blood could well bear.'[2] But was there
not some overstatement in all this ? British journalism and
science had presented Stanley with a generous bouquet. If
there were one or two barbs in it, was it altogether to be
wondered at ? *Of course* the editors were envious of the
Herald's ' scoop.' *Of course* the geographers wished that by
some miracle of telepathy they could have known that
Livingstone was in distress and rescued him betimes themselves. But that did not prevent the great majority of them
from paying Stanley a prompt and unstinted tribute of
gratitude and admiration ; and there the whole matter
might have rested, there might have been no barbs in the
bouquet, if Stanley's personality and conduct had been
other than they were. As it was, his ' headline ' methods,
his almost naïve insistence on taking the front of the public
stage, offered an all too tempting target to cynics and
scandalmongers. Nor is it surprising if some of the geographers betrayed their feelings. Several of them knew
Kirk personally : all of them were aware of his fight
against the Slave Trade: and they regarded Stanley's
public attack on him as an outrage. Most of them must
have resented, moreover, Stanley's identification of himself with Livingstone ; and, while they genuinely respected
his energy and courage and warmly acknowledged the
merit of what he had done, they could not yet regard him
—though in years to come they would—as a great explorer,
a master of African geography, nor accept his description
of Livingstone's discoveries as authentic, until Livingstone's own scientific notes and observations were available
for checking it. It was certainly deplorable that some of
them had not good enough manners to conceal their
resentment or their doubts, but it was not altogether
inexplicable ; and the facts should be seen in their true
proportion before the legend becomes rooted in history
that the behaviour of the British scientific world to Stanley

in 1872 was wholly at variance with British ideas of common decency.*

To plead for a balanced judgment is not to excuse such indecencies as *were* committed, whether in the newspapers or at the Brighton meeting. As to that, it can only be said that they were widely regretted and that some amends were made for them. Anxious, no doubt, as to the effect of Stanley's attitude on American public opinion, the highest authorities gave the lead. About a fortnight after the Brighton meeting Stanley received a letter from Granville conveying the Queen's ' high appreciation ' of his zeal and fearlessness in re-establishing contact with Livingstone and relieving herself and her subjects from the anxiety they had felt as to his fate. A jewelled snuff-box accompanied the letter.[1] Some ten days later, Stanley was presented to the Queen who talked to him ' about Livingstone and Africa '—an experience which, to judge from his journal, made a deep impression on him.[2] This lead was quickly followed in the City. Stanley was received at Guildhall on October 18 and presented with the honorary freedom of the Turners' Company.[3] The resolution was moved by a member of the R.G.S. ; and, three days later, the R.G.S. itself bestowed on Stanley the highest honour in its gift, the Victoria gold medal. The announcement was made at a banquet given to him by the Society, and Rawlinson, who presided, took occasion to make a public apology for that indiscreet remark. ' I ask leave,' he said, ' to do penance for an unhappy expression which I made use of last year in perfect good faith and with no intention of giving offence.' And his praise of Stanley was equally wholehearted. ' I say deliberately that Mr. Stanley's journey from Unyanyembe to Ujiji is one of the most brilliant exploits in the whole history of African travel (cheers) ' ; and he declared his belief that Livingstone owed Stanley his life. In the course of his reply Stanley

* It is part of the legend that Stanley was discredited not only because he was a journalist but because he was an American journalist. But it should be remembered that some of the great British explorers (e.g. Bruce and Speke) had their incredulous critics at home when they first reported their discoveries.

made a guarded allusion to his indictment of Kirk. ' He had been told that Dr. Kirk had received a friendly letter from Dr. Livingstone. He was delighted to hear it. So long as Livingstone thought he was injured by his old friend, he would think so too ; but, if Dr. Livingstone would think that Dr. Kirk was his friend, he would think so too (a laugh).'[1]

That night Stanley left London for the North where the warmth of his reception, following on the banquet and the medal, should have done something at least to salve his wounds. For the British people and, more particularly, Livingstone's own Scottish people had taken no interest in those much-discussed questions of epistolary style and geography. They had enjoyed the notorious letter to the *Herald* ; and it mattered nothing to them whether the Lualaba was or was not the Nile. All they cared about was the rescue of their old national hero, and, without a touch of vulgar chauvinism, they hailed his young American rescuer as a hero too. They liked his striking looks, his self-confidence, his unaffected exuberance, his combativeness : he was, in fact, a 'sportsman' and his adventures a glorious romance. Thus the tour of Scotland in October was an unbroken triumphal progress. At Edinburgh and Glasgow, at Greenock and Helensburgh and Hamilton—where he was introduced to Livingstone's sister and his daughters, Agnes and Anna Mary—everywhere he was given an ovation : cheering crowds at the railway-stations, toasts and tributes at civic banquets, cheers again at crowded public meetings. At these meetings he gave his audiences what they wanted—his story from his own lips—and he told it well, concentrating on the dramatic incidents and leading up to the climax at Ujiji. The reports of his speeches are freely punctuated with ' applause,' ' laughter,' ' loud applause ' ; and again it seems strange that he was not content with the praise so wholeheartedly accorded him because he had befriended Livingstone, that he must needs continue his attack on Kirk. For Kirk, after all, was a Scotsman too. his home was in Scotland. his relations and friends were living there. Yet Stanley devoted nearly half of a speech at Edinburgh—where Kirk had studied for his medical degree—to the old contrast between his own sentiment for Livingstone (' God gave me a heart to feel ') and the indifference of ' the gentleman who had got his fame and position as the friend of Dr. Livingstone ' and ' left him in Africa, silent, alone, deserted and almost at death's door.' And on this occasion he made use of that last conversation he had had with Kirk at Zanzibar. ' Suppose any of you had a friend in Africa, suffering and depending entirely upon you for support, even for life, would you have coolly said, because a formal complaint came against you, " Let the man go to the dogs, I will do no more for him ? " (Applause.)'[1] Nothing was said in Kirk's defence. It was only when, at one of the luncheon-parties, Stanley also attacked the ' easy-chair ' pundits of the R.G.S. that Oswell Livingstone, who was present, felt moved to protest. Some of these men, he said, were his friends ; and, since the Society had made ample apology and since his father, as he knew from his last letter, bore no grudge against them, Mr. Stanley ' should now let that matter drop.'[2]

Speaking at Liverpool and Manchester on the way, Stanley was back in London just in time to attend an important meeting at the Mansion House on November 4. It had been summoned by the Lord Mayor in order to give expression to the public demand for the immediate suppression of the East African Slave Trade. It was now known that an official mission, headed by Sir Bartle Frere, was shortly going to Zanzibar to negotiate with the Sultan to that end ; and Frere and several stalwarts of the anti-slavery crusade, including Waller, were present. Stanley was given a seat beside the Lord Mayor and was received with ' loud and prolonged cheers ' when he rose to make his speech—a long speech, mostly about the horrors of the Trade and their effect on Livingstone's mind, but with one last cut in it at the unhappy Kirk. He made a kindly reference to Frere's diplomatic ' suavity ' : it would be needed at Zanzibar, since ' the Sultan was harassed and annoyed by the energy of Churchill and bore no good will to the present political agent.'[1] Of those two statements the first, as has been seen, was quite true, the second quite false. . . . On November 6 Stanley made his last public appearance at St. James's Hall where his lecture elicited ' vociferous applause.'[2] On November 9 he left for New York.

Some ten days later *How I Found Livingstone* was published. It sold by tens of thousands, and a second large edition was quickly printed off. Stanley had written most of it in the course of his travels and on the voyage home ; it must have gone to press soon after he reached London ; and it would have been mechanically impossible for him to make drastic alterations in the text in view of all that happened between August and November. But he could, and did, add a postscript in which he confessed that there were ' some rough things ' in the book ' respecting certain geographers and others,' that he had written them on the spur of the moment as journalists needs must, and that he was sorry if he had hurt anybody's feelings. He also inserted an appendix containing several letters and dispatches, including those which the Foreign Office had communicated to the press ; and, in commenting on one of these, he deplores the misunderstanding between Livingstone and Kirk and ventures to hope for the restoration of ' the friendly intimacy that formerly characterised the intercourse between the two old friends.' ' As for myself, nothing would delight me more than to see a general shake-hands all round. Dr. Livingstone is well aware of the sentiments I entertain for him, and Dr. Kirk can rest assured that I have a sincere admiration for himself.'[3] In the light of all Stanley had said, some of it quite recently, this was an astonishing, an almost paralysing valedictory. And Stanley presently went further. He seems to have realised that Kirk's prestige in England was greater than he had supposed and that his assault on him had angered a number of respectable and influential people. In the

third edition, therefore, of his book—it was too late to do
it in the second—he cut out almost every reference to Kirk
as well as one or two other passages to which English
reviewers had taken exception.* The 'at-home' at Zanzibar, the 'shooting trip,' the occasional sarcasms, the last
conversation—it was all deleted. The result was curious.
To an uninstructed reader of the third edition or of any
of its many later reprints, there is little left to show that
Kirk existed. His name is only mentioned thrice, and it
does not appear in the index.

31

A few last words must be said about the effect of Stanley's
extraordinary onslaught on Kirk and on his reputation and
career.

When he read in the newspapers what Stanley had said
in Paris and in Scotland, it cannot have hurt his feelings
in the same way as Livingstone had hurt them. He must
have been bewildered rather—and then furiously angry—
and then more than a little anxious. He knew the charges
were unfounded, but he was not in the position of a private
individual who can defend himself publicly against public
attack. He was an officer of the Crown, accused not merely
of betraying a friend but of neglecting his consular duty
towards a fellow-consul. And officials are not expected—
or indeed, as a rule, permitted—to defend themselves in
public. Kirk made one protest. When he saw Fraser's
venomous letter in the *Bombay Gazette*, he wrote at once
to the Bombay Government answering the accusations
seriatim and asking that for once the rule might be broken
and his letter published.[1] 'Government,' came the
answer, 'are not in favour of official replies to attacks of
this sort in the newspapers.'[2] Kirk made no similar appeal

---

* The *Spectator*, for instance, expressed 'disgust' at the story of the screaming
woman. It also 'profoundly regretted' the indictment of Kirk (Nov. 23, 1872).

to the Foreign Office. He never mentioned Stanley's attacks in his dispatches. He did not even talk about them among his friends. Only one expression of his opinion of his assailant is on record—a remark he made to Oswell Livingstone at Zanzibar.[1] ' Stanley,' he said, ' will make his fortune out of your father.'* It was true.

But beneath this silence and self-control Kirk must have been perturbed for the same reason as Waller was perturbed. He was aware that the Government were pleased with his work—they had recently said so—but Governments had been known to sacrifice their trustiest servants to public agitation. And in Edinburgh, it seemed, and elsewhere the public had applauded Stanley's slanders. Happily such anxiety as he felt as to the possibility of losing the work he had now made his life-work was not protracted. The Foreign Office was also perturbed. An open attack by any foreign journalist on any member of its diplomatic staff would have been disconcerting enough ; but in this case the journalist had apparently captured the imagination of the British people, and the diplomatist was the man on whom the Government chiefly relied for the execution of its new policy at Zanzibar. Not only in justice to Kirk, therefore, but in the public interest Granville decided that the issue between Kirk and Stanley must be probed to the roots. Frere was requested, therefore, in the course of his forthcoming mission, to examine the question on the spot ; and in due course he submitted his report.[2]

' After reading,' he wrote, ' with great care and attention ' all the available evidence—Livingstone's complaints, Stanley's accusations, Kirk's reply to Fraser's letter and numerous other official and unofficial documents—and after full inquiry at Zanzibar, he had formed some clear opinions. First, Livingstone's complaints were well-founded. ' The things sent to him did not reach him ; those taken by and sent to Mr. Stanley did reach him.'

* Oswell passed it on to Livingstone who made the characteristic comment : ' He is heartily welcome, for it is a great deal more than I could ever make out of myself.'

Secondly, it was possible, but it could not be certain, that this difference was due to the different types of porters employed. ' Dr. Kirk availed himself of the agency of the largest and most influential Hindu house in Zanzibar. They had been, I believe, with hardly one exception, always employed by the English Consulate on similar work, and have been usually most successful. Mr. Stanley employed the broker of the American Consul who . . . ranks only second to the Hindu house in general estimation. Between the two houses there is no choice other than that between the oldest and largest and the younger and possibly more energetic establishment. But, judging from all I hear and have read, I have little doubt that *Mr. Stanley's own convoy would have failed to reach Ujiji but for his presence with it* and the extraordinary energy with which he pressed it forward. I am not shaken in this opinion by the fact that three separate packets sent up by the American Consul are said to have reached Mr. Stanley after he joined Dr. Livingstone. When Mr. Stanley had once gone on, the place of safety was with him, and the most half-hearted messenger once started from the sea-coast would not willingly stop till he had joined the white man's caravan.'

' On the third and last question, whether Dr. Kirk is in any way to blame for the delays that took place in expediting the stores to Dr. Livingstone, I have no hesitation whatever in stating my conviction that he is not. He seems to me to have done what any one on the spot, *not judging after the event*, would have said was for the best, and his want of success was in no way due to any want of due care, precaution, local knowledge or energy. . . . What appears to me to be conclusive on the subject is the indirect testimony of the great traveller himself. *I judge, of course, simply and entirely from what he has himself written.* Under the pressure of his first disappointment he wrote to Dr. Kirk omitting the habitual forms of personal friendship and in terms expressive of some bitterness and irritation. *Of the precise circumstances and influences under which he wrote, we are but imperfectly informed*. . . . In his subsequent letters, when he found he was regarded as having charged Dr. Kirk with omission to do his duty in a matter of such vital importance to him, Dr. Livingstone explains very clearly and distinctly that he imputed to Dr. Kirk no more than companionship with himself in putting their trust in men who deceived them.'

' With this question,' the report concludes, ' Dr. Kirk's general merits as a public officer have little to do, beyond the obvious fact that a public officer who, I can affirm from my personal observation, is conspicuous for the careful, conscientious, laborious and most efficient discharge of every duty connected with the important offices he holds here, is not likely to have failed in what was to him a labour of love and a duty of long and uninterrupted friendship ; and I cannot conclude this memorandum without expressing my conviction that Dr. Livingstone never had here, possibly not in any part of the world, a truer or warmer friend than Dr. Kirk ; and in saying this I confidently believe that I am only saying what Dr. Livingstone himself would say, if he were here to give us his deliberate testimony.'*

Pronounced by a judge of Frere's capacity, experience and integrity, this complete exoneration of Kirk should have swept away for ever all the mud that had been thrown at him. But some of it stuck—not, of course, in well-informed minds, but in public opinion at large. The report was communicated to the Bombay press and reproduced in the *Times of India*.[1] It was also printed with many other documents in the blue-book published on Frere's mission ; but blue-books are notoriously unreadable or at least unread, and, at Waller's wise request, the full text of the report was given in *The Times*.[2] Even so, for the many thousands who had heard Stanley's dramatic speeches or devoured his exciting book there were relatively few who read Frere's sober judgment ; and, while the charge of betrayal, which had always seemed quite

---

* Italics not in the original.

incredible, was never repeated, the idea that Kirk had been
guilty of culpable negligence was not altogether dissipated.
Dr. Blaikie's *Personal Life of David Livingstone* is a case in
point. It was published in 1880, it is now in its sixth
edition, it is still the fullest and most authoritative bio-
graphy : and, while its praise of ' gallant Stanley ' is
unstinted, it leaves its readers in little doubt that Kirk
failed to do what he ought to have done.[1] Later biographers have intimated that there was something to be
said in Kirk's defence,[2] and have stressed the point that
Livingstone's friendship with him was unbroken ; but they
have not cleared up the mystery as to what actually happened and why. So, beside the exaggerated version of
Stanley's reception in England, the legend of Kirk's
lethargy has lived on ; and for that reason the present
writer has thought it desirable to treat a somewhat disagreeable controversy in considerable detail. It is time
that the memory of a great servant of the British Empire
and of the humanitarian cause should be cleansed, once
for all, from a stain that should never have been cast on it.

32

BEFORE Stanley left for America, Livingstone's friends in
England had made it impossible for any charge of indifference or neglect to be repeated. Though it was clear
from Livingstone's own dispatches that he now had all he
needed to complete his explorations, nevertheless, to make
assurance doubly sure, two expeditions were organised in
the course of 1872 with the object of making contact with
him wherever he might be.

The first was prompted by the belief that he had discovered the source of the Congo, not the Nile. If that were
so, he might never return to Zanzibar. He might find it
easier and much more interesting and scientifically more
useful to follow the Congo to the sea. The R.G.S., accord-

ingly, decided that an expedition should be sent up the river from its mouth. If it ran into Livingstone coming down, it could ease his passage to the coast. If not, it would at least throw some much-needed light on the Congo's course in the interior. A promising young leader was quickly found in Lieutenant W. J. Grandy, R.N. ; and the cost was covered by the munificent offer of £2000 from James Young—a final fruit of the friendship that had begun beside the mechanic's bench at Glasgow in 1837. Grandy sailed from Liverpool on November 30. He reached S. Paolo de Loanda on January 22, 1873 ; and, as soon as he had organised his caravan, struck overland north-eastwards. He was obstructed and delayed by the same troubles which afflicted travellers on the other side of Africa—the difficulty of obtaining porters and the hardships of the rainy season ; and it was not till October that he reached the Congo near Lukangu. The next six months were spent in ' winter quarters ' and in interminable negotiations to obtain the goodwill and guidance of the local chiefs for the journey up the river. A start had just been made when the news arrived of Livingstone's death and on its heels the order of recall from the R.G.S.[1]

The second expedition was also organised by the R.G.S. It was, in fact, a revival of the abortive Search Expedition of the preceding year. Lieutenant V. Lovett Cameron, R.N., who was chosen to command it, was instructed to make a junction with Livingstone, ' to assure him of the unabated admiration and interest with which his proceedings are watched by his countrymen and by the whole civilised world,' and to place himself and the whole expedition ' absolutely and entirely ' at Livingstone's disposal ' to carry out any such work as he may direct or advise.'[2] It was thought that he might wish it to make some explorations subsidiary to his own, perhaps to probe round the north of Lake Tanganyika while he probed round the south of it.

Cameron left England on the same day as Grandy and arrived at Zanzibar, shortly after the Frere Mission, in

January, 1873. It took several weeks, as usual, to obtain porters, but by the end of March the caravan was on its way inland along the Unyanyembe track from Bagamoyo. Cameron had three white companions—W. E. Dillon, a naval surgeon, Lieutenant C. Murphy, R.A., and Robert Moffat. The last was a grandson of the famous missionary and thus a nephew of Livingstone by marriage. When he heard of the projected expedition, he had sold his sugar plantation in Natal—it was all he possessed—and taken the first boat to Zanzibar in the hope of being allowed to take part in the venture. When Cameron accepted him as a recruit, it was, he told him, the 'happiest day of his life.' But for all four of them the succeeding days were far from happy. The porters proved more than usually unreliable. They loitered, they pilfered from their loads, they deserted. And, though the rains had not yet broken, there was water enough about for the breeding of the customary hosts of malarial mosquitoes. All four were repeatedly down with fever. The worst case was Moffat's, and in the latter part of May, at Mohale in Usagara, he died. The survivors reached Unyanyembe in August. They were warmly greeted by the Arabs and lodged in the *tembe* occupied by Stanley and Livingstone. The only news was that the war with Mirambo was still going on in a spasmodic fashion, Mirambo ravaging the countryside and raiding up to the outskirts of Unyanyembe, the Arabs standing timidly on the defensive. Nothing had been heard of Livingstone for many months. The porters sent by Stanley had arrived just about a year ago, and Livingstone had then set off towards Lake Tanganyika. No doubt he had turned southwards in accordance with his declared intentions. But no caravans had come up through that desolate country. Nobody reported having seen him.

At Unyanyembe the expedition was brought to a halt for several weeks. It was not only the perennial problem of porters. Dillon and Cameron were both prostrated with malaria. It affected their eyesight. Dillon, indeed, seemed to be going blind, and Cameron found it difficult to read

the note which was brought him, as he lay dizzy with fever
on his bed, on October 20. He sent for the bearer of the
note. It was Chuma. Livingstone, he said, was dead, and
he and his companions were carrying his body to the
coast.[1]

33

' MR. STANLEY,' says Livingstone's journal for February 18,
1872, ' used some very strong arguments in favour of my
going home, recruiting my strength, getting artificial teeth,
and then returning to finish my task ; but my judgment
said, " All your friends will wish you to make a complete
work of the exploration of the sources of the Nile before
you retire." My daughter Agnes says, " Much as I wish
you to come home, I would rather that you finished your
work to your own satisfaction than return merely to gratify
me." Right and nobly said, my darling Nannie. Vanity
whispers pretty loudly, " She is a chip of the old block."
My blessing on her and all the rest.'

It was a natural decision. Livingstone believed that it
would take him only six or seven months to solve the
problem of the sources of the Nile ;[2] and, if he were to go
home, more than that time would be spent merely in
getting from Unyanyembe to the coast and back. And
that was not the only consideration. Livingstone evidently
felt that to go home now was to go home for good. His
physique, in fact, though vastly improved by the food and
medicine which Stanley had brought, had been incurably
undermined. His real age was much more than fifty-nine,
and he knew it. ' I am terribly knocked up,' he wrote to
Waller a few months later, ' but this is for your own eye
only—in my second childhood, a dreadful old fogie—
doubtful if I live to see you again.'[3] But, if that was a
reason for sticking to his task, it was also a reason for getting
it quickly done. Livingstone, indeed, was thoroughly

home-sick after Stanley left him. When he was last in
Scotland, he had longed to be back in Africa. Now, after
six hard years in Africa, he longed to be back in Scotland.
It was not that Africa had lost its hold on him. In a sense
he was always at home there. It was the loneliness, which
he had positively welcomed in better times but which had
grown less congenial with his growing consciousness of
failing strength. And naturally Stanley's arrival and companionship had made it worse. He felt lonelier, more
home-sick, after Stanley had gone than before he came.

It was with a burning impatience, therefore, that he
who had so often shown such incomparable patience in the
past now waited at Unyanyembe for the arrival of the
new porters from the coast. The fifth day after Stanley's
departure was his birthday, and he made this poignant
entry in his journal. ' 19th March. Birthday. My Jesus,
my king, my life, my all ; I again dedicate my whole self
to Thee. Accept me, and grant, O Gracious Father, that
ere this year is gone I may finish my task. In Jesus' name
I ask it. Amen, so let it be. David Livingstone.' . . . As
the ensuing days go by, he calculates over and over again
how long he will have to wait. Stanley, he thinks, should
reach Zanzibar by May 1. Twenty days might be allowed
for engaging the men. They might start on May 22. That
should bring them to Unyanyembe about the middle of
July. Most of this time-table proved to be not far out.
Stanley, as has been seen, was at Bagamoyo on May 6,
and the caravan left Zanzibar on May 27. But its inland
march took longer than Livingstone had reckoned. It did
not arrive till August 15.

At the end of March the rains which drenched Stanley
in Ugogo broke over the central highlands, first at night
only, then every day and all day. There was nothing for
Livingstone to do but sit in his *tembe* and read and write
and think. He read Baker's *Albert Nyanza*—' artistic and
clever '—and Mungo Park's *Travels*—' they look so truth-
ful '—and Young's *Search after Livingstone*—' thankful for
many kind words about me.' He did not write much :

there are few letters surviving from this time, and the daily
entry in the journal is often very brief and sometimes
altogether omitted. No doubt he thought the more ; and
no doubt, too, it was mainly about the final task, the
crowning of his life work that lay ahead. Thus the dreams
and hopes and prayers of the Manyema period reappear
in the journal. The longest single passage in it is a specula-
tion on the prehistoric geological formation of the heart of
Africa and its effect on the river system. On another page
he maintains that Ptolemy's geography shows him to have
been less well-informed than the Egyptian priests who
talked to Herodotus six centuries before his day. ' They
seem to have been well aware of the accounts of travellers
or traders that a great number of springs contributed to
the origin of the Nile, but none could be pointed at distinctly as the " Fountains " except those I long to discover
or rather rediscover.' ' I pray the good Lord of all to
favour me,' runs another entry, ' so as to allow me to
discover the ancient fountains of Herodotus, and, if there
is anything in the underground excavations to confirm
the precious old documents (τὰ βιβλία), the Scriptures of
truth, may He permit me to bring it to light and give me
wisdom to make a proper use of it.' Somewhere, he
believes, between Lake Tanganyika and the copper-
bearing area of Katanga those elusive springs must lie,
and he plans to march along that line through Fipa and
beyond the Lake until he finds them. But, while he still
pursues his ' dream,' it has lost something of the mystical
power it had over his mind in Manyema. He is beginning,
indeed, to be haunted by an uncomfortable suspicion. He
first mentions it on May 21 and dismisses it with a characteristic jest. ' I wish,' he notes, ' I had some of the assurance
possessed by others, but I am oppressed with the apprehension that after all it may turn out that I have been
following the Congo ; and who would risk being put into
a cannibal pot and converted into black man for it ? '
Ten days later he confesses his ' perpetual doubt and
perplexity.' ' I know too much to be positive.' The

Lualaba *might* be either river. ' The fountains flowing
north and south seem in favour of its being the Nile.
Great westing is in favour of the Congo.' The doubt per-
sists. ' I am even now not at all " cock-sure," ' he notes
towards the end of June, ' that I have not been following
down what may after all be the Congo.'

But far more significant than these moods of doubt as
to the scientific results of his explorations is the recurrence
of his old idea that the ' geographical feat,' whatever it
may prove to be, is not an end in itself. The call that had
come to him twenty years ago in Makalololand, the call to
devote his life to rescuing Central Africa from the Slave
Trade, seems now to have sounded in his heart again with
all its original force. There were times in Manyema when,
though he was still confronted by the horrors of the Trade
and thought and wrote about it, his mind was mainly
occupied with his ' dream.' Now it is the Trade that
obsesses it. ' To overdraw its evils,' he notes, ' is a simple
impossibility. The sights I have seen, though common
incidents of the traffic, are so nauseous that I always strive
to drive them from memory.' But he cannot do it. Other
things can be forgotten but not these. ' The slaving scenes
come back unbidden, and make me start up at dead of
night horrified by their vividness.' Thus, during those
months of waiting, the destruction of the Trade becomes
again his cardinal ambition. If he still passionately desires
to end his work with a great discovery, it is not for its own
sake, but because it will enhance his prestige in Britain
and strengthen the effect on public opinion of his revelations of the Trade's barbarity. In one of the letters to his
friends which Stanley took away with him he had written :
' If indeed my disclosures should lead to the suppression
of the East Coast slave-trade, I would esteem that as a far
greater feat than the discovery of all the sources together.'[1]
And it is now, in May, that he writes, in a letter to the
New York Herald, the famous sentence that was soon to be
inscribed on his grave. ' All I can say in my solitude is,
may Heaven's rich blessing come down on every one—

American, English, Turk—who will help to heal this open sore of the world.'

Another old idea recurs. Exploration, it will be remembered, was to open the way to colonisation as a means of combating the Slave Trade at its source : hence the Zambesi Expedition. When Livingstone discovered the Nyasa highlands, he at once suggested the planting of a colony thereon—not, of course, as he explained, a full-scale British colony in the ordinary sense, but a settlement of a few British farmers and traders who would take the lead in economic development.* Nothing came of that at the time : the only colony was the short-lived mission at Magomero ; and it was only to missions, not as yet to such white settlement as now exists some 200 miles south-east of Unyanyembe, that Livingstone's mind was reverting. He devotes two or three pages of the journal to the means by which a new mission might be founded and the methods it should pursue. And he is not thinking of white missionaries only. In a letter home he suggests the possibility of transferring one of the English settlements which had done so much to destroy the Slave Trade in West Africa over to the East. He does not mean, he explains, a settlement of Englishmen but a voluntary migration of native Christians across the continent.[1] This may not have been a practicable plan, but at least it shows that Livingstone's mind is once more active, inventive, forward-looking. The inertia into which he had drifted before Stanley came to Ujiji has gone. He resumes his crusade in the spirit in which he had entered on it long ago. In ardour and aim, if not in bodily strength, it is the old Livingstone who prepares for his last adventure.

Meantime the days go slowly by at Unyanyembe ; and presently, when the rains are over, Livingstone can find more ways of killing time. He visits his Arab friends. He takes them medicine when the cold winds bring on attacks of fever. He prepares equipment for his coming journey, spreading out the tent which Stanley gave him and tarring

* Kirk on the Zambesi, 271 ; and see p. 11 above.

it, getting milk and making cheeses, buying new-grown rice and converting it into flour. He seems to keep his new-found health : only once in the journal comes the one word, ' ailing ' : but it seems probable that physical effort soon tired him and he was happiest, no doubt, watching children and other creatures in the spring and summer sunshine. The children, he observes, have very few games. They amuse themselves mostly by imitating the occupations of their elders, building huts, laying out gardens, making weapons, shooting locusts with toy-guns. And again, as so often of old, minute observations of animated nature are committed to the journal—how the whydah birds build their nests, the cock bringing the stalks of grass from ' off the top of my *tembe*,' the hen arranging them inside with such vigour as to make the whole nest shake— how the red cock-bird feeds his brood, each chick putting its head on one side to receive its morsel from him, chipruping briskly and ' bothering ' him—how, when full-fledged, they still gladly take a feed, ' putting down the breast to the ground and cocking up the bill and chirruping in the most winning way they know '—how they crouch close together at night for warmth, looking ' like a woolly ball on a branch '—how the sunbirds go for nectar and insects to the pomegranates and pick out the young spiders from their webs. . . . But behind such pastimes and diversions the note of impatience becomes more audible as the weeks turn into months. ' Waiting wearily ' is the refrain and it starts as early as mid-May. ' Stanley 100 days gone,' notes Livingstone a month later, ' he must be in London now.' ' Wearisome waiting this,' he complains on July 3, ' and yet the men cannot be here before the middle or end of this month.' Two days later he only writes two words : ' Weary ! Weary ! ' After another two days : ' Waiting wearily here, and hoping that the good and loving Father of all may favour me and help me to finish my work quickly and well.' July comes, the month in which he calculated that his men should arrive, and creeps along and goes. ' Weary waiting this,' repeats the journal

on the 30th, ' and the best time for travelling passes over
unused.' But at last, on the 31st, there is news of
the men on their way. ' I can think of nothing,' says
the journal on August 6, ' but " When will these men
come ? " ' Then, on the 9th, three men appeared in
advance of their companions. ' Bless the Lord, O my
soul, and all that is within me bless His holy name.
Amen.' On August 15, the rest of the party came in.
' Most thankful to the Giver of all good I am. I have to
give them a rest of a few days, and then start.'

34

LIVINGSTONE'S company now numbered sixty-two. There
were fifty-seven newcomers, mostly the porters hired by
Stanley, but including a few ' Nassick boys ' who had been
sent over from Bombay to join the abortive Search Expedition ; and there were the five trusty survivors of the party
that had set out in 1866 from Mikindani—Susi, Chuma,
Amoda, Mabruki and Gardner. A few days were spent in
packing and weighing the loads, ' an equal load of 50 lbs.
to each and half loads to the Nassickers.' Some bales were
stored at Unyanyembe to provide for the final march to
the coast, and among them by a deplorable accident was
left a precious case of dried milk. On August 25 they
were off.

Like Stanley a year earlier, Livingstone shaped his
course south-west to avoid the war that smouldered across
the Ujiji road ; and for a time he made steady progress
over dry level country covered with ' bush ' or leafless
woods. There were one or two minor mishaps. Two of
the porters decamped with twenty-four lengths of calico,
and a day was wasted in fruitless pursuit of them. The
' Nassickers,' who were charged with the care of the cattle,
proved quite incompetent. They lost ' our best milker '
on the second day out, and on the fourth day the journal

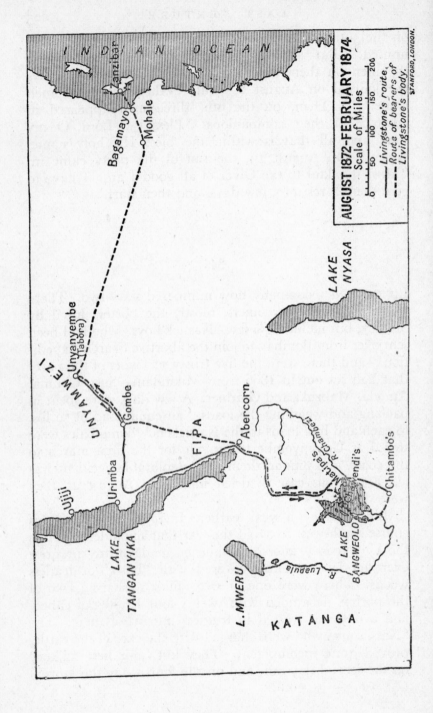

INDIAN OCEAN

Zanzibar

Bagamayo

Mohale

AUGUST 1872–FEBRUARY 1874.
Scale of Miles
0   50   100   150   200

Livingstone's route.
Route of bearers of
Livingstone's body.

STANFORD, LONDON.

LAKE NYASA

UNYAMWEZI

Unyanyembe
(Tabora)

Gombe

FIPA

Abercorn

Ujiji

Urimba

R. Chambezi

Matipa's

Chitambo's

Chowendi's

LAKE TANGANYIKA

L. MWERU

R. Luapula

LAKE BANGWEOLO

KATANGA

records : ' The two Nassickers lost all the cows yesterday
from sheer laziness. They were found a long way off, and
one cow was missing. Susi gave them ten cuts with a
switch.' More serious was the presence of the tsetse fly
which would mean, sooner or later, the death of all the
animals unless they could get beyond its range. On that
account, says the journal, ' we shall have to make forced
marches.' But the torrid, cloudless weather made it hard
to quicken the pace. September 8th : ' Very hot and
people ill.' September 11th : ' Sun very hot and marching
fatiguing for all.' Some time later, when they are farther
south and on lower ground, ' the sun makes the soil so hot
that the radiation is as if it came from a furnace. It burns
the feet of the people and knocks them up. . . . Have been
compelled to slowness very much against my will.' At last,
on October 8, they sighted Lake Tanganyika, at a point
rather more than half-way between Ujiji and its southern
end ; and after two days' rest (' people very tired ') they
began to make their way along the mountain wall that
rises from its waters. It was hard going—like walking
along combe-riven cliffs above the sea—steeply up and
then steeply down. It was too much for some of the remaining cows and they had to be slaughtered. Livingstone, too,
as will be seen, found it tried his strength ; but there were
times when his physical discomfort was almost forgotten in
the beauty of the lake and its surroundings. ' At sunset
the red glare on the surface made the water look like a sea
of reddish gold.' At one point ' we came out on a ledge of
rocks and looked sheer down 500 feet or 600 feet into its
dark green waters.' They were now passing through the
Fipa country, and the hot dry season was coming to an
end. ' It is very hot to-day,' notes the journal on October
24, ' and the first thunder-storm away in the east ' ; and
next day, ' The west coast is very plain to-day ; rain must
have fallen there.'

By this time it was already evident that, despite his long
rest at Unyanyembe, Livingstone's health was quite
unequal to the fatigues and privation of African travel.

The short entry in the journal for September 15, only three weeks from the start, concludes with one disquieting word. 'On to near range of hills. Much large game here. Ill.' Malaria would not have mattered so much, but it was the more dangerous, more persistent enemy, dysentery. September 18. 'Remain at Merera's.' Next day, 'Ditto, ditto, because I am ill with bowels, having eaten nothing for eight days.' Two days later : 'Rest here as the complaint does not yield to medicine or time ; but I begin to eat now, which is a favourable symptom.' The improvement continued. 'Recovering and thankful, but weak.' . . . 'I am getting better slowly.' . . . 'Getting well again—thanks.' . . . But the torrid heat and the steep climbing and the jolting when he took to a donkey, all told against a real recovery. 'It is hot and trying for all,' says the journal on October 4 : 'I feel it much internally and am glad to move slowly.' October 9 : 'This heat makes me useless and I feel constrained to lie like a log. Inwardly I feel tired too.' Any one who has suffered from dysentery knows what that inward tiredness means. But, though Livingstone was well aware of the nature of his trouble, the idea of yielding to it, of admitting that he was attempting something beyond his strength, of giving up and going back seems never to have crossed his mind. 'I am right glad of the rest,' he notes on October 15, 'but keep on as constantly as I can.'

On November 1 the rains began, but for the next week or two there were still intervals of burning sunshine. They were nearing the foot of the Lake now, and presently they emerged from the mountains and struck out across the fairly open, gently undulating country which lies south of the Lake—the country in which the little British township of Abercorn now stands. It was easier going, but food was harder to obtain. 'We tried to get food, but it is very dear and difficult to bargain for.' 'We got very little food, and kill a calf to fill our mouths a little.' Nothing could be worse for Livingstone than lack of milk and fresh vegetables ; and there is an ominous entry on November 9.

'Men sent off to search for a village return empty-handed, and we must halt. I am ill and losing much blood.' There were troubles with the men, too, at this time, not serious, but recalling at this last stage of the long journey similar incidents which had happened in its opening stage. ' I had to punish two useless men for calling out " Posho ! posho ! posho ! " (rations) as soon as I came near. One is a confirmed bange-smoker. The blows were given slightly, but I promised that the next should be severe.' (Those chains, it may be noted by the way, are never mentioned ; it seems more than probable, indeed, that they were left behind at Unyanyembe). Another entry brings back to mind the sepoys' maltreatment of the animals in 1866. ' The donkey died this morning. Its death was evidently caused by tsetse bite and bad usage by one of the men, who kept it forty-eight hours without water. . . . It is a great loss to me.' But these were relatively small things. On the whole the men behaved well. If progress was slow, it was not because they loitered but because some of them were sick. Wearily, but steadily, they followed their weary leader southwards.

35

LIVINGSTONE was now approaching the area of inland waters which he had explored in part in 1867-68. He believed that the two lakes he had then discovered, Bangweolo and Mweru, were connected by a river which flowed out of Mweru northwards to become the Lualaba on whose banks at Nyangwé he had lived so many months. If, as he would fain believe, the Lualaba were the Nile, then the ultimate sources of the Nile must be streams that fed Lake Bangweolo. He planned, therefore, to make his way right round the southern end of it. There, it seemed, the ' fountains ' *must* be found. Unfortunately it was the worst possible time of year to visit that low-lying country.

In the dry season it was swampy enough. In and after the rains vast tracts of it were completely under water. But Livingstone defied the elements. He had survived the ordeal by fiery sun and drought : he would face the ordeal by water and cold. The healthiest man might well have flinched from it, and Livingstone knew that his physical strength was failing ; but his will and his faith had never been stronger, and he trusted that, given one final effort of endurance on his own part, he would be sustained by more than human power just long enough to reach his goal.

By the middle of November he had struck the trail which he had followed northwards in the spring of 1867 ; and for the next fortnight or so he was passing through villages he recognised and meeting chiefs he knew. ' I visited Kampamba. He is still as agreeable as he was before. . . . We made good way with Kiteneha as our guide who formerly accompanied Kampamba and ourselves to Liemba.' But it was still difficult at times to get food. ' I was out of flesh for four days ' (November 24). A characteristic entry appears a few days later. ' Chiwe presented a small goat with crooked legs and some millet flour, but he grumbled at the size of the fathom of cloth I gave. I offered another fathom and a bundle of needles, but he grumbled at this too, and sent it back. *On this I returned his goat and marched.*' A little later he reached a neighbourhood which had recently been ravaged by the notorious slaver, Tippoo Tib. Some villages lay deserted. In others the people fled as the caravan approached. ' No food to be got on account of raids.' (December 3.) ' We hasten along as fast as hungry men can go ' (December 6.) ' Send off men to a distance for food, and wait of course. Here there is none for either love or money.' (December 9.)

Meantime the rains had set in steadily. ' We were soon overwhelmed in a pouring rain,' says the journal on November 18, ' and had to climb up a slippery red path. . . . One of the men picked up a little girl who had been deserted by her mother. As she was benumbed by cold

and wet he carried her ; but when I came up he threw her
into the grass. I ordered a man to carry her and we gave
her to one of the childless women.' Soon the whole
country was drenched with moisture. 'Started at daybreak. The grass was loaded with dew, and a heavy mist
hung over everything' (November 26.) 'Very heavy rain
and high gusts of wind which wet us all.' (November 27.)
Day by day the innumerable streams which crossed their
path ran deeper and swifter and began to overflow their
banks. 'Cross the River Lithabo, thirty yards wide and
thigh deep, moving fast to the S.W.' (December 15.)
'Crossed the Lipanza, twelve yards wide and waist deep,
being now in flood' (December 16.) Presently they came
to rivers too deep for wading and had to wait till canoes
could be borrowed from the nearest village. And still the
rain fell, sometimes in sheets, sometimes in a steady drizzle.
Livingstone, one imagines, was seldom dry. 'A wet bed
last night,' he notes on December 20, 'for it was in a
canoe that was upset. It was so rainy that there was no
drying it.'

Early in December he left his old route and struck westwards, apparently not following a deliberate course but
simply making for the next inhabited village in the hope
of obtaining food. In any case he could not determine
exactly where he was, since the blanket of rain-clouds, day
and night, made scientific observations quite impossible.
About December 20, when he was some eighty miles
north of Lake Bangweolo, he turned south. 'We crossed
a rivulet ten yards wide and thigh deep, and afterwards
in an hour and a half came to a sedgy stream which we
could barely cross. We hauled a cow across bodily'
(December 22.) Christmas Eve was 'very wet and drizzling.' The entry for Christmas Day is as follows : 'I thank
the good Lord for the good gift of His Son Jesus Christ
our Lord . . . Slaughtered an ox, and gave a *fundo* and
a half to each of the party. This is our great day, so we
rest. It is cold and wet, day and night.' A few days later
the sky cleared. 'New moon last night . . . it may be a

real change to drier weather.' 'The rains have ceased for a time,' says the journal on New Year's Day. But that is all. Only once before since the start from Mikindani—at the beginning of 1869 when he was very ill with lung trouble—had Livingstone omitted to note down a prayer or a hope for what the coming year might bring. And this time he was again very ill. The relief from dysentery had been short. As early as November 9, as has been seen, he was losing blood. On December 13 comes the one word, 'Ill.' And nothing, of course, could have been worse for him in that condition than the lack of good food and the constant exposure to damp and cold. On January 3 'our last cow' was fatally injured in crossing a river—a disastrous loss since that case of dried milk had been left at Unyanyembe. It seems probable, indeed, that only by keeping a goat or two, of the few that could be purchased, for milk instead of the meat which the rest of the party needed that Livingstone kept alive.

The hope of a change in the weather proved false. The nearer they got to the lake, the more heavily the rain streamed down. It becomes a regular refrain in the journal. 'A cold rainy day keeps us in a poor village very unwillingly.' 'Detained by heavy continuous rains.' 'No observations can be made from clouds and rain.' 'Cold and rainy weather: never saw the like.' 'Storm-stayed. . . . Never was in such a spell of cold rainy weather except in going to Loanda in 1853.' It goes on all through January. 'Rain, rain, rain as if it never tired on this watershed' (January 23.) 'A dreary wet morning, and no food that we know of near. It is drop, drop, drop and drizzling from the north-west' (January 28.) Even the rivulets now were running deep, and alongside all the streams as well as the rivers the ground was so waterlogged as to constitute great belts of what the journal calls 'sponge'—a sort of sticky swamp in which men sank almost as easily as in water. So widespread, too, was the flooding that, unless the porters watched for the swirl of the current that alone betrayed a river's course, they might

be out of their depth in a moment. And out of their depth
they were in any case if they came to the hidden pot-holes
left by the weight of some wandering elephant. To plunge
and stagger through such a watery waste was now quite
beyond Livingstone's strength, and from time to time he
had to be carried pick-a-back on his men's shoulders.
' Carrying me across one of the broad sedgy rivers,' he
calmly observes, ' is really a very difficult task. One we
crossed was at least 2000 feet broad. . . . The main
stream came up to Susi's mouth and wetted my seat and
legs.' Five others took their turn after Susi. ' Each time
I was lifted bodily and put on another pair of stout willing
shoulders, and fifty yards put them out of breath, no
wonder ! . . . It took us full an hour and a half. . . .
The water was cold, and so was the wind.' ' Our progress
is distressingly slow,' that same day's entry (January 24)
not unnaturally complains. ' Wet, wet, wet ; sloppy
weather, truly, and no observations.' And so it goes on,
day after day, till at last on February 13 they sight Lake
Bangweolo. It had taken nearly two months of their
splashing, meandering progress to cover a distance of
eighty miles. Measured in a straight line, that meant
about 1½ miles a day.

36

ALL this time the dysentery was gaining a stronger hold
on Livingstone. He was never free of it, and the pain was
often acute and the intestinal hæmorrhage severe. He
made light of it at first, as he had two years before in
Manyema. ' I lose much blood,' he notes on January 28,
' but it is a safety-valve for me, and I have no fever or
other ailments.' A fortnight later, however, he seems to
realise the danger. He records a day of inaction ' because
of an excessive hæmorrhagic discharge ' ; and then
immediately follows this prayer—' If the good Lord gives

me favour, and permits me to finish my work, I shall thank and bless him, though it has cost me untold toil, pain and travel ; this trip has made my hair all grey.' But, though he was steadily growing weaker, he was not yet incapacitated. He could walk unaided on dry ground, he could think clearly, and he could write. During those tedious waits enforced by illness or the weather or the search for food, he kept his journal regularly and wrote several letters.

The entries in the journal are never so long, it is true, as they often were in earlier days ; but they bear witness to the old reflecting mind and the old observant eye. He suddenly jots down, for instance, a plea for the missionary calling which he had chosen himself so long ago. ' The spirit of Missions is the spirit of our Master : the very genius of His religion. A diffusive philanthropy is Christianity itself. It requires perpetual propagation to attest its genuineness.' And, even when he is exhausted or in pain, he never fails to mark the beauties or the curiosities of nature. During those scorching days beside Lake Tanganyika he had observed how the flowers defied the heat. ' Though all the plants are burnt off or quite dried, the flowers persist in breaking out of the hot dry surface, generally without leaves. A purple ginger, with two yellow patches inside, is very lovely to behold, and it is alternated with one of a bright canary yellow ; many trees, too, put on their blossoms.' And now, in the rain and cold, he describes minutely the rich variety of flowers growing beside his sodden track—marigolds, orchids, pink asclepias, clematis, polygalas, blue-flowering bulbs, blood-red balsams, blue and yellow spiderworts, flowery aloes, yellow and red, ' in one whorl of blossoms,' and so on. . . . There had been birds in plenty above Tanganyika, and he had watched flocks of swifts and swallows circling over the lake ; but he found comparatively little bird-life in the watery country. Less pleasant living things abounded. Snakes were met with from time to time : he killed one himself that was seven feet long. ' He reared up before

me and turned to fight.' And, of course, there were leeches.
' In one place I counted nineteen leeches in our path in
about a mile. Rain had fallen, and their appearance out
of their hiding places suddenly after heavy rain may have
given rise to the idea of their fall with it as fishes do.'
And there were worse enemies than leeches. He was
attacked one night, as he lay in bed, by an army of red
ants. ' The first came on my foot quietly, then some began
to bite between the toes, then the larger ones swarmed over
the foot and bit furiously and made the blood start out.'
He staggered out of the tent, but there the enemy were in
greater force and he was covered with them in a moment
from head to foot. Grass fires were lighted to smoke them
off, and some of the men helped him to pick them from
his body. ' After battling for an hour or two they took me
into a hut not yet invaded, and I rested till they came,
the pests, and routed me out there too ! ' It was scarcely
an occasion, one would have thought, for scientific observation ; but Livingstone closely watched the insects' movements and their order of battle and entered in his journal
a minute description of the way they bit, driving home
the needle-points of their mandibles with all the force of
their six legs.

Of the letters he wrote at this time the longest was to
Waller. He began it soon after leaving Unyanyembe, continued it at intervals, but never finished it. There is little
new in it. He tells over again the story of his wanderings
and troubles and harps again on his grievances ; but
towards the end he picks up the old personal threads and
reverts to the old affectionate badinage which had been so
constant a feature of his correspondence with that particular friend. ' I hope you will yet be a missionary bishop
of Bembatouk Bay or elsewhere, and I shall give you
osculum pacis with a smack that will make the rafters ring,
and girls all giggle, and Mrs. Waller jealous.' And he goes
on to ask Waller to prepare for his home-coming. Will he
speak to a dentist about a speedy fitting of artificial teeth ?
And will he secure some lodgings—' say, anywhere near

Regent's Park : comfortable and decent, but not excessively dear. Agnes will come up, and will need accom-
modation at the same place : one sitting-room will do for
both.'[1]

Another letter, written in December to his brother in
Canada, shows what is still his ultimate, dominant objective. ' If the good Lord permits me to put a stop to the
enormous evils of the inland slave-trade, I shall not grudge
my hunger and toils. . . . The Nile sources are valuable
to me only as a means of enabling me to open my mouth
with power among men.'[2] Nor does he forget his debt
to Stanley. ' I am perpetually reminded,' he writes to
him ' that I owe a great deal to you for the men you sent.
With one exception the party is working like a machine.'[3]
He repeats this testimonial in a joint letter to his old
friend, Macleod, the Astronomer Royal at the Cape, and
Mann, his assistant, written on the shore of Lake Bangweolo. ' The men have behaved as well as Makalolo. I
cannot award them higher praise.' In another letter to
' Paraffin ' Young he writes : ' *Opere peracto ludemus*—the
work being finished, we will play—you remember in your
Latin Rudiments lang syne. It is true for you, and I
rejoice to think it is now your portion, after working nobly,
to play. May you have a long spell of it ! I am differently
situated ; I shall never be able to play. . . . I have been
led, unwittingly, into the slaving field of the Banyans and
Arabs in Central Africa. I have seen the woes inflicted
and I must still work and do all I can to expose and mitigate
the evils.' So retirement no longer means inaction. He
will never go ' on the shelf.' He will work on to influence
public opinion when he gets back to those lodgings near
Regent's Park. That he will get back he now seems confident. ' During a large part of this journey,' he goes on,
' I had a strong presentiment that I should never live to
finish it. It is weakened now, as I seem to see the end
towards which I have been striving looming in the
distance.'[4]

37

AT the beginning of February Livingstone was brought to
a halt on the north-east shore of Lake Bangweolo some
fifteen miles above the point at which the River Chambezi
enters it. Around him stretched a great waste of water,
covering the level country to a depth of four to seven feet
and merging imperceptibly into the deeper lake. A
bleaker, gloomier, more monotonous scene could scarcely
be imagined. Here and there a patch of rising ground had
not been submerged, and on some of these islets there were
little groups of huts. Elsewhere the surface of the flood
was only broken by the crown of some great ant-hill or a
clump of reeds or lotus plants or the scraggy branches of a
leafless thorn. The watery wilderness was as silent as it
was bare. The only sounds were the call of the birds at
daybreak, the occasional scream of a fish-eagle, the rare
cry of some lost wild beast, the noise of the wind in the
rushes, the steady splashing of the rain.

In these desolate surroundings Livingstone was held up
for several weeks. It was impossible for his party to make
its way round the southern fringe of the lake entirely on
foot. Most of the baggage, at any rate, would have to be
taken in canoes. And it was difficult to get canoes. They
could only be got, it seemed, from Matipa, the leading
chief of the neighbourhood, and that proved a long and
tedious business. The first messengers sent to him failed
to reach his village and returned ' with a most lame story.'
The next lot broke their undertaking to go. ' They have
no honour,' Livingstone complains. ' It is so wet we can
do nothing. . . . I was never in such misty cloudy weather
in Africa.' Another messenger was obtained, and, to make
sure this time that he did what he promised to do, Susi
and Chuma went with him. They were back in four days
with good news. For five bundles of brass wire Matipa
would transport the party across the water to the country

of his brother, Kabende, from whom, no doubt, they could get further help. But nothing happened. No canoes arrived. The delay was the more exasperating because the living conditions would have been intolerably uncomfortable even for a healthy man, and all this time Livingstone was very ill. Once or twice he shifted camp. One night they slept ' in a most unwholesome ruined village. Rank vegetation had run over all, and the soil smelled offensively.' Another night was spent on ' a miserable dirty fishy island. . . . All are damp.' Finally Livingstone decided to see Matipa himself. ' I purpose to go near him to-morrow,' he notes at the end of February ; ' the good Lord help me.' On March 2 he landed on the island on which Matipa's big village stood, and next morning he paid him a visit. He found him ' an old man, slow of tongue and self-possessed.' They had a long talk, and amongst other things Livingstone asked him about the mountains southwards of the Lake, where, if anywhere, the ' fountains ' he sought must lie. But, while Matipa knew of mountains to the south-east and to the west, he had never heard of any to the south. On the whole he seemed friendly and professed himself very willing to convey the party to Kabende's, where there were ' few rivers and plenty to eat.' Next day, since the village ' swarms with mice and is very closely built and disagreeable,' the camp was moved to a pitch on the highest part of the island, ' where we can see around us and have the fresh breeze from the lake. . . . Rainy as we went up, as usual.' . . . Ten days passed. . . . ' Matipa says "Wait." . . . Time is no value to him.' The entry in the journal for Sunday, March 16, is as follows : ' Service. I spoke sharply to Matipa for his duplicity. He promises everything and does nothing. . . . Ill all day with my old complaint.' ' The delay is most trying,' he writes next day : and then, as if ashamed of grumbling, ' So many detentions have occurred they ought to have made me of a patient spirit.' On March 19 he was sixty and set down his last birthday-prayer. ' Thanks to the Almighty Pre-

server of men for sparing me thus far on the journey of
life. Can I hope for ultimate success ? So many obstacles
have arisen. Let not Satan prevail over me, Oh ! my
good Lord Jesus.'

The birthday seems to have spurred him to action ;
for, in the course of it, he came nearer to treating peaceful
Africans with violence than ever in his life. He left ten
men to guard his camp. With the rest he took ' quiet
possession ' of Matipa's house and village. Then he fired
a pistol—through the roof. This *coup de main* was brilliantly
successful. Matipa himself ran away ; but, before noon
his people brought three canoes in which Livingstone
promptly dispatched some of his men across the water to
build a camp on the farther bank of the Chambezi. On
the morrow Matipa returned and presented Livingstone
with two large baskets of flour, a sheep and a cock. ' I
gave Matipa a coil of thick brass wire and his wife a string
of large neck beads, and explained my hurry to be off. He
is now all fair, and promises largely : he has been much
frightened by our warlike demonstration. I am glad I had
nothing to do but make a show of force.'

So, at last, on March 24, with all the goods packed in
canoes, they started slowly across the flood. ' We punted
six hours to a little islet without a tree, and no sooner did
we land than a pitiless pelting rain came on. We turned
up a canoe to get shelter. . . . The wind tore the tent
out of our hands and damaged it too. The loads are all
soaked, and with the cold it is bitterly uncomfortable. A
man put my bed into the bilge, so I was safe for a wet
night.' Yet, suffering though he often was, from hæmorrhage and agonising pain, Livingstone would not yield an
inch. The very next entry in the journal is a last defiance
of misfortune. ' *Nothing earthly will make me give up my work
in despair. I encourage myself in the Lord my God and go
forward.*'

On March 25 they again punted for six hours. ' The
flood extends for twenty or thirty miles, far too broad to
be seen across. Fish abound and ant-hills alone lift up

their heads. . . . The wind on the rushes makes a sound
like the waves of the sea.' Next day they crossed the
Chambezi and camped beyond it. Messengers were sent
to bring on some of the men for whom there had not been
room in the canoes. March 30 : 'A lion roars nightly.
The fish-hawk utters his weird voice in the morning, as if
he lifted it up to a friend at a great distance, in a sort of
falsetto key.' April 3 : 'Very heavy rain last night. Six
inches fell in a short time. The men at last have come
from Matipa's.' On April 5 they were off again, with a
few canoes and food obtained from a local chief, most of
the men going by land, if so it could be called, the rest
with Livingstone and the 'luggage' by water. 'The
amount of water spread out over the country,' says the
journal of the 6th, 'constantly excites my wonder : it is
prodigious. . . . It is the Nile apparently enacting its
inundations even at its sources.' Next day they skirted a
stretch of drier ground or shallower flood. 'Men were
hunting, and we passed near large herds of antelopes
which made a rushing, plunging sound as they ran and
sprang away among the waters. A lion had wandered into
this world of water and ant-hills, and roared night and
morning, as if very much disgusted : we could sympathise
with him !' That evening the canoes lost all touch with
the land-party. They were 'lost in stiff grassy prairies
from three to four feet deep in water. . . . We fired a gun
in the stillness of the night, but received no answer.' Two
villagers appeared in the morning and told them that their
comrades were away to the south-east. Since the floods in
that direction were shallower, most of the day was spent
in dragging the heaviest of the canoes through reeds and
mud. 'All hands could move her only a few feet. Putting
all their strength to her, she stopped at every haul with a
jerk, as if in a bank of adhesive plaster.' Another day and
then, on April 9, they reached a river-crossing where they
heard that the land-party has recently passed by. 'My
men were all done up.'

So was their leader. On April 10 the journal at last

admits the gravity of the persistent hæmorrhage. 'I am pale, bloodless and weak from bleeding profusely ever since the 31st of March last : an artery gives off a copious stream and takes away my strength. Oh ! how I long to be permitted by the Over Power to finish my work.' Livingstone, in truth, had begun to bleed to death ; and, now that he had caught up the landsmen and was stumbling and splashing with them, ankle-deep or more, along such tracks as they could find, he was soon unable to keep it up. ' Great loss of αἱμα made me so weak I could hardly walk, but tottered along nearly two hours and then lay down quite done. Cooked coffee—our last—and went on, but in an hour I was compelled to lie down. Very unwilling to be carried, but on being pressed I allowed the men to help me along by relays ' (April 12). He must have realised, one imagines, how critical his condition now was : but, after that last *cri de coeur*, he allows no sign of foreboding to appear in the journal. On the contrary the entry he makes on the very morrow of his breakdown is the most cheerful he has made for weeks ! ' Fish and other food are abundant, and the people civil and reasonable. . . . The sky is clearing, and the S.E. wind is the lower stratum now. It is the dry season well begun.' There follows another of those fascinating pages of natural observation —the last—and it ends on a note so eerie as almost to suggest that Livingstone, who had Highland blood in him, was displaying the Gael's reputed gift of ' second sight.' Though the land, he observes, beneath the shallow flood is grassland, the water itself is full of ' purely aquatic subaqueous plants which send up their flowers only to fructify in the sun. Others, with great cabbage-looking hearts, seem to remain always at the bottom. The young fish swarm and bob in and out from the leaves. A species of soft moss grows on most plants, and seems to be good fodder for fishes. . . . One species of fish has the lower jaw turned down into a hook, which enables the animal to hold its mouth close to the plant as it glides up or down, sucking in all the soft pulpy food.' He notes, too, that the

south-east aerial current has raised the temperature. It is
so warm, indeed, that a blanket is scarcely needed till the
early hours of the morning, when the noise of birds begins.
First ' the turtle doves and cocks give out their warning
calls,' and then ' the fish-eagle lifts up his remarkable
voice. . . . Once heard, his weird unearthly voice can
never be forgotten—it sticks to one through life. . . . *It
seems as if he were calling to someone in the other world.*'

38

THE end was near now. ' I, being very weak,' says the
journal on April 15, ' had to be carried part of the way.'
Only part of the way ! Did he insist on walking for the
rest of it, although, as the entry goes on to admit, ' αἱμα
flowed copiously ' the previous night ? Two days later ' a
tremendous rain '—so much for the dry season !—' burst
all our now rotten tents to shreds,' and in the confusion and
the downpour and the dark Livingstone lay ' suffering
severely all night.' Yet, next day, they ' went on at 6.35
a.m.,' and they had marched for three hours before Livingstone was obliged to stop and rest. On April 18 they forded
a river ' seventy yards broad and waist to breast deep,'
and pushed on for two hours south-westwards, when again
Livingstone was ' forced to stop.' ' Very ill all night, but
remembered that the bleeding and most other ailments in
this land are forms of fever. Took two scruple doses of
quinine and stopped it quite.' So on again next morning.
' A fine bracing S.E. breeze kept me on the donkey across
a broad sponge and over flats of white sandy soil and much
cultivation for an hour and a half when we stopped at a
large village. . . . I am excessively weak, and but for the
donkey could not move a hundred yards. . . . No observations now, owing to great weakness ; I can scarcely hold
the pencil, and my stick is a burden. Tent gone ; the
men build a good hut for me and the luggage.' That is

his first admission of the full extent of his physical exhaustion ; and, since he is Livingstone to the very end, he takes the edge off the confession, so to speak, with the last of those dry, intensely characteristic comments with which he so often salted what he said and wrote. ' It is not all pleasure,' he feebly scrawls, ' this exploration.'

The remaining entries in the journal were as follows.

' 20th April, 1873. S[unday]. Service. Cross over the sponge, Moenda, for food and to be near the headman of these parts, Moanzambamba. I am excessively weak. Vil[lage] on Moenda sponge, 7 a.m. Cross Lokulu in a canoe. R[iver] is about thirty yards broad, very deep and flowing in marshes two knots from S.S.E. to N.N.W. into Lake.'

' 21st. Tried to ride but was forced to lie down and they carried me back to vil. exhausted.'

' 22nd. Carried in *kitanda* [litter] over sponge S.W. 2¼ [miles].

' 23rd. Do. 1½.'
' 24th. Do. 1.'
' 25th. Do. 1.'
' 26th. Do. 2½. To Kalunganjofu's, total 33=8¼.'

27th. Knocked up quite and remain : recover, sent to buy milch goats. We are on the banks of R. Molilamo.'

He could write no more, and our knowledge of what happened in the following week as well as for a fuller account of what had happened in the preceding days are derived from the information given to Waller by Chuma and Susi when they came to England.

It was evident, they said, that after April 21, when he had failed to keep his seat on the donkey and fallen to the ground, he was steadily growing weaker. There seemed, indeed, no likelihood of his being able to walk or ride again. So, since he insisted on going on, they made a *kitanda*—a wooden framework, seven feet long by three wide, covered with grass and a blanket, and slung on a pole borne on the shoulders of two men. Another blanket was hung from the pole to keep off the heat of the sun.

Progress was very slow, for the least movement seemed to aggravate the sufferer's pain. Purging meant frequent halts, and Livingstone was now too weak to put his feet to the ground without Chuma's support. The men would have wished him to stop for a week or more on the bare chance that complete rest might give him back a little strength. But he would not have it. He forced himself on, still hoping against hope that suddenly he would find what he was seeking. At the village they reached on the 25th, while he was lying in the shade on his *kitanda* and the men were building a hut for the night, he asked that one of the villagers should be brought to him. Several of them came ; for, unlike most of the people they had recently encountered, they were not afraid of the newcomers but friendly and inquisitive. Livingstone roused himself to question them. ' Did they know of a hill on which four rivers took their rise ? ' ' No,' said the spokesman : ' we ourselves are not travellers, and all those who used to go on trading expeditions are now dead.' And he went on talking till Livingstone could not bear it any longer and politely dismissed the party.

He was not thinking only of the ' fountains ' during those last days. He was actually making plans for the return march to the coast. On the day after that talk with the villagers he told Susi to count over the bags of beads, and, when it appeared that there were still twelve of them, he instructed him, if he had a chance, to buy two large ivory tusks which they could exchange with the Arabs at Ujiji for the cloth they would need for *hongo* on their way down to Bagamoyo.

On the 29th Livingstone was too weak to be moved from his bed in the hut to the *kitanda* outside : so, since the door was too narrow, the wall of the hut was broken down to enable the *kitanda* to be brought to his side. That day was the most difficult of all ; for there was the usual river to cross, and it now proved impossible for Livingstone to be helped to a canoe as heretofore. They laid his bed in the bottom of the strongest canoe, and tried to lift him

off the *kitanda*. But he could not bear the pressure of a
hand under his back. ' Beckoning to Chuma, in a faint
voice he asked him to stoop down over him as low as
possible, so that he might clasp his hands together behind
his head, directing him at the same time how to avoid any
pressure on the lumbar region of the back. In this way he
was deposited in the bottom of the canoe and quickly
ferried across.' As that day went on, he suffered such pain
that several times he begged his bearers to stop and put
the *kitanda* down. Once, when spoken to, he was too faint
to answer. Step by step, they carefully carried him on.
After a time he was strong enough to speak and pleaded
again to be left motionless ; but, just at that moment, a
village was seen in the distance and he allowed himself
to be borne to it. It was Chief Chitambo's village, some
four miles from the Bangweolo floods and not far east
of the southern tip of the lake. There Livingstone's last
journey came to an end.

He was laid under the eaves of one of the village huts
while his own frail lodging was quickly built with branches
and reeds and grass, banked round with earth. The men
worked at it in a drizzle of rain, while the villagers came
and stood watching the half-conscious white man whose
fame, it seemed, had somehow reached their ears. By
nightfall the hut was ready, the bales and boxes stowed in
it, and Livingstone laid on his bed. Outside, near the
door, a fire was lighted. Just inside sat the boy, Majwara,
whose duty it was to call Susi or Chuma if Livingstone
woke and wanted anything.

Early next morning (April 30), Chitambo came to pay
his respects, but Livingstone was obliged to ask him to
come again on the morrow when he hoped he would have
the strength to talk. . . . In the course of the afternoon
he asked Susi to bring his watch and showed him how to
hold it while he slowly wound it up. . . . When night
came on, some of the men went to their huts to sleep ;
others stayed watching round their fire. About eleven,
there was a noise of villagers scaring a wandering buffalo

off their crops, and Susi was sent for to tell Livingstone what it was. . . . ' Is this the Luapula ? ' he asked a little later. Susi told him they were at Chitambo's. ' How many days is it to the Luapula ? ' he asked, speaking this time in Swaheli. ' I think it is three days, master,' replied Susi in the same tongue. Presently he gave a sigh of pain and then seemed to fall asleep. . . . About an hour later Majwara summoned Susi again. Livingstone told him to boil some water, and, when he brought it, he asked for his medicine chest and with great difficulty—he could hardly see—he selected a dose of calomel. Then he told Susi to put a cup with a little water in it by his bed and another empty cup beside it. That done, ' All right,' he murmured faintly ; ' you can go out now. . . .'

Some time later, Livingstone seems to have realised that the end had come ; and, since he meant to die as he had lived, with a last, perhaps a fatal, effort of his unconquerable will he somehow got himself from the bed to his knees.

About four in the morning Majwara woke up Susi. He was afraid, he said. Before falling asleep he had seen the ' master ' kneeling at his bedside. He did not know how long he had slept, but he had looked again when he woke and the ' master ' had not moved. Susi summoned Chuma and two or three others and they went together to the hut. A candle, stuck on a box with its own wax, was burning, and by its dim light they could see Livingstone still kneeling ' by the side of his bed, his body stretched forward, his head buried in his hands upon the pillow.' He was praying, apparently, and for a moment they hesitated to go in. They watched. There was no motion, no sign of breathing. Then one of them went quietly and touched his cheek. It was nearly cold. He had been dead, it seemed, for some long time.

39

For the little band of 'faithfuls' who had followed
Livingstone for so many years, and especially for Chuma
and Susi, the death of the 'master' they had worshipped
must have been a grievous blow ; and for the whole party
it might well have seemed a catastrophe. They were
stranded in the heart of the African wilderness, hundreds
of miles from their homes in space, months away in time ;
and the great white man, who had led them there, whom
they had trusted to lead them back, on whose bravery
and wisdom and prestige they had relied to see them
safely through all the hardships and dangers of the march,
was dead. The conduct of these Africans in this critical
situation can only be described as astonishing. Most of
them were simple tribesmen, without a particle of education or knowledge of the world. Civilised folk in those
days would have called them ' savages.' They might have
lost their heads, hastily buried the body, and leaving it
and—what was perhaps more important—the journal and
notes and letters in the wilds, made off homewards in a
desperate and disorderly flight. But, if we can trust, as
certainly we can, the circumstantial story told by Chuma
and Susi,* they did not for a moment lose their heads.
There was no panic, nor even useless lamentation. They
behaved with quite remarkable coolness, courage and
discipline. It was as if the incomparable power which
Livingstone in his prime had exerted over Africans was
still at work on them.

The news of his death was spread at once through the
camp, and in the dusk of dawn they all assembled to discuss
what they should do. Two decisions were taken without

* Waller cross-questioned them on every detail and had no doubt that they told
the truth.

hesitation or dissent. First, they must carry Livingstone's body and his personal belongings back to Zanzibar. Second, Susi and Chuma, not so much because they had been Livingstone's closest companions as because of their long experience of African travel, must be the leaders. Nothing could have proved the strength of their devotion more plainly than the first of those decisions. All primitive peoples are haunted by superstitious fears of death and the dead ; and to carry a stranger's corpse from village to village across Africa was bound to be difficult and might well be very dangerous. They thought that Chitambo himself, at the outset, might forbid the removal of the body or levy so exorbitant a fine as to rob them of the means of paying their way later on ; and they decided to move at once a little distance from his village and to pretend that Livingstone, though too ill to be seen, was still alive. Happily, when the truth leaked out, Chitambo was friendly and sympathetic. ' Why did you not tell me ? ' he said. ' I know that you have no bad motives in coming to our land, and death often happens to travellers in their journeys.' He urged them to bury the body on the spot ; to take it to the coast, he said, was plainly impossible ; but, when they could not be dissuaded, he freely granted them permission to set up a camp near the village, in which the body could be prepared for the journey.

One of the men, Farijala, had been a servant in a surgeon's house at Zanzibar and had seen enough of *post-mortem* examinations to perform the simple operation that was needed. The heart and *viscera* were cut out and buried in a tin box. Jacob Wainwright, one of the ' Nassick boys,' who possessed a prayer-book and spoke English well, read the burial service. The body was left to dry for a fortnight in the sun and was then wrapped up in calico and fitted into a cylinder of bark neatly stripped from a tree. Sail-cloth was sewn round this, and the package lashed to a pole so that, like the *kitanda*, it could be carried by two men. Finally, an inscription was carved by Wainwright on a neighbouring *myonga* tree—' Livingstone, May 4,

1873 '*—and two strong posts with a cross-piece were erected to mark the spot where the body had lain.†

Soon after the middle of May they started—a long procession in single file, mostly with loads on their heads, the drummer-boy at the head, close behind him the Union Jack and the Sultan's scarlet flag, the precious burden half-way down the line. They had chosen to continue on the course which Livingstone had set. They knew that the River Luapula flowed not very far ahead, and they doubtless argued that to complete Livingstone's design and follow round the west side of the Lake might take less time than to return on their tracks round the east side. The going, too, might be better : it certainly could not be worse. . . . For a day or two all went well, but then they were smitten by a strange disease—severe pain in the limbs, prostration, and in the worst cases a kind of paralysis. They attributed it themselves to the constant wading through cold water which had been their almost daily lot for weeks before Livingstone died. Whatever its cause, almost all of them went down with it. Two of the women died, and one of the men only just pulled through. Susi himself was seriously ill. It was at least a month before they were fit to resume the march.

Then all went smoothly. The dry season had now really set in. The floods were subsiding, and they found no big river in their path—thus answering the question that Livingstone had so passionately wanted to be answered otherwise—till they reached the Luapula where it left the Lake. It was so broad that ' a man could not be seen on the opposite bank,' and they were lucky to be able to obtain canoes without difficulty at a neighbouring village. Beyond the river they had to traverse another long stretch

* The only certain date is that of the last entry in the journal, April 27. According to Susi's and Chuma's reckoning the death occurred in the early hours of May 1 and this was accepted by Waller and Blaikie. The date on the tree may have been that of the burial. May 4 was also adopted for the gravestone in Westminster Abbey.

† A photograph of the tree with the inscription is given in R. J. Campbell's *Livingstone*, p. 333. The tree has since perished, but shoots from its root have sprung up round the memorial which has been erected on the spot. The part of the trunk bearing the inscription was cut out and brought to England in 1900 and is now to be seen at the headquarters of the R. G. S. in Kensington Gore.

of flood and swamp ; but they were used to that, and the only mishap was the loss of the donkey on which Livingstone had ridden as long as he could ride—it was carried off one night by a hungry lion. Nor was there any trouble with the people of the country except at one village, Chawendi's, near the northern end of the Lake. Here they found the villagers, who had been indulging, as it happened, in a bout of beer-drinking, suspicious and unfriendly ; and, when their request for shelter for the night was flatly refused, they did what Livingstone would never have done : they tried to push their way inside the stockade. A scuffle ensued which soon developed into a serious fight. Arrows were let fly and spears thrown. Drums were beaten, other villagers came running from the fields, and the party would soon have been overwhelmed if they had not had guns. As it was, their assailants fled when they opened fire, killing two and wounding several. Their own casualties were only three men slightly wounded. They remained in undisturbed occupation of the village for several days, resting and eating the food they found there. An ugly incident, but it was the only one. Elsewhere the party was regarded as an innocent trading-caravan, returning to its Arab masters in the north. More difficulty might have been expected when they came again to the track they had followed southwards in the previous winter and could no longer conceal their identity. But there was none. When their real purpose was known and what it was they carried, there was no superstitious excitement, no obstruction, no blackmail. The villagers accorded to the dead the same respect which Africans had almost invariably accorded to the living man. And it was further proof of the interest his wanderings had excited far and wide through the heart of Africa that, while the party was still a long way south of Lake Tanganyika, they heard the news that an expedition had landed at Bagamoyo and was preparing to set out inland in quest of Livingstone. This was Cameron and his comrades, of course ; but by a natural confusion with the earlier Search

Expedition the leader was reported to be Livingstone's son.

On arrival at the Lake, Susi and Chuma wisely decided to avoid the route along its eastern wall which had cost so much time and toil on the outward march and to strike straight for Unyanyembe. They found only one range of mountains in their path. Thenceforward it was easy going over a vast level plain, part of it a great bare salt-pan, part open grassland thronged by all sorts of big game, part dry wooded country. As they traversed the outskirts of Fipa, *hongo* was levied for the first time, but not at excessive rates. There were no other difficulties, no serious misadventures. On October 20 Chuma met Cameron at Unyanyembe. The journey from Chitambo's had taken five months.

On November 9 the party started on its march to the sea, followed by Murphy, who had resigned from the Expedition now that its primary purpose was no longer operative, and by Dillon, who was far too ill to accompany Cameron farther. On the same day Cameron set out westward. Susi had told him that Livingstone had left a box of books and papers at Ujiji and had said, one day towards the end, that, if anything happened to him, that box must be recovered and dispatched to England. Cameron, therefore, decided to go direct to Ujiji ; but he had not got far before he was recalled by tragic news. Delirious with fever, virtually blind, and suffering from an acute attack of dysentery, Dillon had shot himself. ' The day on which I received the news,' wrote Cameron, ' was the saddest of my life.' He made his way to Kasakera, where the tragedy had happened, and then once more shaped his course for Ujiji. It was a toilsome journey, and its natural hardships were aggravated, as usual, by the behaviour of the porters. When he reached Ujiji in February, 1874, and examined the bales, he had brought with him, he discovered that the contents of only one were intact : something or other had been pilfered from all the rest. Livingstone's box was found safe in the custody of Mohammed bin Salib.[1]

At about the same time that Cameron arrived at Ujiji the bearers of Livingstone's body reached Bagamoyo. The ' rains ' had not yet broken, and they had had an unobstructed, uneventful journey except at a very early stage. Dillon's suicide had not been the only untoward event at Kasakera. There, for the first time, the force of primitive superstition, which had nowhere proved the obstacle it had been expected to be, made itself felt. The party were refused admission to the village ; and, since the news of what they were carrying was bound to run ahead of them all the way down to the coast, the prospect, though now the end was so near, seemed less favourable than at any time since they had left Chitambo's. They determined to try what trickery could do. They put it about that, in view of the difficulty of getting it to Zanzibar, the body would be taken back for burial at Unyanyembe. It was then taken from its shell, sheathed in a fresh strip of bark, wrapped in cloth and so tied up as to resemble a large bale of ordinary goods. The original shell was packed up again to look as it had before, and towards sundown six men bore it reverently off along the backward track to Unyan-yembe. In the darkness of the night they halted in a patch of jungle, broke up the package, carefully hid or destroyed all vestiges of it, and stealthily rejoined their companions. The ruse was completely successful. The party was now given shelter in the village and in due course continued their journey bearing their bales. There was no trouble at any other village. Nothing else happened worth recording. On February 15, just about nine months since they had started from Chitambo's, they arrived at Bagamoyo.

Chuma had pushed on to Zanzibar a few days in advance of the rest. He found that Kirk had gone home on leave and it was to Captain W. F. Prideaux, acting in his place, that Chuma made his report. A cruiser, H.M.S. *Vulture*, was in harbour at the time, and her captain promptly offered to fetch the body from Bagamoyo. It was taken on board on February 16, enclosed in a new double coffin of zinc and wood, and transported the same day to Zanzibar. A medical examination revealed a skull of European shape, big cheekbones, a broad high forehead, and white straight hair. Though the features were no longer recognisable, there could be no reasonable doubt that the body in fact was Livingstone's. On instructions from the Foreign Office, the coffin was put on board the next mailboat for England. Wainwright was sent with it. It reached Southampton on April 15, and was thence brought in a special train to London and lodged at the headquarters of the Royal Geographical Society in Savile Row. On April 18 it was interred in Westminster Abbey, near the centre of the nave.[1]

It was a day of national mourning. The streets through which the funeral procession passed were lined with people, and the Abbey itself was full. The pall-bearers were Sir Thomas Steele, whose lifelong friendship with Livingstone had begun when, on leave from his regiment, he was hunting big game in the Bakhatla country in 1843, W. C. Oswell, his companion on the expedition to Lake Ngami, E. D. Young, W. F. Webb of Newstead Abbey, Waller, Kirk, Stanley and Wainwright.

It was fitting that the ' Nassick boy ' should have had his place that day beside those others in the national shrine of England. Those others were men of Livingstone's own race. He alone belonged to the people for whom Livingstone had lived and died. It would have been still more fitting if Chuma and Susi, who were brought home a few weeks later and introduced by Waller to Livingstone's friends, could have followed their master all the way and stood beside his grave. They had a better right to be there than any one else in all the great congregation, better even than Waller or Kirk. It was thirteen years since Chuma had been rescued from the slaves and Susi set to cutting wood beside the Shiré. It was eight years since they had mislaid their master's spoons and forks and forgotten about his breakfast, and, growing to manhood in those eight years, they had served him with indomitable devotion to the end of his life and after it.

40

THE immediate sequel* to the story of Livingstone's last journey opens with a curious historical coincidence. On May 1, 1873, when Livingstone died or lay on the point of death at Chitambo's, the first blow was struck in a campaign which in three short years brought to its final triumph the cause to which he had given his life.

The Frere Mission, which was mainly due, as has been seen, to the growing revolt of British public opinion against the Arab Slave Trade which in turn had been mainly due to Livingstone's work and fame, arrived at Zanzibar in mid-January. It was charged with the task of persuading Sultan Barghash to conclude a new treaty with the British Crown under which all export of slaves from the coast of his African dominions would be prohibited and all markets for the sale of imported slaves closed. Only by such drastic measures, it was thought, could the Arab Slave Trade in East Africa be effectively suppressed, and the British Government were determined to secure their adoption. For nearly a month Frere, ably supported with facts and arguments by Kirk, tried to persuade Barghash to acquiesce. It was no easy task ; for the stoppage of the import of slaves to Zanzibar would soon result in a shortage of slave-labour for the Arab clove-plantations on the island and its neighbour, Pemba ; and, while Barghash appreciated the value of British friendship, he knew that, if he committed himself too far against the wishes and interests of his Arab sheikhs and their excitable followers, he might quickly provoke one of those rebellions which had long been a familiar feature of the history of Arab countries. He temporised, therefore, and protracted the discussion and refused to say yes or no. And Frere for his part, though the lives and liberty of many thousands of Africans were at stake, was unwilling to use more than moral pressure.

* Details in *The Exploitation of East Africa*, chaps. x and xi.

Several ships of the British navy were within call. No violent action was needed. There was no question of bombarding Zanzibar. The mere threat of a blockade would have brought Barghash at once to submission. But Frere did not use that weapon ; and for that reason, and because he was led to believe that he could count on French support, Barghash finally repudiated the treaty. So, when Frere left for home in March, he had failed to achieve the purpose of his mission. The immediate result was a sharp fall in British prestige all down the coast. The British Government, it was said, were not strong enough to get their way.

Frere had argued that the sea-trade in slaves could be stopped by treating their shipment as piracy and by a stricter interpretation of the old treaty of 1845. And it was on his orders that on May 1, when the annual trading-season opened, the British naval patrol was instructed to prevent the export of slaves from the coastal ports. But by now Frere's dispatches had reached London, and the Government had decided that the legality and effectiveness of Frere's policy were equally dubious and that the only clean method of gaining their end and satisfying public opinion was to get the new treaty signed. Kirk was accordingly instructed to inform the Sultan that, unless he accepted the treaty without delay, Zanzibar would be cut off from the world by a naval blockade. Kirk received these orders on June 2. Next day he presented the ultimatum. When Barghash tried to argue, ' I have not come to discuss,' he said, ' but to dictate.' Turning to the sheikhs of the Sultan's council, whose presence he had requested for this very purpose, he insisted that they must share the responsibility for the decision. If they did not like it, they must not turn against the Sultan after it. He urged them to submit. The alternative, he said, was war—the only kind of war that England could wage against a defenceless state.

That night Barghash invited Kirk again to the palace and asked him to explain the situation to another group

of Arab notables. The same thing happened the following
night, and on this occasion Barghash finally and fully
surrendered. Next morning, June 5, the treaty was signed,
sealed and ratified by the Sultan and signed on the British
Government's behalf by Kirk. On that same day, on the
Sultan's orders, the great slave-market at Zanzibar was
closed for ever.

Thus, almost within a month of Livingstone's death,
the prime object of his life had been more than half
attained. More than half, but not completely ; for the
slavers, unable now to move their slaves by sea, moved
them by land instead. Almost as many as before were
brought down from the Nyasa country to Kilwa, thence
marched right up the coast as far as Somaliland, and sold
off at the coast-towns as they went. When they came
abreast of Pemba, several of them were regularly smuggled
over to the island by night. It soon became clear that it
was no good abolishing the Trade by sea unless it were
also abolished by land.

It was Kirk who got this done. His prestige at Zanzibar
had been greatly enhanced by the sequel to the Frere
Mission, and on Frere's recommendation he had been
raised to the status of a Consul-General and provided at
last with an adequate staff. He had more time now for
touring up and down the coast and for making personal
contacts with some of the leading chiefs. Before long the
name of the ' great *balozi* (consul) ' was known and
honoured throughout East Africa. As early as 1875,
indeed, Cameron reported that the Arabs in the heart of
the continent regarded him as ' a sort of second Sultan.'
And, since Kirk was careful always to use his growing
power to strengthen the Sultan's authority, it was not in
the least resented by Barghash. On the contrary he came
to rely on Kirk not merely as a shrewd adviser but as a
friend, the best and trustiest, perhaps, of all his friends.
And it was this that made it possible for Kirk to bring
about the abolition of the trade in slaves by land. Barghash had observed the treaty with scrupulous loyalty :

he had done all he could to help the naval patrols ; he had punished those few of his subjects who had ventured to defy his orders ; and now when, with the cordial backing of the Foreign Office, Kirk pointed out that the Trade was by no means dead and that there was only one way of killing it, he made no difficulty at all. On April 13, 1875, he signed two proclamations, drafted for him by Kirk, forbidding ' all conveyance of slaves by land under any conditions ' and declaring in particular that any slaves brought down from the Nyasa country would be confiscated.

Those proclamations, Kirk told Lord Derby, were ' the most effectual step yet taken ' to stop the steady devastation and depopulation of mid-East Africa. It was true. The Arab Slave Trade between the Great Lakes and the Indian Ocean had received a mortal blow. A trickle of smuggling continued for some years, but as a regular organised business the infamous Trade was dead. The ' open sore ' had been healed at last.

NOTES AND REFERENCES

8   [1] W. G. Blaikie, *Personal Life of David Livingstone* (6th ed., London, 1925), 46.

    [2] *Ibid.*, 69.

14   [1] *Ibid.*, 221.

15   [1] *Ibid.*, 115.

    [2] *Ibid.*, 190.

    [3] *Ibid.*, 253.

    [4] *Ibid.*, 261.   [5] *Ibid.*, 263.

16   [1] *Kirk on the Zambesi*, 242-44.

    [2] *Ibid.*, 105-6.

    [3] *Ibid.*, 242-45.

    [4] E.g., R. & T. Lander, *Niger Journal* (London, 1832), iii. 74-7 ; Grant, *A Walk Across Africa* (1864), 211 ; Thomson, *To the Central African Lakes and back* (1881), ii. 133-34, 162-63, 201-2.

17   [1] *Kirk on the Zambesi*, 192.

    [2] *Ibid.*

18   [1] *Ibid.*, 240.

    [2] Baines denied the charge, and Kirk's diary confirms the view that he was, to say the least, ungenerously treated. See *Kirk on the Zambesi*, 158-62 ; J. P. R. Walls, *Thomas Baines* (London, 1941), chap. iv.

    [3] *Kirk on the Zambesi*, 181.

    [4] *Ibid.*, 180.

19   [1] E. D. Young, *The Search after Livingstone* (London, 1868), 15.

20   [1] *Kirk on the Zambesi*, 190.

    [2] *Ibid.*, 250.

21   [1] *Ibid.*, 183.

    [2] *Ibid.*, 247.

    [3] These and other letters are in the Kirk Papers in the Bodleian.

22   [1] *The Zambesi and its Tributaries*, 583-4.

23   [1] Blaikie, 284-6.

    [2] *Ibid.*, 287.

    [3] *Ibid.*, 264.

25   [1] Writing to Waller in 1872, Livingstone says that, on his recommendation, the leadership of the expedition was offered to Kirk who refused it. (For his reasons see p. 26 above.) L. to W., 1872-3, unfinished. Waller Papers.

    [2] Blaikie, 293-4.

    [3] *The Zambesi and its Tributaries*, vi.

26   [1] L. to K., 13, v. 65. Kirk Papers.

    [2] Blaikie, 301.

27   [1] L. to W., 27, ix. 65. Waller Papers.

28   [1] Livingstone, *Missionary Travels and Researches in South Africa* (London, 1912 ed.), 164-65. Only two of the 27 were Makololo by blood : the rest were men from neighbouring districts who had been incorporated in the Makololo tribe.

PAGE
29 [1] Blaikie, 304.
    [2] L. to W., 27, ix. 65. Waller Papers.
    [3] L. to W., 27, ix. 65 and 26, x. 65. Waller Papers.
30 [1] L. to Layard, 28, ix. 65. B. M. add. MS. 39117, f. 190.
31 [1] W. E. Oswell, *William Cotton Oswell* (London, 1900), ii. 91.
    [2] L. to K., 1, i. 66. Kirk Papers.
33 [1] L. to W., 26. x. 15, xi. 2, xii. 65. Waller Papers.
    [2] L. to Agnes L., 29, i. 66. Blaikie, 311.
34 [1] Translated from the Arabic. *Last Journals*, i. 6.
    [2] Blaikie, 311.
35 [1] *The Search after Livingstone* (London, 1868), 22-4.
    [2] W. F. W. Owen, R.N., *Narrative of Voyages to explore the shores
       of Africa, Arabia and Madagascar* (London, 1833), i. 184. For
       their amusing relations with British naval officers calling at
       Johanna, see R. Coupland, *East Africa and its Invaders* (Oxford,
       1938), 163-64, 173.
    [3] *Zanzibar* (London, 1872), i. 341-42.
    [4] L. to W., 15, xi. 65. Waller Papers.
36 [1] L. to K., 13, v. 65. Kirk Papers.
    [2] *What led to the Discovery of the Source of the Nile* (London, 1864),
       357.
    [3] *Ibid.*, 252-53.
37 [1] See *East Africa and its Invaders*, 324-25.
    [2] *Last Journals*, i. 8. Livingstone does not name the ' old man,'
       but it must have been Ludha Damji (for whom see *East Africa
       and its Invaders*, 325). The information as to ' Koorji's ' status
       was kindly obtained for me by Mr. R. H. Crofton from an
       old Indian resident at Zanzibar in 1931. It was the firm, of
       course, not Koorji personally, that farmed the customs. The
       Banians are the traders' caste.
    [3] *Zanzibar*, i. 485.
46 [1] *Kirk on the Zambesi*, 207.
48 [1] Eight sepoys arrived at Zanzibar in October, 1866. (Seward
       to Chief Sec. Bombay, 25, x. 66 ; K.P., Ia, 244.) Seward
       notes : ' Their unfitness for African travel might have been
       predicted ' (Seward to Stanley, 10, xii. 66. ; *Ibid.*, 236).
       According to Musa's story (see pp. 60-2 above) the *havildar* died
       of dysentery on the way to the coast (K.P. Ia, 235). Four
       sepoys remain unaccounted for.
49 [1] For his meeting with E. D. Young in 1875, see p. 65, note, above.
    [2] L. to W., 3, xi. 66. Waller Papers.
50 [1] *Last Journals*, i. 115. L. to Kirk, 5, ii. 71. Kirk Papers.
    [2] For the naming of this range, see *Kirk on the Zambesi*, 256. It
       is to be hoped that the name will be perpetuated in modern
       maps of Nyasaland.
53 [1] Writing to Seward, eight months after the event, Livingstone
       gives a rather different version of the loss of his medicine.
       The culprit is now one of the Nassick boys who had given
       trouble from the start. ' He was determined not to work

when we left the coast and told me to take my gun and shoot him if I insisted on the very easy work of leading a mule and did not allow him to load it with a big bag of maize he had bought as private stores. I tried a simple instrument in the shape of a stick to his back. He did not venture to rebel again, but was a nuisance by remaining behind in the march, and at last gave his load to a country lad, and went off to collect mushrooms ; came up with his bonnet full of them, but minus his bundle which contained all our medicines, tools, and six large tablecloths. This was in a part so densely covered with forest no pursuit could be made.' Livingstone allowed the boy to go back to Zanzibar with the bearer of this letter. L. to Seward, 25, ix. 67 ; K.P., Ib., 153.

54   [1] Writing to Sir Roderick Murchison (2. ii. 67), Livingstone speaks of the loss of the medicine as ' the sorest loss of goods I ever sustained.' ' I am hoping, if fever comes, to fend it off by native remedies and trust in the watchful care of a Higher Power.' *Proceedings of the Royal Geographical Society*, xii. 175.
[2] L. to Seward, Bemba, 1, ii. 67. K.P. Ib, 131-32.

57   [1] Hamees and some of the other Arab traders started back for Zanzibar in September 1867, and Livingstone entrusted them with a letter to Seward which was received by Churchill in August, 1868. In this letter Livingstone warmly commended his Arab friends. ' I send a note to His Highness Seyed Majid by this same opportunity, acknowledging the kindness of his people. I also give notes to the three head Arabs as sort of testimonials. They have behaved like gentlemen all through.' In the same letter Livingstone casually refers to the ' tedious process ' of peace-making, which ' detained me one-and-a-half months, drinking blood. Don't shudder, my dear fellow ; it is in homeopathic doses. My love to Mrs. Seward and Dr. Kirk.' L. to Seward, 25, ix. 67. K.P. Ib, 153.

58   [1] This dispatch was never sent for lack of writing-paper : it was incorporated in the journal : i. 254-268. Writing to Seward from Casembe's on December 14, Livingstone says, ' I am going to Ujiji in two days.' K.P. Ib, 154.

59   [1] L. to Frere, July 1868 : *P.R.G.S.*, xiv. 13. He started with five men, but Amoda ran away back after one day. He left his ' bundle ' behind ; so Livingstone characteristically sent it after him by a messenger.

60   [1] Cited by Seward to Lord Stanley, 10, xii. 66 ; K.P. Ia, 234.

62   [1] Seward to Lord Stanley, 10. xii, 66, and 23, xii. 66, K.P. Ia, 234, 236. K.'s report, 237-39. Seward to Stanley, 26, i. 67 (*re* Kilwa traders), 240 ; 22, iii. 67 (*re* examination at Johanna), 245. Sunley's report, 246-47. Sultan of Johanna to Political Agent, Zanzibar, iii. 9, 67, Zanzibar Archives, *Inward Miscellaneous*, Oct. 1865 to Dec. 1868.
[2] Kirk had written these words earlier to Murchison, but his

letter had gone *via* the Cape and arrived later than the letter
to Asst. Sec. Bates which went *via* Aden.

63 [1] K. to M., 19, xii, 66. *P.R.G.S.*, xi, 142.

[2] *P.R.G.S.*, xi. 144-46.

[3] E. D. Young's letter to Murchison communicated to *The Times*,
18, iii. 67.

64 [1] See Murchison's presidential address to the R.G.S., May 27,
1867 (*Journal*, vol. xxxvii, pp. cxxvii-cxxx).

[2] When Young traversed this route again in 1875, on the way
to found a mission-station on Lake Nyasa (Livingstonia), he
found that these graves had been carefully protected by the
local natives. *Nyassa, a Journal of Adventures, etc.* (London,
1877), 26, 31, 38, 168.

65 [1] The Expedition is described by Young in his report to the
R.G.S. (*Journal*, xxxviii. 111-118) and with more detail in
The Search after Livingstone. The finding of the evidence, pp.
139-201. H. Faulkner in *Elephant Haunts* (London, 1868) gives
a better and fuller account, with digressions on sport, especially in ' Elephant Marsh.' The evidence, pp. 112-18, 150-51.

66 [1] Churchill to Stanley, 28, ix. and 5, x. 67, enclosing depositions :
K.P. Ia, 257-262. K.'s official report on the evidence, 260-61.
—Bundouky's arrival and statement, Churchill to Stanley, 27,
i. 68 ; K.P. Ib, 129-31. Bundouky (gun) was more properly
called Maguru Mafupee (short legs) : *ibid.*, 129. He was
given the letters because he claimed to be in the service of
the British Consul at Zanzibar. Ludha Damji explained that
he had accompanied Burton and Speke on their first journey
to Tanganyika (K.P. Ia, 258-59).—Refusal of wages, *ibid.*,
259. Another reason for not paying them was that the amount
claimed exceeded the small sum left by Livingstone at
Zanzibar for current expenses (*ibid.*, 246).—Sultan of Johanna's letter. ' I have made up my mind that those wreches
(sic) shall be punished with as much severity as I am able to
inflict. . . . I thought of putting them to death, but the law
will not allow me as it was no capital crime they were guilty
of.' Sultan of J. to P.A., Zanzibar, 13, iii. 68 ; Zanzibar
Archives, *Inward Miscellaneous*, Oct. 1865—Dec. 1868.—After
eight months in irons (a severe punishment in a Johanna gaol)
Musa was sent by the Sultan to Zanzibar for further punishment or liberation. The P.A. (Kirk ?) released him with a
caution not to return to Johanna without the Sultan's permission, Jan. 1869. Zanzibar Archives, *Bombay to Agency*,
1868-72.

67 [1] *R.G.S. Journal*, vol. xxxviii, pp. cxciv-cxcviii.

70 [1] Churchill to Stanley, 27, i. 68. (K.P. Ib, 129).

71 [1] *Ibid.* Livingstone had said, ' We may be at Tanganyika by
May.' (1867). As has been seen, he reached the Lake in
April, but, instead of proceeding to Ujiji, turned west and
south for nearly two years.

PAGE

2 Churchill to Stanley, 19, viii. 68. L. to Seward, 25, ix. and 14, xii. 67. K.P. Ib, 152-54.

72   1 L. to K., 17, xi. 71, India Office Records.

73   1 L. to K., 130, v. 69, *East Coast of Africa, Correspondence respecting the Slave Trade*, 1869, C. 141, 16-17.
     2 Seward to Stanley, 23, xii. 66. K.P. a, 236-37.
     3 K. to Churchill, 12, ix. 68 (K.P. Ib, 160) on private information from Mozambique.

75   1 L. to K., 30, v. 69, *Slave Trade Correspondence*, cited above, p. 17.

91   1 R. J. Campbell, *Livingstone* (London, 1929), 317.

92   1 *The Exploitation of East Africa*, 58-9.
     2 See p. 72 above.

93   1 K.P. Ic, 63. Kirk says that he had received another letter from Livingstone on September 7 and had done what it asked of him. Presumably this was one of several letters dispatched by Livingstone before he reached Ujiji, asking for goods but not for money ; and the goods, no doubt, were sent off by Arab caravan. There is no record of what became of them.

96   1 K. to Sec. to Govt. of Bombay, Political Dept., 11, v. 72 : India Office Records. Churchill to Granville, 18, viii. 70 : *East Coast of Africa, Correspondence respecting the Slave Trade*, 1871, p. 42.

99   1 The story is told in detail in Livingstone's ' Complaint,' see p. 185 above, and less fully in sundry letters. It is based on information extracted by Livingstone from the seven men and on what he learned from Sherif and others on his return to Ujiji in 1871. Kirk did not question the facts : K. to Govt. of Bombay, 11, v. 72. The five deaths from cholera were reported by Churchill to Granville, 18, viii. 70 : cited p. 96 note above.

100 1 L. to K., 17, xi. 71 : India Office Records.

107 1 For this document see p. 72, note above.

109 1 Blaikie, 342.
     2 Campbell, 335.
     3 Originals in the Kirk Papers in the Bodleian (Rhodes House Library).

114 1 Kirk himself noted this evidence that some at least of the quinine he sent had reached Livingstone in the margin of his copy of the *Last Journals*, ii. 129.

133 1 H. M. Stanley, *How I found Livingstone* (New York, 1872), 411-12. The date given by Stanley for his arrival at Ujiji, Nov. 10, must clearly be accepted in place of that given in Livingstone's journal, Oct. 28. Similarly, the date which Stanley, after hearing a full account from Livingstone of his travels, gives for Livingstone's arrival at Ujiji (Oct. 16), though obviously less certain, may be taken as probable.

134 1 *Autobiography of Sir Henry Morton Stanley*, ed. Lady Stanley (London, 1909), vi.

PAGE

136   [1] *Ibid.*, 213.

138   [1] *Ibid.*, 244.

139   [1] *The Times*, 1869 ; Jan. 20, April 19, 20, July 16, Sept. 6, 7, 15, Oct. 1.

141   [1] H. M. Stanley, *How I found Livingstone* (1st ed., London, 1872), xviii-xix. The last sentence of this paragraph is one of several passages in the book which, though purporting to have been written or spoken at the time, seem more like 'afterthoughts.'

143   [1] *The Times*, Nov. 6, 24, Dec. 9, 1869 ; Jan. 7, 1870.
      [2] *P.R.G.S.*, xiv. 39.
      [3] *The Times*, Feb. 5, 6, March 15, Dec. 24, 1870.

144   [1] K. to Murchison, 14, vi. 70 : *The Times*, July 19, 1870.
      [2] K. to Pol. Sec. Govt. of Bombay, 11, v. 72. India Office Records.

145   [1] K. to G. of B., 13, ix. 72. India Office Records.

146   [1] K. to G., 18, ii. 71 ; K P. I. f., 56-7. K. to G. of B., 13, ix. 72 ; India Office Records.

147   [1] *East Africa and its Invaders*, 295 ff.

149   [1] *Select Committee's Report on East African Slave Trade* (No. 420 of 1871), xi. *The Exploitation of East Africa*, 60.

150   [1] *The Exploitation of East Africa*, 98-9.

151   [1] *How I found Livingstone*, 18. Fraser's initials were H. A., not H. C.
      [2] At the outset his company was subsidiary to the respectable Bombay firm of Nicol & Co., whose managers were assumed, later on, to have been unaware of Fraser's subsequent conduct.

152   [1] For further details and references to dispatches, see *The Exploitation of East Africa*, 178-81.

154   [1] *How I found Livingstone*, 14-15. According to Stanley, Kirk said that Livingstone was now too old to keep a scientific record of his explorations and, asked if he were a modest man, admitted that he was ' not quite an angel ' and knew the value of his discoveries. If Kirk did say such things, it was unlike his usual shrewdness ; but of course he had no notion that what he said would be published without any further reference to him.

158   [1] Frere's memorandum, cited below.

163   [1] *The Exploitation of East Africa*, 67-8.

164   [1] *Ibid.*, 263-65, 363.

170   [1] Reprinted in the *Daily Telegraph*, 29, vii. 72.

176   [1] *Autobiography*, 279-280.
      [2] Blaikie, 359.

177   [1] L. to W. ix. 72. Waller Papers.
      [2] Blaikie, 438-52.
      [3] *Autobiography*, 284.

178   [1] *Ibid.*, 276.
      [2] *Autobiography*, 277.

183   [1] *Ibid.*, 274-75.

PAGE
184 [1] K. to M. 22, ix. 71 ; *P.R.G.S.*, xvi. 103 ; K. to Granville, 22, ix. 71 ; K.P., I. f, 143 ; K. to Rawlinson, 15, i. 72 ; *P.R.G.S.*, xvi. 226.

184 [1] L. to W., xi. 71 : Waller Papers.

185 [1] L. to M., 13, iii. 72 : *P.R.G.S.*, xvi. 433.
[2] L. to Murchison, 13, iii. 72 : *loc. cit.*
[3] This and other letters were published in *The Times* and other London newspapers on September 27, 1872, and also in an appendix to Stanley's book.

186 [1] *How I found Livingstone*, 663.
[2] See last note but one.

187 [1] L. to K. vi. 72 Kirk Papers.

189 [1] *The Exploitation of East Africa*, 55-57.

190 [1] *P.R.G.S.*, xv. 116, 206, 335.
[2] *Ibid.*, 310. Mr. C. R. Markham's address (Jan. 22) : *P.R.G.S.*, xv. 158-63.

191 [1] *P.R.G.S.*, xvi. 159-64.
[2] *Ibid.*, 184-87.

192 [1] Quoted in K. to G. of B., 13, ix. 72 : India Office Records.

193 [1] J. Christie, *Cholera Epidemics in East Africa* (London, 18), 427.
[2] L. to Granville, 1, vii. 72.

194 [1] *The Times*, 27, vii. 72.
[2] *P.R.G.S.*, xvi. 419-33.

195 [1] *Life, Wanderings and Labours in Eastern Africa* (London, 1873), 517-19.
[2] *P.R.G.S.*, xvi. 425.
[3] *How I found Livingstone*, 712.

196 [1] K. to Granville, 28, v. 72. *How I found Livingstone*, 709-10.

198 [1] *Daily Telegraph*, 25 and 27, vii. 72.
[2] *Daily Telegraph* and *The Times*, 2, viii. 72.

199 [1] *D.T.*, 26, vii. 72 ; *The Times*, 3, viii. 72.
[2] *D.T.*, 29, vii. 72.
[3] *Bombay Gazette*, 25, vi. 72.
[4] *Standard*, 26, vii. 72.

200 [1] W. to L., begun 12, viii. continued 28, viii. 72. Waller Papers.

202 [1] L. to G., i., vii. 72.

203 [1] *T.T.*, 29. vii. 72.
[2] *Echo*, 26, vii. 72.
[3] *Standard*, 27. vii. 72.
[4] *T.T.*, 3, viii. 72.
[5] *E.S.*, 30, vii. 72.

204 [1] *S.R.*, 3. viii. 72.
[2] *S.R.*, 'Reviler' : *Letters of J. R. Green* (London, 1901), 182.
[3] *T.T.*, 14, ix. 71.
[4] R. to S., 6, viii. 72 ; *T.T.*, 8, viii. 72.

205 [1] *Nature*, vi. May to Oct., 1872, p. 347.
[2] *How I found Livingstone*, 684.
[3] Report of the *British Association for the Advancement of Science*, 1872 : Proceedings of Sections, 209-14.

PAGE
206 [1] *Nature*, loc. cit. ; *T.T.*, 16, viii. 72.
     [2] *T.T.*, 23, viii. 72.
     [3] *How I found Livingstone*, 680-82.
     [4] *Ibid.*, 684. The text of Rawlinson's letter has been quoted
         above. It was published on August 6 and would have been
         written earlier, as Rawlinson afterwards explained, if he and
         his colleagues had not left London for the August Holiday.
         Stanley left Paris for London on August 1.
     [5] *Ibid.*, 683-88. Grant is accused of disliking, as Speke's friend,
         ' to hear any other person claiming to have discovered another
         Nile source.'
207 [1] *Autobiography*, 289.
     [2] *T.T.*, 13, ix. 72.
208 [1] G. to S., 27, viii. 72. *How I found Livingstone*, 719.
     [2] *Autobiography*, 289-91.
     [3] *T.T.*, 19, x. 72.
209 [1] *T.T.*, 22, x. 72.
210 [1] *Scotsman*, 1, xi. 72.
     [2] *North British Mail*, 21, x. 72.
211 [1] *T.T.*, 5, xi. 72.
     [2] *T.T.*, 7, xi. 72.
     [3] *How I found Livingstone*, 712-13.
212 [1] K. to Government of Bombay, 13, ix. 72 : India Office.
     [2] *Correspondence respecting Sir Bartle Frere's Mission*, 1873 (C.—820),
         49.
213 [1] L. to W., 9, ix. 72 : Waller Papers.
     [2] *Correspondence respecting Sir Bartle Frere's Mission*, 1873 (C.—820),
         49-51.
215 [1] 29, viii. 73.
     [2] *T.T.*, 13, viii. 73.
216 [1] Blaikie, 355-64.
     [2] E.g., R. J. Campbell, *Livingstone* (London, 1929), 323 ; J. I.
         Macnair, *Livingstone the Liberator* (London, 1940), 323, 329,
         342-43.
217 [1] *P.R.G.S.*, xvii. 13, 56, 137, 204-5 ; xix. 79-104. Young ulti-
         mately gave over £3000. *Ibid.*, 79.
     [2] *Ibid.*, 158.
219 [1] V. L. Cameron, *Across Africa* (London, 1877), i. chaps. i.-ix.
     [2] *How I found Livingstone*, 436.
     [3] L. to W., 10, i. 72 : Waller Papers.
222 [1] L. to Maclear and Mann ; Blaikie, 359. Similar passage in
         Livingstone's first letter to Bennett ; Stanley, *How I found
         Livingstone*, 618.
223 [1] L. to I. B. Braithwaite, Jan., 1872 ; *P.R.G.S.*, xviii. 279.
236 [1] L. to W., 2, ix. 72 (unfinished) : Waller Papers.
     [2] Blaikie, 374.
     [3] *Ibid.*, 370.
     [4] *Ibid.*, 373-4.
251 [1] Cameron, i. 171-241.

PAGE
253   [1] Prideaux to Granville, 10, ii. and 8 and 12, iii. 74. *Correspondence, etc.*, 41-8. Final certainty as to the identity of the body was attained when a further examination in London showed the un-united fracture of the shoulder which had resulted from Livingstone's being mauled by a lion in 1844. Blaikie, 381.

INDEX

Abyssinia, 25, 39.

Africa, its exploration, 23-25 ; topography, 39-41, 101-102 ; native population, 41-43 ; effects of slave raids, 42, 51, 78, 102.

Ajawa, 29, 64 ; conflict with the, 13, 16.

Albert Nyanza Lake, 24, 40, 67.

Amoda, 35, 50, 225.

Angola, 11, 14.

Arab trade routes, 36, 43 ; " colony " at Unyanyembe, 36, 43, 163 ; Slave Trade, 10, 27, 42, 43, 48, 87-88, 102-103, 110-111, 148-150, 151, 254-257 ; Livingstone's dependence on, 56-59, 65, 67-70, 81 ; obstruction, 48, 54, 73, 93, 119, 145, 195 ; cruelty, 86-87, 128 ; the Mirambo conflict, 163-164.

Bagamoyo, 36, 40, 54, 66, 144, 145, 159, 190, 192, 195, 252.

Baggage—animals, 38, 41 ; almost useless, 27-28 ; buffaloes as, 30, 35 ; purchase, 35 ; maltreatment and death of, 47, 229.

Baines, 18, 183.

Baker, Sir Samuel, 24, 63, 75, 139.

Bambarré, 77, 78, 79, 80, 81, 82-91, 130.

Bangweolo, Lake, 59, 60, 67, 68, 229, 233, 237.

Bantus, 41.

" Banyan slaves," 92 ; story on recruitment, 95-96 ; their private trading, 97-98 ; truculent attitude, 100, 103, 107-108, 115, 117 ; increase native's distrust, 103-104, 118-119 ; at Ujiji, 132. See also Sherif.

Barghash, relations with Kirk, 149-150, 254-256.

Bates, 139.

Batoka highlands, 8-9 ; settlement, 11.

Bedingfeld, 18, 183.

Beke, 205.

Bemba, Lake. See Bangweolo Lake.

Bennett, J. G., 137, 138, 170, 176 ; interview with Stanley, 140-141.

Blaikie, W. G., 249 ; Personal Life of David Livingstone, 11, 216.

Bogharib, Mohamad, 68, 69, 81, 89, 100, 102, 110, 118, 129.

Bombay Marine Battalion, 28, 30.

Bombay, voyage to, 22 ; preparations in, 27-33.

British Anti-Slavery Movement, The (Coupland), 9.

British Government and the Slave Trade, 9-10, 148-149, 254-257.

Buckley, Patrick, 64.

Bundouky, 66.

Burton, 24, 36, 37, 74 ; on Johanna men, 35.

Buxton's "positive" policy, 9, 11.

Cambridge lecture (1857), 15.

Cameron, Lt. V. Lovett, 174, 217-219, 250-252.

Cape Delgado, 25.

Cape of Good Hope, 10, 11, 39.

Caseme's, 58, 59, 71.

Chambezi, River, 52, 66, 237, 250.

Chawendi's, fight at, 250.

Chitamba's, 56, 57.

Chitambo's, 245-246, 248, 251, 252.

Chobe, River, 8.

Cholera epidemic, 83, 91, 94-95, 96, 145.

Chonaune, 8.

Chuma, 22, 29, 49, 50, 80, 108, 176, 225, 237, 243, 244, 245, 246, 247, 248, 249, 251, 252, 253.

Churchill, H. A., 55, 66, 70-71, 92, 139, 144, 149-150, 153, 198-199.

Clarendon, Lord, 58, 92.

Columbine, H.M.S., 144, 145.

Comoro Islands, 35.

Congo, River, 8, 24, 43, 59, 66, 75.

Cook, Helen, 32.

Cooley, W. D., 108, 113, 115-116, 139.

Coupland, Sir Reginald, The British Anti-Slavery Movement, 9 ; Kirk on the Zambesi, 12, 22, 104, 223 ; The Exploitation of East Africa, 20, 42, 94, 148, 150, 191, 254 ; East Africa and its Invaders, 30, 163.

Damji, Ludha, 95, 97, 99, 186 ; Livingstone on, 37, 185.

Dawson,, Lt. L. S., 191-193, 194.

Dickinson, 64.

Dillon, W. E., 218, 251, 252.

Dugumbé, Hassani, 78, 89, 100, 116-117, 118-120 ; and the massacre at Nyangwé, 120-127.

East Africa and its Invaders (Coupland), 30, 163.

Expedition, Niger (1841), 9 ; across Africa (1853-55), 11, 17, 28 ; Zambesi, (1858-63), 12-13, 17-22, 24, 28, 35, 50, 63 ; Young (1867), 63-66, 67, 90 ; Search (1872), 190-193 ; Grandy,

217 ; Search (1873), 217-219, 250-
252. *See also* Personnel *and* Supplies.
Exploitation of East Africa, The (Coupland)
20, 42, 94, 148, 150, 191, 254.

Farijala, 248.
Farquhar, W. L., 158, 161-162, 185, 188.
Faulkner, Lt. H., 64.
Food, in Ujiji, 36 ; scarcity, 51, 54, 57,
145, 228-229, 230, 232.
Fort Jameson, 50.
Fraser, H. C., " hire " of slaves, 151-
152 ; letter to the *Bombay Gazette*, 199,
212.
Frere, Sir Bartle, 27, 28, 31, 32, 33, 34,
200 ; Mission, 210, 254-256 ; report,
213-215.

Gardner, 80, 225.
Garforth, Lt., 38.
Gladstone, W. E., 23.
Grandy, Lt. W. J., 217.
Grant, 24, 205.
" Great Rift Valley," 40.

Habib, Syde bin, 68, 70, 87, 89.
Hamees, 57.
Hassani, incident on the Lualaba, 104.
Henn, Lt. W., 190-192, 194.
Hongo, 42, 161, 172, 187, 251 ; evaded
by Stanley, 167-168.
How I Found Livingstone (Stanley), 140,
156-157, 204, 206-207, 211.

Indian merchants, 37, 43 ; in Slave
Trade, 93.
Ivory Trade, 43, 68, 78, 86-87.

Johanna men, 47 ; their character, 35 ;
desertion, 49-50, 54 ; account of
Livingstone's " death," 60-62 ; punishment, 66 ; Sultan of, 62, 66.

Kalahari Desert, 8, 11, 14.
Karungu's, 57.
Kasakera, 251, 252.
Katanga copper belt, 43, 85-86.
Katonga's, 87.
Kenya, 39 ; Mt., 8.
Kilimanjaro, Mt., 8, 191.
Kilwa, 50, 53, 60, 63, 66, 73, 256.
Kirk, John, 14, 17, 25, 73, 92, 101, 142,
191, 193, 194, 195, 252, 253 ; char-
acter, 15, 16, 31 ; on Livingstone, 15,
18, 20-21 ; early career, 19-20 ; the
Zambesi Expedition, 20-21, 63 ; rela-
tions with Livingstone, 21-22, 26, 31-
32, 63, 182 ; and the Slave Trade,
31-32, 109, 112, 149-150, 201, 254,
255-257 ; and Musa's story, 61, 62,

63, 66 ; **and** supplies to Livingstone,
71, 72, 74-75, 90, 92-93, 95-96, 100,
116, 143, 146, 163 ; and cholera, 91,
95, 96 ; Livingstone's letters to, 109-
117 ; Stanley's prejudice against, 147,
150-151, 152-156, 157 ; Stanley's
attack on 182-187, 198 *et seq.* ; the
defence, 199-202, 210, 212-213 ;
Frere's report, 213-215.
Kirk on the Zambesi (Coupland), 12, 22,
104, 223.
Kolobeng, 8.
Koorji (Kooverji Valabdhas), 72, 95 ;
Livingstone on, 37, 70-71.
Kuruman, 8.

Lacerda, 58.
Lady Nyassa, 22, 35 ; its sale, 27.
Layard, A. H., 30.
Letters, difficulties of transmission, 48,
60, 70, 72-73, 91 ; to Kirk, 109-117.
Lipanza, River, 231.
Lithabo, River, 231.
Livingstone, Agnes, 23, 29, 109, 110,
209, 219.
Livingstone, Charles, 18, 20, 21, 23.
Livingstone, David, *The Zambesi and its
Tributaries*, 12, 14, 23 ; *Missionary
Travel and Researches in South Africa*, 14 ;
early travels (1842-51), 8-9 ; march
across Africa, 11, 14, 17, 28 ; Zambesi
Expedition, 12-14, 18-19, 24 ; voyage
to Bombay, 22 ; return home, 22-23 ;
last expedition, finances, aims and
status, 24-26 ; massacre at Nyangwé,
120-127 ; ambushed, 128-129 ; the
coming of Stanley, 133, 169 ; failing
strength, 233 *et seq.* ; death, 246 ;
return to Zanzibar, 247 *et seq.* ; on
African settlement, 10-11, 12, 223 ;
on Slave Trade, 32, 34, 45, 73, 110-
111, 222-223, 236 ; on Ujiji, 36, 73 ;
on travel, 38-39 ; on the Lualaba, 102,
103, 112, 117, 221-222 ; on Nyangwé
markets, 106-107 ; resolution, 14-16,
50, 53-54, 56, 84, 172, 219, 228 ;
humanity, 13, 16, 67, 178-179, 231 ;
physical endurance, 16-17, 131 ; disappointments at Ujiji, 70-73, 131-132 ;
health, 17, 21, 23, 51, 52-53, 55-56,
68-70, 74, 77, 79, 81, 82, 126, 128,
130, 131, 169, 173, 219, 224, 227-229,
232 *et seq.* ; isolation, 89-91, 169, 220 ;
dreams, 83-86, 221 ; grievances, 107-
108, 183, 184-186, 235 ; rumours of
his whereabouts, 137-138, 139, 142-
144 ; dependence on Arabs, 56-59, 65,
67-70, 81, 89, 100, 117, 118-120 ; and
Kirk, 19-22, 109-117, 184-186, 187 ;
and Stanley, 169, 176-181 ; Stanley
on, 180-181, 183.

Livingstone, Mary, her death, 14, 15, 64, 69.
Livingstone, Oswell, 23, 187, 199, 210, 213 ; and the Search Expedition (1871), 191-195.
Loanda to Makololand (1854-55), 11.
Loangwa, River, 50, 51.
Lofuko, River, 68.
Lomamé, 117, 118.
London Missionary Society, 8.
Lualaba, River, 59, 67, 77-78, 79, 80, 81, 82, 101, 102, 103, 112, 222, 229 ; its narrows, 104-105, 117.
Luamo, River, 78.
Luapanya, battle with Bogharib, 102.
Luapula, River, 246, 249.
Lueki, River, 103, 105.
Lukangu, 217.
Lusizé, River, 172.

Mambotsa, 8.
Mabruki, 225.
Mackenzie, Bishop, 12-13, 48, 52, 64 ; on Livingstone, 17 ; on Kirk, 20.
Magomero, 29, 64.
Majid, Seyd bin, 132, 133.
Majid, Seyyid, 30, 33, 38, 48, 66, 75, 147, 149 ; connections with Slave Trade, 33-34, 148 ; his authority, 34, 48, 56, 58, 93-94.
Majwara, 245, 246.
Makololand to Loanda (1853-54), 11, 28.
Makololo, 19, 28, 50, 64, 65 ; Livingstone's visits to the, 9, 15 ; involved in slavery, 10.
Mamohela, 80.
Manganja, 64.
Manyema, 67, 77-81 ; Livingstone on, 74-75, 86-87, 88.
Marenga, Chief, 49, 65.
Massacre at Nyangwé, 120-127.
Matabele, 51.
Mataka, Chief, 45, 47, 51, 189.
Matipa, 237-239.
Mazitu raids, 45-46, 49-50, 51, 52, 61, 64, 73.
Medicines, 69, 71, 74, 75, 145 ; loss of, 52-54, 55 ; request for, 54-55, 70.
Merera's, 228.
Mikindani, 38, 39, 40, 53, 73 ; departure from, 45, 46, 47.
Mirambo, 163-164, 174.
Missionary Travel and Researches in South Africa (Livingstone), 14.
Moffat, Robert, 218.
Molilamo, River, 243.
Mozambique revolt, 73.
Mpapwa, 188.
Mponda's, 49.
Mpweto's, 59, 67.
Muanampunda, 129.

Mulundini, Mt. of " Kirk's Range," 50.
Murchison Falls, 64.
Murchison, Sir Roderick, 24-25, 62-64, 66, 139, 142-143, 185, 190, 200.
Murphy, Lt. C., 218, 251.
Murray, Mungo, 8.
Musa, 51 ; his character, 35, 63 ; his desertion, 49-50 ; account of Livingstone's " death," 60-62, 64, 65 ; punishment, 66.
Masunya, Lake, 168.
Mweru, Lake, 56, 58, 59, 229.

Nasangwa, Chief, 80, 81.
Nassick boys, 29, 46, 47, 50, 225.
Ndonde, 29.
New, Rev. Charles, 191-193, 194.
New York Herald, 137 ; Livingstone's letters to, 170-171, 197, 203-204, 209.
Ngami, Lake, 8.
Niger Expedition (1841), 9.
Niger, River, 8.
Nile, River, 8, 24, 53, 67, 75, 103.
Nsama, 57.
Nyangwé, journey to, 99-103 ; sojourn at, 103-107, 118-127 ; letters from, 109-117.
Nyasa, Lake, 25, 34, 36, 40, 42, 43, 45, 48, 55, 56, 60, 61, 63, 64-65, 66, 74 ; its discovery, 12, 13, 49.

Oswell, W. C., 8, 31, 253.
Owen, Captain, on Johanna men, 35.

Palmerston, Lord and Lady, 22-23.
Pamalombe, Lake, 49.
Penguin, H.M.S., 7, 34, 38.
Personal Life of David Livingstone (Blaikie), 11, 216.
Personnel (Livingstone), recruitment, 27-29, 30, 35 ; defection and dismissal, 46-50, 52, 59, 80, 92, 103 ; on the last journey, 225-227, 229, 233, 236, 243 et seq. See also " Banyan slaves " (Stanley), recruitment, 158-159 ; at Unyanyembe, 165 ; mutiny, 166-167 ; European companions, see Farquhar and Shaw.
Pioneer, The, 35.
Playfair, Colonel, 30, 31.
Portuguese and the Slave Trade, 10, 42, 64, 73, 78.
Portuguese East Africa, 25.
" Positive " policy in slave trade, 9, 11.
Preparations in Bombay, 27-33 ; in Zanzibar, 33-39.
Prideaux, 252 ; on Fraser, 152.
Problems of exploration, 27-28.

Quilimane, 11, 21.

Racoon, H.M.S., 65.

Rains, 40-41, 50, 54, 59, 75, 79, 80, 103, 161, 188 *et seq.*, 220, 228 *et seq.*
Rawlinson, Sir Henry, 190-191, 204, 205-206, 208.
Records of Livingstone's expeditions, 14 ; unauthorised accounts, 112-113, 154.
Reid, John, 64.
Rhodesia, 50.
Ripon Falls, 24.
Roscher, 42.
Rovuma, River, 7, 16, 18, 24, 25, 29, 30, 34, 36 ; arrival at, 38, 45, 60.
Royal Geographical Society, 24, 25, 62, 63, 64, 190, 191, 193, 194, 205-206, 208, 216-217, 253.
Rugufo River, 168.
Russell, Earl, 23, 25.
Rusugi, River, 167.

S. Paolo de Loanda, 217.
Said, Seyyid, 30, 34, 147, 148.
Saleh, Mohamad bin, 58, 59, 67, 75, 112, 131, 133.
Salim, Said bin, 146, 163.
Scudamore, 64.
Search Expedition (1872), 190-193 ; (1873), 217-219, 250-252.
Sepoys, recruitment, 28-29 ; dismissal, 46-48, 54.
Seward, G. E., 31, 54, 66, 70, 73, 112, 151-152 ; and Musa's story, 61, 62, 63, 66.
Sewji, Jairam, 37.
Shaw, J. W., 158-159, 161-162, 165-166, 185.
Sherif, 107, 108, 116, 117, 132, 144, 145 ; his private trading, 97-98 ; pilfers Livingstone's stores, 98, 111-112, 114, 131 ; retires to Ujiji, 99.
Shiré, River, 12, 13, 19, 35, 49, 64.
Shupanga, 14, 35, 69.
Slave Trade, 9-11, 12-13, 23, 25, 31-34, 48-51, 73, 87-88, 93, 94, 102-103, 110-111, 148-150, 199-200, 201, 207, 210, 222-223, 254-257. *See also* Arab *and* Portuguese.
South America, 10.
Speke, 24, 36, 37, 74, 75, 95.
Stanley, H. M., *How I found Livingstone*, 140, 156-157, 204, 206-207, 211 ; early career, 134-137 ; first investigation, 137-138 ; commissioned for the search, 138-141 ; preliminary tour, 141-142 ; at Zanzibar, 146-147 ; preparations, 157-159 ; speed of travel, 159-160 ; at Unyanyembe, 163-165 ; arrival at Ujiji, 133, 169 ; departure from Unyanyembe, 175, 176-181 ; to Bagamoyo, 187-190 ; reception in Britain, 202-212 ; attitude towards natives, 136, 157, 177-179 ; discipline,

160, 166-167, 168, 195 ; health, 161, 164, 165, 173, 174 ; and the Search Expedition, 190-195 ; and Kirk, 147, 151, 153-159 ; attack on Kirk, 182-187, 198 *et seq.* ; and Livingstone, 169-181.
Stanley, Lord, 62, 152.
Suelim, Thani bin, 37, 75.
Sunley, William, 35 ; and Musa's story, 62.
Supplies (Livingstone), preliminary arrangements, 37-38 ; pilfered, 49, 51, 174-175 ; appeal for, 54-55 ; at Ujiji, 70-74, 131-132 ; the "Banyan slaves," 97-99, 131-132 ; lost when attacked, 130 ; sent by Stanley, 195, 197 ; on the last journey, 225-227, 228-229, 230 ; Stanley's version, 182-187, 198, 210 ; Frere's report, 213-215 ; (Stanley), 158, 165, 167, 174-175 ; (Search Expedition, 1871), 192, 193 ; (Search Expedition, 1872), 218.
Susi, 35, 50, 80, 108, 176, 225, 227, 233, 237, 243, 244, 245, 246, 247, 248, 249, 251, 253.

Tanganyika, Lake, 24, 36, 37, 40, 43, 52, 54, 55, 56, 59, 67, 68, 75, 131, 172, 227, 250-251.
Tete, 50.
Thornton, 18, 64.
Thule, The, 33.
Tozer, Bishop, 13, 32-33, 143, 183.
Transportation of provisions. *See* Personnel *and* Baggage animals.

Uganda, 41, 43.
Ujiji, 24, 25 ; as an advanced base, 36-37, 54, 56, 58, 59, 60, 67, 68, 69, 70-75, 77, 118-120 ; unsuitability, 93, return to, 127-131 ; Stanley at, 133, 169.
Ulimengo, 177-178.
United Universities Mission, 12 ; on Kirk, 20.
Unyanyembe, 24, 72, 74, 75, 188, 195, 220-225, 251 ; Arab trading "colony," 36, 43, 93, 144, 145, 146 ; the Arab-Mirambo conflict, 163-164, 174.
Urimba, 173.
Usambara, 41.
Uzegula, 189.

Victoria, Lake, 24.

Wainwright, Jacob, 248-249, 253.
Waiyau "boys," desertion with medicines, 52, 59.
Waller, Horace, 19, 23, 26, 27, 29, 32, 33, 49, 63, 109, 113, 139, 143, 177, 184,

210, 243, 247, 249, 253 ; and Stanley's indictment, 199-202, 213, 215, 235-236.

Webb, F. R., 146, 147, 192, 196.
Webb, W. F., 23, 253.
Webb's River. *See* Lualaba.
Wikitani, 22, 29, 49, 65.
Wilberforce, William, 9, 22.
Wilson, Dr., 29.

Young, E. D., 21, 253 ; on Livingstone, 19 ; on Musa, 35, 63 ; Expedition, 63-66, 67, 90.
Young, James, 25, 112, 217, 236.

Zambesi and its Tributaries, The (Livingstone), 12, 23.
Zambesi, River, 8, 11, 18, 26, 63 ; Expedition (1858-63), 16-17, 28, 35, 50 ; its misfortunes, 12-13, 24 ; personal relationships during, 17-22, 63.
Zanzibar, 7, 10, 13, 27, 48, 53, 54, 57, 60, 65, 66, 67, 148, 195 ; to Bombay (1863), 22, 29 ; base for the expedition, 30 ; final preparations at, 32, 33-38 ; and slavery, 33-34, 94, 254-256 ; the cholera epidemic, 94-95, 96 ; rivalry amongst foreign residents, 147, 150-151 ; hurricane, 179.